T0118146

Shadow and Light

and Light

An Autobiography

Shadow
and Light
An Autobiography

Mifflin Wistar Gibbs

MINT EDITIONS

Shadow and Light: An Autobiography was first published in 1902.

This edition published by Mint Editions 2020.

ISBN 9781513266459 | E-ISBN 9781513266893

Published by Mint Editions®

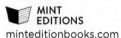
MINT
EDITIONS
minteditionbooks.com

Publishing Director: Jennifer Newens
Project Manager: Gabrielle Maudiere
Design & Production: Rachel Lopez Metzger
Typesetting: Westchester Publishing Services

Contents

Preface

During the late years abroad, while reading the biographies of distinguished men who had been benefactors, the thought occurred that I had had a varied career, though not as fruitful or as deserving of renown as these characters, and differing as to status and aim. Yet the portrayal might be of benefit to those who, eager for advancement, are willing to be laborious students to attain worthy ends.

I have aimed to give an added interest to the narrative by embellishing its pages with portraits of men who have gained distinction in various fields, who need only to be seen to present the career of those now living as worthy models, and the record of the dead, who left the world the better for having lived. To enjoy a life prominent and prolonged is a desire as natural as worthy, and there have been those who sought to extend its duration by nostrums and drinking-waters said to bestow the virtue of "perpetual life." But if "to live in hearts we leave behind is not to die," to be worthy of such memorial we must have done or said something that blessed the living or benefited coming generations. Hence autobiography is the record, for "books are as tombstones made by the living, but destined soon to remind us of the dead."

Trusting that any absence of literary merit will not impair the author's cherished design to "impart a moral," should he fail to "adorn a tale."

Little Rock, Ark., January, 1902.

Introduction

It is seldom that one man, even if he has lived as long as Judge M. W. Gibbs is able to record his impressions of so many widely separated parts of the earth's surface as Judge Gibbs can, or to recall personal experiences in so many important occurrences.

Born in Philadelphia, and living there when that city—almost on the border line between slavery and freedom—was the scene of some of the most stirring incidents in the abolition agitation, he was able as a free colored youth, going to Maryland to work, to see and judge of the condition of the slaves in that State. Some of the most dramatic operations of the famous "Underground Railroad" came under his personal observation. He enjoyed the rare privilege of being associated in labor for the race with that man of sainted memory, the Hon. Frederick Douglass. He met and heard many of the most notable men and women who labored to secure the freedom of the Negro. As a resident of California in the exciting years which immediately followed the discovery of gold, he watched the development of lawlessness there and its results. A few years later he went to British Columbia to live, when that colony was practically an unknown country. Returning to the United States, he was a witness to the exciting events connected with the years of Reconstruction in Florida, and an active participant in the events of that period in the State of Arkansas. At one time and another he has met many of the men who have been prominent in the direction of the affairs of both the great political parties of the country. In more recent years he has been able to see something of life in Europe, and in his official capacity as United States Consul to Tamatave, Madagascar, adjoining Africa, has resided for some time in that far-off and strange land.

It would be difficult for any man who has had all these experiences not to be entertaining when he tells of them. Judge Gibbs has written an interesting book.

Interspersed with the author's recollections and descriptions are various conclusions, as when he says: "Labor to make yourself as indispensable as possible in all your relations with the dominant race, and color will cut less figure in your upward grade."

"Vice is ever destructive; ignorance ever a victim, and poverty ever defenseless."

"Only as we increase in property will our political barometer rise."

It is significant to find one who has seen so much of the world as Judge Gibbs has, saying, as he does: "With travel somewhat extensive and diversified, and with residence in tropical latitudes of Negro origin, I have a decided conviction, despite the crucial test to which he has been subjected in the past, and the present disadvantages under which he labors, that nowhere is the promise along all the lines of opportunity brighter for the American Negro than here in the land of his nativity."

I bespeak for the book a careful reading by those who are interested in the history of the Negro in America, and in his present and future.

BOOKER T. WASHINGTON.

Chapter 1

In the old family Bible I see it recorded that I was born April 17, 1823, in Philadelphia, Pa., the son of Jonathan C. Gibbs and Maria, his wife. My father was a minister in the Wesleyan Methodist Church, my mother a "hard-shell" Baptist. But no difference of religious views interrupted the even tenor of their domestic life. At seven years of age I was sent to what was known as the Free School, those schools at that time invaluable for colored youth, had not graded studies, systematized, and with such accessories for a fruitful development of the youthful mind as now exist. The teacher of the school, Mr. Kennedy, was an Irishman by birth, and herculean in proportions; erudite and severely positive in enunciation. The motto "Spare the rod and spoil the child" had no place in his curriculum. Alike with the tutors of the deaf and the blind, he was earnest in the belief that learning could be impressively imparted through the sense of feeling. That his manner and means were impressive you may well believe, when I say that I yet have a vivid recollection of a bucket with an inch or two of water in it near his desk. In it stood an assortment of rattan rods, their size when selected for use ranging in the ratio of the enormity, of the offence or the age of the offender.

Among the many sterling traits of character possessed by Mr. Kennedy was economy; the frequent use of the rods as he raised himself on tiptoe to make his protest the more emphatic—split and frizzled them—the immersion of the tips in water would prevent this, and add to the severity of the castigation, while diminishing the expense. A policy wiser and less drastic has taken the place of corporal punishment in schools. But Mr. Kennedy was competent, faithful and impartial. I was not destined to remain long at school. At eight years of age two events occurred which gave direction to my after life. On a Sunday in April, 1831, my father desired that the family attend his church; we did so and heard him preach, taking as his text the 16th verse of Chapter 37 in Genesis: "I seek my brethren; tell me, I pray thee, where they feed their flocks."

On the following Sunday he lay before the pulpit from whence he had preached, cold in death, leaving my mother, who had poor health, with four small children, and little laid by "for a rainy day." Unable to remain long at school, I was "put out" to hold and drive a doctor's horse at three dollars a month, and was engaged in similar employment until I reached sixteen years of age. Of the loving devotion and self-sacrifice of an invalid mother I have not words to express, but certain it is, that should it ever appear that I have done anything to revere, or aught to emulate, it should be laid on the altar of her Christian character, her ardent love of liberty and intense aspiration for the upbuilding of the race. For her voice and example was an educator along all the lines of racial progress.

Needing our assistance in her enfeebled condition, she nevertheless insisted that my brother and myself should learn the carpenter trade. At this period in the career of youth, the financial condition of whose parents or sponsors is unequal to their further pursuit of scholastic studies, it is not without an anxious solicitude they depart from the parental roof. For the correct example and prudent advice may not be invulnerable to the temptation for illicit pleasures or ruinous conduct. Happy will he be who listens to the admonitions of age. Unfortunately by the action of response, sad in its humor, too often is: I like the advice but prefer the experience.

The foundation of the mechanical knowledge possessed by the Negro was laid in the Southern States. During slavery the master selecting those with natural ability, the most apt, with white foremen, had them taught carpentering, blacksmithing, painting, boot and shoe making, coopering, and other trades to utilize on the plantations, or add to their value as property. Many of these would hire themselves by the year from their owners, contract on their own account, and by thrift purchase their freedom, emigrate and teach colored youths of Northern States, where prejudice continues to exclude them from the workshops, while at the South the substantial warehouse and palatial dwelling from base to dome, is often the creation of his brain and the product of his handiwork.

James Gibbons, of the class above referred to, and to whom we were apprenticed, was fat, and that is to say, he was jolly. He had ever a word of kind encouragement, wise counsel or assistance to give his employees. Harshness, want of sympathy or interest is often the precursor and stimulator to the many troubles with organized labor that continue to paralyze so many of our great industrial concerns at the present time, resulting in distress to the one and great material loss to the other. Mr. Gibbons had but a limited education, but he possessed that aptitude, energy, and efficiency which accomplishes great objects, that men call genius, and which is oftimes nothing more than untiring mental activity harnessed to intensity of purpose. These constituted his grasp of much of the intricacies of mechanical knowledge. His example was ever in evidence, by word and action, that only by assiduous effort could young men hope to succeed in the battle of life.

Mr. Gibbons was competent and had large patronage. We remained with him until we reached our majority. During a religious revival we both became converted and joined the Presbyterian Church. My brother entered Dartmouth College, under the auspices of the Presbyterian Assembly, graduated and ministered in the church at Philadelphia. After a brief period as a journeyman, I became a contractor and builder on my own account. It is ever a source of strength for a young person to have faith in his or her possibilities, and as soon as may be, assume mastership.

While remaining subject to orders, the stimulus is lacking for that aggressive energy, indispensable to bring to the front. Temporary failure you may have, for failure lies in wait for all human effort, but sneaks from a wise and unconquerable determination. We read of the military prisoner, alone, dejected, and despairing, looking to the walls of his cell; he watches a score of attempts and failure of a spider to scale the wall, only to renew an attempt crowned with success. The lesson was fruitful for the prisoner.

Mr. Gibbons built several of the colored churches in Philadelphia, and in the early forties, during my apprenticeship, he was a bidder for the contract to build the first African Methodist Episcopal brick church of the connection on the present site at Sixth and Lombard streets in Philadelphia. A wooden structure which had been transformed from a blacksmith shop to a meeting house was torn down to give place to the new structure. When a boy I had often been in the old shop, and have heard the founder, Bishop Allen, preach in the wooden building. He was much reverenced. I remember his appearance, and his feeble, shambling gait as he approached the close of an illustrious life.

The A. M. E. Church was distinctively the pioneer in the career of colored churches; its founders the first to typify and unflinchingly assert the brotherhood of man and the Fatherhood of God. Dragged from their knees in the white churches of their faith, they met exclusion by cohesion; ignorance by effort for culture, and poverty by unflinching self-denial; justice and right harnessed to such a movement, who shall declare its ultimatum.

Out from that blacksmith shop went an inspiration lifting its votaries to a self-reliance founded on God, a harbinger of hope to the enslaved.

From Allen to Payne, and on and on along lines of Christian fame, its missionaries going from triumph to triumph in America, and finally planting its standard on the isles of the sea.

A distinct line is ever observable between civilization and barbarism, in the regard and reverence for the dead, the increase of solicitude is evidence of a people's advancement. Until the year 1848 the colored people of Philadelphia used the grounds, always limited, in the rear of their churches for burial. They necessarily became crowded, with sanitary conditions threatening, without opportunity to fittingly mark and adorn the last resting place of their dead.

In the above year G. W. Gaines, J. P. Humphries, and the writer purchased a tract of land on the north side of Lancaster turnpike, in West Philadelphia, and were incorporated under the following act by the Legislature of the State of Pennsylvania: "An Act to incorporate the Olive Cemetery Company," followed by the usual reservations and conditions in such cases provided. Among reasons inducing me to refer to this are, first, to give an idea of the propriety and progress of the race fifty years ago, and secondly, for the further and greater reasons, as the following will show, that the result of the project was not only a palladium for blessed memory of the dead, but was the nucleus of a benefaction that still blesses the living.

The land was surveyed and laid out in lots and avenues, plans of gothic design were made for chapel and superintendent's residence, and contract for construction was awarded the writer. The project was not entirely an unselfish one, but profit was not the dominating incentive. After promptly completing the contract with the shareholders as to buildings and improvements of the ground, the directors found themselves in debt, and welcomed the advent of Stephen Smith, a wealthy colored man and lumber merchant, to assist in liquidating liabilities. To him an unoccupied portion of the ground was sold, and in his wife's heart the conception of a bounteous charity was formed. The "Old Folks' Home," so beneficent to the aged poor of Philadelphia, demands more than a passing notice.

"The Harriet Smith Home for Aged and Infirm Colored Persons" is a continuation of a charity organized September, 1864, and the first board of managers (a noble band of humanitarians) elected. The preamble was as follows: "For the relief of that worthy class of colored persons who have endeavored through life to maintain themselves, but who, from various causes, are finally dependent on the charity of others, an association is hereby organized." The work of this home was conducted in a large dwelling house on South Front street until the year 1871, when, through the munificence of Stephen Smith and his wife, the land on the corner of Belmont and Girard avenues, previously purchased from the Olive Cemetery Company, together with a large four-story building, valued at $40,000, was given to the Board. In 1871 it was opened as the "Harriet Smith Home," where it still stands as an enduring monument to the original donors, and other blessed friends of the race, who have continued to assist with generous endowments. Edward T. Parker, who died in 1887, gave $85,000 for an annex to the building. Colored people since its incipiency have given $200,000. The board is composed of white and colored persons. On a recent visit I found the home complete, convenient, and cleanly in all its appurtenances, with an air of comfort and contentment pervading the place. From many with bent and decrepit bodies, from wrinkled and withered faces, the sparkling eye of gratitude could be seen, and prayer of thankfulness read; for this product of a benign clemency that had blessed both the giver and receiver. There can be no one with filial affection happy in the thought that it is in their power to assuage the pain or assist the tottering steps of their own father or mother, but will recognize the humanity, Christian character, and unselfishness of the men and women organized for giving the helping hand to the "unfortunate aged, made dependent by blameless conditions."

During my apprenticeship, aware of my educational deficiencies, having been unable to pursue a consecutive course of study in earlier life, I spent much of the night and odd times in an endeavor to make up the loss. In joining the Philadelphia Library Company, a literary society of colored men, containing men of such mental caliber as Isaiah C. Wear, Frederick Hinton, Robert Purvis, J. C. Bowers, and others, where questions of moment touching the condition of the race were often discussed with acumen and eloquence, I was both benefited and stimulated. It was a needed help, for man is much the creature of his environments, and what widens his horizon as to the inseparable relations of man to man and the mutuality of obligation, strengthens his manhood in the ratio he embraces opportunity.

Pennsylvania being a border State, and Philadelphia situated so near the line separating the free and slave States, that city was utilized as the most important adjunct or way-station of the "underground railroad," an organization to assist runaway slaves to the English colony of Canada. Say what you will against old England, for, like all human polity, there is much for censure and criticism, but this we know, that when there were but few friends responsive, and but few arms that offered to succor when hunted at home, old England threw open her doors, reached out her hand, and bid the wandering fugitive slave to come in and "be of good cheer."

As one of the railroad company mentioned, many cases came under my observation, and some under my guidance to safety in Canada. One of the most peculiar and interesting ones that came under by notice and attention, was that of William and Ellen Craft, fugitives from the State of Georgia. Summoned one day to a colored boarding house, I was presented to a person dressed in immaculate black broadcloth and silk beaver hat, whom I supposed to be a young white man. By his side stood a young colored man with good features and rather commanding presence. The first was introduced to me as Mrs. Craft and the other as her husband, two escaped slaves. They had traveled through on car and boat, paying and receiving first-class accommodations. Mrs. Craft, being fair, assumed the habit of young master coming north as an invalid, and as she had never learned to write, her arm was in a sling, thereby avoiding the usual signing of register on boat or at hotel, while her servant-husband was as obsequious in his attentions as the most humble of slaves. They settled in Boston, living very happily, until the passage of the fugitive slave law in 1850, when they were compelled to flee to England.

The civil war of 1861 and proclamation of freedom followed. In 1870, arriving in Savannah, Georgia, seeking accommodation, I was directed to a hotel, and surprised to find the host and hostess my whilom friends of underground railroad fame. They had returned to their old home after emancipation. The surprise was pleasant and recognition mutual.

One other, and I shall pass this feature of reminiscence. It was that of William Brown, distinguished afterward as William Box Brown, the intervening "Box" being a synonym of the manner of his escape. An agent of the underground railroad at Richmond, Virginia, had placed him in a box two feet wide and four feet long, ends hooped, with holes for air, and bread and water, and sent him through the express company to Philadelphia. On the arrival of the steamboat the box was roughly tumbled off as so much dead freight on the wharf, but, unfortunately for Brown, on the end, with his feet up and head down. After remaining in such position for a time which seemed to him hours, he heard a man say to another, "Let's turn that box down and sit on it." It was done, and Brown found himself "right side up," if not "with care." I was called to the anti-slavery office, where the box was taken. It had been arranged that when he arrived at his destination, three slow and distinct knocks should be given, to which he was to respond. Fear that he was crippled or dead was depicted in the faces of Miller McKim, William Still and a few others that stood around the box in the office. Hence it was not without trepidation the agreed signal was given, and the response waited for. An "all right" was cheerily given; the lifting of suspense and the top of the box was almost simultaneous. Out sprang a man weighing near 200 pounds. Brown, though uneducated, it is needless to say, was imbued with the spirit of liberty, and with much natural ability, with his box he traveled and spoke of his experience in slavery, the novelty of his escape adding interest to his description. Many similar cases of heroism in manner of escape of men and women are recorded in William Still's "Underground Railroad."

Chapter 2

The immortal bard has sung that "there's a destiny that shapes our ends." At eight years of age, as already stated, two events occurred which had much to do in giving direction to my after life. The one the death of my father, as formerly mentioned; the other the insurrection of Nat Turner, of South Hampton, Virginia, in August, 1831, which fell upon the startled sense of the slaveholding South like a meteor from a dear sky, causing widespread commotion. Nat Turner was a Baptist preacher, who with four others, in a lonely place in the woods, concocted plans for an uprising of the slaves to secure their liberty. Employed in the woods during the week, a prey to his broodings over the wrongs and cruelties, the branding and whipping to death of neighboring slaves, he would come out to meetings of his people on Sunday and preach, impressing much of his spirit of unrest. Finally he selected a large number of confederates, who were to secretly acquire arms of their masters. The attack concocted in February was not made until August 20, when the assault, dealing death and destruction, was made.

All that night they marched, carrying consternation and dread on account of the suddenness, determination and boldness of the attack. The whole State was aroused, and soldiers sent from every part. The blacks fought hand to hand with the whites, but were soon overpowered by numbers and superior implements of warfare. Turner and a few of his followers took refuge in the "Dismal Swamp," almost impenetrable, where they remained two or three months, till hunger or despair compelled them to surrender. Chained together, they were taken to the South Hampton Court House and arraigned. Turner, it is recorded, without a tremor, pleaded not guilty, believing that he was justified in the attempt to liberate his people, however drastic the means. His act, which would have been heralded as the noblest heroism if perpetrated by a white man, was called religious fanaticism and fiendish brutality.

Turner called but few into his confidence, and foolhardy and unpromising as the attempt may have been, it had the ring of an heroic purpose that gave a Bossarius to Greece, and a Washington to America. A purpose "not born to die," but to live on in every age and clime, stimulating endeavors to attain the blessings of civil liberty.

It was an incident as unexpected in its advent as startling in its terrors. Slavery, ever the preponderance of force, had hitherto reveled in a luxury heightened by a sense of security. Now, in the moaning of the wind, the rustling of the leaves or the shadows of the moon, was heard or seen a liberator. Nor was this uneasiness confined to the South, for in the border free States there were many that in whole or in part owned plantations stocked with slaves.

In Philadelphia, so near the line, excitement ran high. The intense interest depicted in the face of my mother and her colored neighbors; the guarded whisperings, the denunciations of slavery, the hope defeated of a successful revolution keenly affected my juvenile mind, and stamped my soul with hatred to slavery.

At 12 years of age I was employed at the residence of Sydney Fisher, a prominent Philadelphia lawyer, who was one of the class above mentioned, living north and owning a plantation in the State of Maryland. Over a good road of 30 miles one summer's day, he took me to his plantation. I had never before been that distance from home and had anticipated my long ride with childish interest and pleasure. After crossing the line and entering "the land of cotton and the corn," a new and strange panorama began to open, and continued to enfold the vast fields bedecked in the snowy whiteness of their fruitage. While over gangs of slaves in row and furrough were drivers with their scourging whip in hand. I looked upon the scene with curious wonder. Three score of years and more have passed, but I still see that sad and humbled throng, working close to the roadway, no head daring to uplift, no eye to enquiringly gaze. During all those miles of drive that bordered on plantations, as machines they acted, as machines they looked. My curiosity and youthful impulse ignoring that reticence becoming a servant, I said: "Mr. Fisher, who are these people?" He said, "They are slaves." I was startled but made no reply. I had not associated the exhilaration of the drive with a depressing view of slavery, but his reply caused a tumult of feeling in my youthful breast. The Turner episode of which I had heard so much, the narratives of whippings received by fugitives, slaves that had come to my mother's house, the sundering of family ties on the auction block, were vividly presented to my mind. I remained silent as to speech, as to feelings belligerent. A few moments elapsed and Mr. Fisher broke the silence by saying, "Mifflin, how would you like to be a slave?" My answer was quick and conformed to feeling. "I would not be a slave! I would kill anybody that would make me a slave!" Fitly spoken. No grander declaration I have ever made. But from whom did it come—from almost childish lips with no power to execute.

I little thought of or knew the magnitude of that utterance, nor did I notice then the effect of its force. Quickly and quite sternly came the reply: "You must not talk that way down here." I was kept during our stay in what was known during slavery as the "great house," the master's residence, and my meals were eaten at the table he had quit, slept in the same house, and had, if desired, little or no opportunity to talk or mingle with the slaves during the week's visit. I did not understand at that time the philosophy of espionage, but in after years it became quite apparent that from my youthful lips had came the "open sesame to the door of liberty," "resistance to oppression," the slogan that has ever heralded the advent of freedom.

As I passed to manhood the object lesson encountered on the Maryland plantation did much to intensify my hatred of slavery and to strengthen my resolution to ally myself with any effort for its abolition. The burning of Pennsylvania Hall by a mob in Philadelphia, in 1838, built and used by anti-slavery people, the ravages of what was known as the "Moyamensing Killers," who burned down the churches and residences of the colored people and murdered their occupants, did much to increase the anti-slavery feeling.

Old Bethel Church, then the nursery of the present great A. M. E. Church, was guarded day and night by its devoted men and women worshipers. The cobble street pavement in front was dug up and the stones carried up and placed at the windows in the galley to hurl at the mob. This defense was sustained for several weeks at a time. Every American should be happy in the thought that a higher civilization is making such acts less and less frequent. It is not strange that our present generation enjoying a large measure of civil and political liberty can but faintly comprehend the condition fifty years ago, when they were persistently denied. The justice of participation seems so apparent, it is not easy to fully conceive, when all were refused, in quite all that were denominated free States.

When street cars were first established in Philadelphia "the brother in black" was refused accommodations. He nevertheless persisted in entering the cars. Sometimes he would be thrown out, at others, after being "sized up" the driver with his horses would leave his car standing on switch, while its objectionable occupant was "monarch of all he surveyed."

The "man and brother" finding his enemy impervious to direct attack, commenced a flank movement. As he was not allowed to ride inside, he resolved to ride alongside; bought omnibuses and stock and established a line on the car route at reduced rates. The cars were not always on time, and many whites would avail themselves of its service. I remember one of this class accosting a driver: "What 'Bus is this?" The simple driver answered, "It is the colored peoples!" "I don't care whose in the —— it is, does it go to the bridge? I am in a hurry to get there," and in he got. I thought then and still think what a useful moral the incident conveyed to my race. Labor to make yourself as indispensable as possible in all your relations with the dominant race and color will cut less and less figure in your upward grade. The line was kept up for some time, often holding what was called "omnibus meetings" in our halls, always largely attended, make reports, hear spirited speeches, and have a deal of fun narrating incidents of the line, receiving generous contributions when the horses or busses needed replenishing. But the most exciting times were those when there had been interference with the running of the "underground railroad," and the attempt to capture passengers in transit, or at the different way-stations, of which as previously stated, Philadelphia was the most prominent in forwarding its patrons to Canada.

Before the passage of the fugitive slave law, in 1850, if the fugitive was taken back it was done by stealth—kidnapped and spirited away by clandestine means. Sometimes by the treachery of his own color, but this was seldom and unhealthy. The agent of the owner was often caught in the act, and by argument more emphatic than gentle, was soon conspicuous by his absence. At others local anti-slavery friends would appeal to the courts, and the agent would be arrested. Slavery in law being local before the passage of the "Act of 1850," making it national, we were generally successful in having the fugitives released. We were extremely fortunate in having for our chief counsel David Paul Brown, a leader of the Philadelphia bar, who, with other white friends, never failed to respond to our call; learned in Constitutional law, eloquent in expression, he did a yeoman's service in behalf of liberty.

The colored men of Pennsylvania, like their brethren in other Northern States, were not content in being disfranchised. As early as 1845 a committee of seven, consisting of Isaiah C. Wear, J. C. Bowers, and others, including the writer, were sent to the capitol at Harrisburg to lay a petition before the Legislature asking for enfranchisement and all rights granted to others of the commonwealth. The grant was tardy, but it came with the cannon's boom and musketry's iron hail, when the imperiled status of the nation made it imperative. Thus, as ever, with the immutable decrees of God, while battling for the freedom of the slave, we broadened our consciousness, not only as to the inalienable rights of human nature, but received larger conceptions of civil liberty, coupled with a spirit of determination to defend our homes and churches from infuriated mobs, and to contend for civil and political justice.

They were truly a spartan band, the colored men and women. The naming of a few would be invidious to the many who were ever keenly alive to the proscription to which they were subject, and ever on the alert for measures to awaken the moral sense of the border States.

Meetings were nightly held for counsel, protests and assistance to the fugitive, who would sometimes be present to narrate the woes of slavery. Sometimes our meetings would be attended by pro-slavery lookers-on, usually unknown, until excoriation of the Northern abettors of slavery was too severe to allow them to remain incognito, when they would reply: It is a sad commentary on a phase of human nature that the oppressed often, when vaulted into authority or greater equality of condition, become the most vicious of oppressors. It has been said that Negro drivers were most cruel and unsparing to their race. The Irish, having fled from oppression in the land of their birth, for notoriety, gain, or elevation by comparison, were nearly all pro-slavery. At one of our meetings during the narration of incidents of his life by a fugitive, one of the latter class interrupted by saying, "Aren't you lying, my man? I have been on plantations. I guess your master did not lose much when you left." Now, it is a peculiarity of the uneducated, when, puzzled for the moment, by the tardiness of an idea, to scratch the head. Jacobs, the fugitive, did so, and out it came. "I dunno how much he lost, only what master said. I was the house boy, one day, and at dinner time he sent me to the well to get a cool pitcher of water. I let the silver pitcher drop in the well. Well, I knowed that pitcher had to be got out, so I straddled down and fished it up. Master was mad, 'cause I staid so long, so I up and tells him. He fairly jumped and said "Did you go down that well? Why didn't you come and tell me and I would made Irish Mike, the ditcher, go down. If you had drowned I'd lost $800. Don't you do that agin.""

It is needless to say that this "brought down the house," and shortly the exit of the son of the Emerald Isle. At another time the interrupter said: "Will you answer me a question or two? Did you not get enough to eat?" "Yes." "A place to sleep?" "Yes." "Was your master good or bad to you?" "Marster was pretty good, I must say." "Well, what else did you want? That is a good deal more than a good many white men get up here." The man stood for a moment busy with his fingers in a fruitless attempt to find the fugitive ends of a curl of his hair, temporarily nonplussed at his palliating concessions, half apologetically said: "Well, I think it a heap best to be free." Then suddenly and gallantly strengthening his defense; "but, look here, Mister, if you think it so nice down there, my place is still open." The questioner good naturedly joined in the general merriment.

Very frequently we were enthused and inspired by Frederick Douglass, Henry Highland Garnett, Marten R. Delaney, and Charles L. Remond, an illustrious quartet of the hallowed band in the anti-slavery crusade, whose eloquence, devotion, and effectiveness stood unsurpassed.

There were few, if any, available halls for these meetings. The only resort was the colored churches. Those under the auspices of white denominations had members who objected to their use for such a purpose. Craven and fawning, content with the crumbs that fell from these peace-loving Christians, who deprecated the discussion of slavery while they ignored the claim of outraged humanity, these churches were more interested in the physical excitement of a "revival" than in listening to appeals in behalf of God's poor and lonely. Their prototypes that "passed by on the other side" have been perpetuated in many climes, in those who believe that it is the formalities of contact with the building that blesses a people and not the Godliness and humanity of the worshippers that give glory and efficacy to the church. An antagonism thus created resulted in a crusade against such churches styled "Come-Outerism," and many left them on account of such apathy to carry on the warfare amid congenial association.

It has been said that citizenship was precipitated upon the Negro before he was fit for its exercise. Without discussing the incongruity of this, when applied to the ignorant native Negro and not to the ignorant alien emigrant, it may be conceded that keeping them in abject bondage with no opportunity to protest, made slavery anything but a preparatory school for the exercises of civic virtues, or the assumption of their responsibilities. It was not true, however, with the mass in the free, or many in the slave States. Always akin and adjunct are the yearnings indestructible in human nature for equal rights. And in every age and people the ratio of persistency and sacrifice have been the measure of their fitness for its enjoyment. During 25 years preceding the abolition of slavery the colored people of the free States, though much proscribed, were active in their protests against enslavement, seizing every chance through press and forum "to pour the living coals of truth upon the nation's naked heart," setting forth in earnest contrast the theory upon which the government was founded with its administration as practiced.

In 1848 Philadelphia Square, whereon the old State House of historic fame still stands, was made resonant by the bell upon whose surface the fathers had inscribed "Proclaim liberty throughout the world and to all the inhabitants thereof," and was bedecked with garlands and every insignia of a joyful people in honor of the Hungarian patriot, Louis Kossuth. Distinctive platforms had been erected for speakers whose fatherland was in many foreign lands. Upon each was an orator receiving the appreciation and plaudits of an audience whose hearts beat as one for success to the "Great Liberator." The "unwelcome guests," the colored men present, quickly embraced the opportunity, utilizing for a platform a dry goods box, upon which I was placed to give the Negro version of this climax of inconsistency and quintessence of hypocrisy. This was the unexpected. All the people, both native and foreign, had been invited and special places provided for all except the Negro, and on the native platform he was not allowed space. The novelty of the incident and curiosity to hear what the colored man had to say quickly drew a crowd equal to others of the occasion. Then, as now, and perhaps forever, there was that incalculable number of non-committals whose moral sense is disturbed by popular wrong, but who are without courage of conviction, inert, waiting for a leader that they may be one of the two that take place behind him, or one of three or four, or ten, who follow in serried ranks, that constitute the wedge-like motor that splits asunder hoary wrong, proximity to the leader being in ratio to their moral fibre. Most of the audience listened to the utterance of sentiments that the allurements of trade, or the exactions of society, forbade them to disseminate.

The occasion was an excellent one to demonstrate the heartlessness of the projectors, who, while pretending to glorify liberty in the distance, were treating it with contumely at home, where 3,000,000 slaves were held in bondage, and feeling keenly the ostracism of the slave as beyond the pole of popular sympathy or national compassion, with words struggling for utterance, I spoke as best I could, receiving toleration, and a quiet measure of approbation, possibly on the supposition, realized in the fruition of time, that such discussion might eventuate in the liberation of white men from the octopus of subserviency to the dictum of slavery which permeated every ramification of American society. I heard Hon. Cassius M. Clay, of Kentucky, sometime in the forties, while making a speech in Philadelphia, say: "Gentlemen, the question is not alone whether the Negroes are to remain slaves, but whether we white men are to continue free." So bitter was the onslaught on all, and especially on white men, politically and socially, who dared denounce slavery.

Chapter 3

An event that came under my notice of startling character, attracting national attention, was the arrival of the schooner "Amistad" at Philadelphia in 1840. This vessel had been engaged in the slave trade. With a cargo of slaves from Africa was destined for one of the West India Islands. Cinguez, one of, and at the head of the captives, rebelled while at sea, killing a number of the crew and taking possession of the ship.

In the concluding scene of the foregoing drama, Mr. Douglass was an actor, I an observer. After the decision giving them their liberty, the anti-slavery society, who had been vigilant in its endeavors to have them liberated ever since their advent on American shores, held a monster meeting to receive them.

Frederick Douglass introduced "Cinguez" to the meeting. I cannot forget or fail to feel the inspiration of that scene. The two giants locked in each others embrace, looked the incarnation of heroism and dauntless purpose, equal to the achievement of great results. The one by indomitable will had shaken off his own shackles and was making slavery odius by his matchless and eloquent arraignment; the other, "a leader of men," had now written his protest with the blood of his captors. Cinguez, with unintelligible utterance in African dialect with emphatic gesture, his liberty loving soul on fire, while burning words strove for expression, described his action on the memorable night of his emancipation, with such vividness, power, and pathos that the audience seemed to see every act of the drama and feel the pulsation of his great heart. Through an interpreter he afterwards narrated his manner of taking the vessel, and how it happened to reach American shores. How, after taking the ship, he stood by the tiller with drawn weapon and commanded the mate to steer back to Africa. During the day he complied, but at night took the opposite course. After sometime of circuitous wandering the vessel ran into Long Island Sound and was taken possession of by the United States authorities. Cinguez, as hero and patriot, ennobled African character.

When majority and the threshold of man's estate is attained, the transition from advanced youth to the entry of manhood is liable to casualties; not unlike a bark serenely leaving its home harbor to enter unfrequented waters, the crew exhilarated by fresh and invigorating breezes, charmed by a genial sky, it moves on "like a thing of beauty" with the hope of "joy forever." The chart and log of many predecessors may unheeded lie at hand, but the glorious present, cloudless and fascinating, rich in expectation, it sails on, fortunate if it escapes the rocks and shoals that ever lie in wait. It is unreasonable to expect a proper conception, and the happiest performance of life's duties at such a period, especially from those with easy and favorable environments, or who have been heedless of parental restraint, for even at an advanced stage in life, there have been many to exclaim with a poet:

"Ne'er tell me of evening serenely adorning
The close of a life richly mellowed by time,
Give me back, give me back the wild freshness of morning
Her smiles and her tears are worth evening's best light."

Twenty-one years of age found me the possessor of a trade, an attainment, and a capital invaluable for a poor young man beginning the race of life. For whether seen smutted by the soot of the blacksmith shop, or whitened by the lime of the plasterer or bricklayer; whether bending beneath tool box of the carpenter or ensconced on the bench of the shoemaker, he has a moral strength, a consciousness of acquirement, giving him a dignity of manhood unpossessed by the menial and those engaged in unskilled labor. Let it never be forgotten that as high over in importance as the best interest of the race is to that of the individual, will be the uplifting influence of assiduously cultivating a desire to obtain trades. The crying want with us is a middle class. The chief component of our race today is laborers unskilled. We will not and cannot compete with other races who have a large and influential class of artisans and mechanics, and having received higher remuneration for labor, have paved the way for themselves or offsprings from the mechanic to the merchant or to the professional. These three factors, linked and interlinked, an ascending chain will be strong in its relation, as consistent in construction.

In 1849 Frederick Douglass, Charles Lenox Remond and Julia Griffith, an English lady prominent in reform circles in England, attended the National Anti-slavery Convention held in Philadelphia, and presided over by that apostle of liberty, Wm. Lloyd Garrison. At its close Mr. Douglass invited me to accompany him to his home at Rochester, and then to join him in lecturing in the "Western Reserve."

Without salary, poor in purse, doubtful of useful ability, dependent for sustenance on a sentiment then prevailing, that for anti-slavery expression was as reserved as the "Reserve" was Western. I have often thought of my feelings of doubt and fear to go with Mr. Douglass, as an epoch in my life's history. The parting of the ways, the embarkation to a wider field of action, the close connection between obedience to an impulse of duty (however uninviting or uncertain the outcome), and the ever moral and often material benefit.

Rochester proved to be my pathway to California. Western New York, 50 years ago, then known as the "Western Reserve," was very unlike the present as to population, means of travel, material developments, schools of learning, and humanizing influences. Mr. Douglass, in the Baptist Church in Little Rock, Ark., a short time before his death, told how, in 1849, we there traveled together; that where now are stately cities and villages a sparsely settled wilderness existed; that while we there proclaimed abolition as the right of the slave, the chilling effect of those December days were not more cold and heartless than the reception we met when our mission as advocates for the slave became known; churches and halls were closed against us. Stables and blacksmith shops would sometimes hold audiences more generous with epithets and elderly eggs than with manly decorum. God be thanked, Douglass, the grandest of "our grand old men," lived to see "the seeds of mighty truth have their silent undergrowth, and in the earth be wrought." A family, however poor, striving as best they may to give the rudiments of knowledge to their children, should have, if but few, books descriptive of the hopes and struggles of those no better situated, who have made impress on the age in which they lived. We seldom remember from whence we first received the idea which gave impulse to an honorable action; we received it, however, most probably from tongue or pen. For impressible youth such biography should be as easy of access as possible.

It has been said that "a man's noblest mistake is to be born before his time." This will not apply to Frederick Douglass. His "Life and Times" should be in the front rank of selection for blessing and inspiration. A blessing for the high moral of its teaching; an inspiration for the poorest boy; that he need not "beg the world's pardon for having been born," but by fostering courage and consecration of purpose "he may rank the peer of any man."

Frederick Douglass, born a slave, hampered by all the depressing influences of that institution; by indomitable energy and devotion; seizing with an avidity that knew no obstacle every opportunity, cultivated a mind and developed a character that will be a bright page in the history of noble and beneficent achievements.

For the conditions that confronted him and the anti-slavery crusade, have been well and eloquently portrayed by the late George William Curtis. That how terribly earnest was the anti-slavery agitation this generation little knows. To understand is to recall the situation of the country. Slavery sat supreme in the White House and made laws at the capitol. Courts of Justice were its ministers, and legislators its lackeys. It silenced the preacher in the pulpit; it muzzled the editor at his desk, and the professor in his lecture-room. It sat a price on the heads of peaceful citizens; robbed the mails, and denounced the vital principles of the declaration of independence as treason. In the States where the law did not tolerate slavery, slavery ruled the club and drawing room, the factory and the office, swaggered at the dinner table, and scourged with scorn a cowardly society. It tore the golden rule from the school books, and from the prayer books the pictured benignity of Christ. It prohibited schools in the free States for the hated race; hunted women who taught children to read, and forbade a free people to communicate with their representatives.

It was under such conditions so pungently and truthfully stated that Douglass appeared as a small star on the horizon of a clouded firmament; rose in intellectual brilliancy, mental power and a noble generosity. For his devotion was not only to the freedom of the slave with which he was identified, but for liberty and the betterment of humanity everywhere, regardless of sex or color. His page already luminous in history will continue to brighten, and when statuary, now and hereafter, erected to his memory, shall have crumbled "neath the beatings of time;" the good fame of his name, high purpose and unflinching integrity to the highest needs of humanity, will remain hallowed "foot prints in the sands of time." Eminently fit was the naming of an institution in Philadelphia "The Frederick Douglass Hospital and Freedman's School;" the assuaging of suffering and the giving of larger opportunity for technical instruction were cherished ideals with the sage of Anacostia; also the lives of Harriet Beacher Stowe, Lucretia Mott and Francis E. Harper, and the noble band of women of which they were the type, who bravely met social ostracism and insult for devotion to the slave, will ever have a proud place in our country's history. Of this illustrious band was Julia Griffith, hitherto referred to, a grand representative of those renowned women, who at home or abroad, did so much to hasten the downfall of slavery and encourage the weak and lowly to hope and effort. Thackery has said that, "Could you see every man's career, you would find a woman clogging him, or cheering him, or beckoning him on."

Having finished my intended tour with Mr. Douglass, and returned to Rochester, the outlook for my future, to me, was not promising. The opportunities for advancement were much, very much less than now. With me ambition and dejection contended for the mastery, the latter often in the ascendant. To her friendly inquiry I gave reasons for my depression. I shall never forget the response; almost imperious in manner, you could already anticipate the magnitude of an idea that seemed to struggle for utterance. "What! discouraged? Go do some great thing." It was an inspiration, the result of which she may never have known. We are assured, however, that a kind act or helpful word is inseparably connected with a blessing for the giver. To earnest youth I would bequeath the excelsior of the "youth mid snow and ice," and the above injunction, "upward and onward;" "go do some great thing."

The war with Mexico, discovery of gold in California in 1848, the acquisition of new territory, and the developments of our hitherto undeveloped Western possessions, stimulated the financial pulse, and permeated every avenue of industry and speculative life. While in New York State I met several going and returning gold seekers, many giving dazzling accounts of immense deposits of gold in the new Eldorado; and others, as ever the case with adventurers, gave gloomy statements of peril and disaster. A judicious temperament, untiring energy, a lexicon of endeavor, in which there is no such word as "fail," is the only open sesame to hidden opportunities in a new country. Fortune, in precarious mood, may sometime smile on the inert, but she seldom fails to surrender to pluck, tenacity and perseverance. As the Oxford men say it is the one pull more of the oar that proves the "beefiness of the fellow;" it is the one march more that wins the campaign; the five minutes more persistent courage that wins the fight.

I returned to Philadelphia, and with some friendly assistance, sailed, in 1850, from New York, as a steerage passenger for San Francisco. Arriving at Aspinwall, the point of debarkation, on the Atlantic side, boats and boatsmen were engaged to transport passengers and baggage up the "Chagress," a small and shallow river. Crossing the Isthmus to Panama, on the Pacific side, I found Panama very cosmopolitan in appearance, for mingled with the sombrero-attired South American, could be seen denizens from every foreign clime. Its make up was a combination of peculiar attributes. It was dirty, but happy in having crows for its scavengers; sickly, but cheery; old, but with an youthful infusion. The virtues and vices were both shy and unblushing. A rich, dark foliage, ever blooming, and ever decaying; a humid atmosphere; a rotting vegetation under a tropical sun, while fever stalked on from conquest to conquest.

The sudden influx, the great travel from ocean to ocean, had given much impetus to business as well as to local amusements. For the latter, Sunday was the ideal day, when bull and cock fights secured the attendance of the elite, and the humble, the priest and the laity.

The church, preaching gentleness and peace in the morning, in the afternoon her minister, with sword spurred "bolosed" bantams under their arms, would appear on the scene eager for the fray.

After recovering from the Panama fever I took passage on the steamship "Golden Gate" for San Francisco. Science, experience, and a greatly increased demand have done much during the intervening fifty years to lessen risk and increase the comfort of ocean travel. Yet it is not without a degree of restless anticipation that one finds himself and baggage finally domiciled on an ocean-going steamer. Curiosity and criticism, selfishness and graciousness each in turn assert themselves. Curiosity in espionage, criticism in observation, while selfishness and graciousness alternate. You find yourself in the midst of a miniature world, environed, but isolated from activities of the greater, an epitome of human proclivities. A possible peril, real, imaginary or remote; a common brotherhood tightens the chain of fellowship and gradually widens the exchange of amenities.

We had a stormy passage, making San Diego with the top of smoke stack encrusted with the salt of the waves, paddle wheel broken and otherwise disabled, finally arriving at San Francisco in September.

Chapter 4

Having made myself somewhat presentable upon leaving the steerage of the steamer, my trunk on a dray, I proceeded to an unprepossessing hotel kept by a colored man on Kearny street. The cursory view from the outside, and the further inspection on the inside, reminded me of the old lady's description of her watch, for she said, "it might look pretty hard on the outside, but the inside works were all right." And so thought its jolly patrons. Seated at tables, well supplied with piles of gold and silver, where numerous disciples of that ancient trickster Pharaoh, being dubious perhaps of the propriety of adopting the literal orthography of his name, and abbreviated it to Faro.

Getting something for nothing, or risking the smaller in hope of obtaining the greater, seems a passion inherent in human nature, requiring a calm survey of the probabilities, and oftimes the baneful effects to attain a moral resistance. It is the "ignis fatuus" that has lured many promising ones and wrecked the future of many lives.

The effervescent happiness of some of the worshipers at this shrine was conspicuous. The future to them seemed cloudless. It was not so with me. I had a secret not at all complacent, for it seemed anxious to get out, and while unhappy from its presence, I thought it wise to retain it.

When I approached the bar I asked for accommodation, and my trunk was brought in. While awaiting this preparatory step to domicile, and gazing at the prints and pictures more or less "blaser" that adorned the bar, my eye caught a notice, prominently placed, in gilt letters. I see it now, "Board twelve dollars a week in advance." It was not the price, but the stipulation demanded that appalled me. Had I looked through a magnifying glass the letters could not have appeared larger. With the brilliancy of a search light they seemed to ask "Who are you and how are you fixed?" I responded by "staring fate in the face," and going up to the bar asked for a cigar. How much? Ten cents. I had sixty cents when I landed; had paid fifty for trunk drayage, and I was now a moneyless man—hence my secret.

Would there be strict enforcement of conditions mentioned in that ominous card. I was unacquainted with the Bohemian "song and dance" parlance in such extremities, and wondered would letting my secret come out let a dinner come in. Possibly, I may have often been deceived when appealed to, but that experience has often been fruitful to friendless hunger.

Finally the bell rang, and a polite invitation from the landlord placed me at the table. There is nothing so helpful to a disconsolate man as a good dinner. It dissipates melancholy and stimulates persistency. Never preach high moral rectitude or the possibilities of industry to a hungry man. First give him something to eat, then should there be a vulnerable spot to such admonition you will succeed. If not, he is an incorrigible.

After dinner I immediately went out, and after many attempts to seek employment of any kind, I approached a house in course of construction and applied to the contractor for work. He replied he did not need help. I asked the price of wages. Ten dollars a day. I said you would much oblige me by giving me, if only a few days' work, as I have just arrived. After a few moments thought, during which mayhap charity and gain held conference, which succumbed, it is needless to premise, for we sometimes ascribe selfish motives to kindly acts, he said that if I choose to come for nine dollars a day I might. It is unnecessary for me to add that I chose to come.

When I got outside the building an appalling thought presented itself; whoever heard of a carpenter announcing himself ready for work without his tools. A minister may be without piety, a lawyer without clients, a politician impolitic, but a carpenter without tools, never! It would be prima facia evidence of an imposter. I went back and asked what tools I must bring upon the morrow; he told me and I left. But the tools, the tools, how was I to get them. My only acquaintance in the city was my landlord. But prospects were too bright to reveal to him my secret. I wended my way to a large tent having an assortment of hardware and was shown the tools needed. I then told the merchant that I had no money, and of the place I had to work the next morning. He said nothing for a moment, looked me over, and then said: "All right take them." I felt great relief when I paid the merchant and my landlord on the following Saturday.

Why do I detail to such length these items of endeavor; experiences which have had similarity in many lives? For the reason that they seem to contain data for a moral, which if observed may be useful. Never disclose your poverty until the last gleam of hope has sunk beneath the horizon of your best effort, remembering that invincible determination holds the key to success, while advice and assistance hitherto laggard, now with hasty steps greets you within the door.

I was not allowed to long pursue carpentering. White employees finding me at work on the same building would "strike." On one occasion the contractor came to me and said, "I expect you will have to stop, for this house must be finished in the time specified; but, if you can get six or eight equally good workmen, I will let these fellows go. Not that I have any special liking for your people. I am giving these men all the wages they demand, and I am not willing to submit to the tyranny of their dictation if I can help it." This episode, the moral of which is as pertinent today as then, and more apparent, intensifies the necessity of greater desire upon the part of our young men and women to acquire knowledge in skilled handicraft, reference to which I have hitherto made. But my convictions are so pronounced that I cannot forbear the reiteration. For while it is ennobling to the individual, giving independence of character and more financial ability, the reflex influence is so helpful in giving the race a higher status in the industrial activities of a commonwealth. Ignorance of such activities compel our people mostly to engage in the lower and less remunerative pursuits. I could not find the men he wanted or subsequent employment of that kind.

All classes of labor were highly remunerative, blacking boots not excepted.

I after engaged in this, and other like humble employments, part of which was for Hon. John C. Fremont, "the pathfinder overland to California."

Saving my earnings, I joined a firm already established in the clothing business. After a year or more so engaged, I became a partner in the firm of Lester & Gibbs, importers of fine boots and shoes. Just here a thought occurs which may be of advantage to ambitious but impecunious young men. Do not hesitate when you are without choice to accept the most humble and menial employment. It will be a source of pleasure, if by self-denial, saving your earnings, you keep a fixed intent to make it the stepping stone to something higher.

The genius of our institutions, and the noblest of mankind will estimate you by the ratio of distance from the humblest beginning to your present attainment; the greater the distance the greater the luster; the more fitting the meed of praise.

Our establishment on Clay street, known as the "Emporium for fine boots and shoes, imported from Philadelphia, London and Paris," having a reputation for keeping the best and finest in the State, was well patronized, our patrons extending to Oregon and lower California. The business, wholesale and retail, was profitable and maintained for a number of years. Mr. Lester, my partner, being a practical bootmaker, his step to a merchant in that line was easy and lucrative.

Thanks to the evolution of events and march of liberal ideas the colored men in California have now a recognized citizenship, and equality before the law. It was not so at the period of which I write. With thrift and a wise circumspection financially, their opportunities were good; from every other point of view they were ostracised, assaulted without redress, disfranchised and denied their oath in a court of justice.

One occasion will be typical of the condition. One of two mutual friends (both our customers) came in looking over and admiring a display of newly arrived stock, tried on a pair of boots, was pleased with them, but said he did not think he needed them then; lay them aside and he would think about it. A short time after his friend came in, was shown the pair the former had admired; would he like such a pair? He tried on several and then asked to try on his friend's selection; they only suited, and he insisted on taking them; we objected, but he had them on, and said we need not have fear, he would clear us of blame, and walked out. Knowing they were close friends we were content. Possibly, in a humorous mood, he went straight to his friend, for shortly they both came back, the first asking for his boots; he would receive no explanation (while the cause of the trouble stood mute), and with vile epithets, using a heavy cane, again and again assaulted my partner, who was compelled tamely to submit, for had he raised his hand he would have been shot, and no redress. I would not have been allowed to attest to "the deep damnation of his taking off."

The Magna Charter, granted by King John, at Runney Mead, to the Barons of England, in the twelfth century, followed by the Petition of Right by Charles I, has been rigidly preserved and consecrated as foundation for civil liberty. The Continental Congress led the van for the United States, who oftimes tardy in its conservatism, is disposed to give audience to merit and finally justice to pertinacity of purpose.

In 1851, Jonas P. Townsend, W. H. Newby, and other colored men with myself, drew up and published in the "Alto California," the leading paper of the State, a preamble and resolutions protesting against being disfranchised and denied the right of oath, and our determination to use all moral means to secure legal claim to all the rights and privileges of American citizens.

It being the first pronouncement from the colored people of the State, who were supposed to be content with their status, the announcement caused much comment and discussion among the dominant class. For down deep in the heart of every man is a conception of right. He cannot extinguish it, or separate it from its comparative. What would I have others do to me? Pride, interest, adverse contact, all with specious argument may strive to dissipate the comparison, but the pulsations of a common humanity, keeping time with the verities of God never ceased to trouble, and thus the moral pebble thrown on the bosom of the hitherto placid sea of public opinion, like its physical prototype, creating undulations which go on and on to beat against the rock and make sandy shores, so this our earnest but feeble protest contributed its humble share in the rebuilding of a commonwealth where "a man's a man for all that."

The committee above named, with G. W. Dennis and James Brown, the same year formed a company, established and published the "Mirror of the Times," the first periodical issued in the State for the advocacy of equal rights for all Americans. It has been followed by a score of kindred that have assiduously maintained and ably contended for the rights and privileges claimed by their zealous leader.

State conventions were held in 1854, '55 and '57, resolutions and petitions passed and presented to the Legislature of Sacramento. We had friends to offer them and foes to move they be thrown out the window. It is ever thus, "that men go to fierce extremes rather than rest upon the quiet flow of truths that soften hatred and temper strife." There was that unknown quantity, present in all legislative bodies, composed of good "little men" without courage of conviction, others of the Dickens' "devilish sly" type, who put out their plant-like tendrils for support; others "who bent the pliant servile knee that thrift may follow fawning"—all these the make-weight of a necessary constituent in representative government conservatism. The conservative majority laid our petition on the table, most likely with the tacit understanding that it was to be "taken up" by the janitor, and as such action on his part is not matter for record, we will in this happier day with "charity to all," over this episode on memory's leaf, simply wrote "lost or stolen."

Among the occasions continually occurring demanding protests against injustice was the imposition of the "poll tax." It was demanded of our firm, and we refused to pay. A sufficient quantity of our goods to pay tax and costs were levied upon, and published for sale, and on what account.

I wrote with a fervor as cool as the circumstances would permit, and published a card from a disfranchised oath-denied standpoint, closing with the avowal that the great State of California might annually confiscate our goods, but we would never pay the voters tax. The card attracted attention, the injustice seemed glaring, the goods were offered. We learned that we had several friends at the sale, one in particular a Southern man. Now there was this peculiarity about the Southern white man, he would work a Negro for fifty years for his victuals and clothes, and shoot a white man for cheating the same Negro, as he considered the latter the height of meanness. This friend quietly and persistently moved through the crowd, telling them why our goods were there, and advising to give them a "terrible letting alone." The auctioneer stated on what account they were there, to be sold, asked for bidders, winked his eye and said "no bidders." Our goods were sent back to our store. This law, in the words of a distinguished Statesman, was then allowed to relapse "into innocuous desuetude." No further attempts to enforce it upon colored men were made.

Chapter 5

A rush to newly discovered gold fields bring in view every trait of human character. The more vicious standing out in bold relief, and stamping their impress upon the locality. This phase and most primitive situation can be accounted for partly by the cupidity of mankind, but mainly that the first arrivals are chiefly adventurers. Single men, untrammeled by family cares, traders, saloonists, gamblers, and that unknown quantity of indefinite quality, ever present, content to allow others to fix a status of society, provided they do not touch on their own special interests, and that other, the unscrupulous but active professional politician, having been dishonored at home, still astute and determined, seeks new fields for booty, obtain positions of trust and then consummate peculation and outrage under the forms of law. But the necessity for the honest administration of the law eventually asserts itself for the enforcement of order.

It was quaintly said by a governor of Arkansas, that he believed that a public official should be "reasonably honest." Even should that limited standard of official integrity be invaded the people with an honest ballot need not be long in rectifying the evil by legal means. But cannot something be said in palliation of summary punishment by illegal means, when it is notorious and indisputable that all machinery for the execution of the law and the maintenance of order, the judges, prosecuting attorneys, sheriff and drawers of jurors, and every other of court of law are in the hands of a despotic cabal who excessively tax, and whose courts convict all those who oppose them, and exonerate by trial the most farcical, the vilest criminal, rob and murder in broad day light, often at the bidding of their protectors. Such a status for a people claiming to be civilized seems difficult to conceive, yet the above was not an hypothesis of condition, but the actual one that existed in California and San Francisco, especially from 1849 to 1855. Gamblers and dishonest politicians from other States held the government, and there was no legal redress. Every attempt of the friends of law and order to elect honest men to office was met at the polls by vituperation and assault.

One of the means for thinning out the ranks of their opponents at the polls they found very efficient. It was to scatter their "thugs" along the line of waiting voters and known opposers, and quickly and covertly inject the metal part of a shoemaker's awl in the rear but most fleshy part of his adversary's anatomy, making sitting unpleasant for a time. There was usually uncertainty as to the point of compass from which the hint came to leave, but none as to the fact of its arrival. Hence the reformer did not stand on the order of his going, but generally left the line. These votes, of course, were not thrown out, for the reason they never got in. It diminished, but did not abolish the necessity of stuffing ballot boxes. In the West I once knew an old magistrate named Scott, noted for his impartiality, but only called Judge Scott by non-patrons of his court, who had never came within the purview of his administration, to others he was known as "old Necessity," for it was said he knew no law. Revolutions, the beneficial results of which will ever live in the history of mankind, founded as they were on the rights of human nature and desire for the establishment and conservation of just government, have ever been the outgrowth of necessity.

Patient in protest of misgovernment, men are prone to "bear the ill they have" until, like the accumulation of rills on mountain side, indignation leaps the bounds of legal form and prostrate law to find their essence and purpose in reconstruction. At the time of which I write, there seemed nothing left for the friends of law, bereft as they were of all statutary means for its enforcement, but making a virtue of this necessity by organizing a "vigilance committee" to wrench by physical strength that unobtainable by moral right. There had been no flourish of trumpets, no herald of the impending storm, but the pent up forces of revolution in inertion, now fierce for action, discarded restraint. Stern, but quiet had been the preparation for a revolution which had come, as come it ever will, with such inviting environments. It was not that normal status, the usual frailties of human nature described by Hooker as "stains and blemishes that will remain till the end of the world, what form of government, soever, may take place, they grow out of man's nature." But in this event the stains and blemishes were effaced by a common atrocity.

Sitting at the back of my store on Clay street a beautiful Sunday morning, one of those mornings peculiar to San Francisco, with its balmy breezes and Italian skies, there seemed an unusual stillness, such a quiet as precedes the cyclone in tropical climes, only broken occasionally by silvery peals of the church bells. When suddenly I heard the plank street resound with the tramp of a multitude. No voice or other sound was heard but the tramp of soldiery, whose rhythm of sound and motion is ever a proclamation that thrills by its intensity, whether conquest or conservation be its mission. I hastened to the door and was appalled at the sight. In marching column, six or eight abreast, five thousand men carrying arms with head erect, a resolute determination born of conviction depicted in linament of feature and expression.

Hastily improvised barracks in large storehouses east of Montgomery street, fortified by hundreds of gunny sacks filled with sand, designated "Fort Gunney," was the quarters for committee and soldiers. The committee immediately dispatched deputies to arrest and bring to the Fort the leaders of this cabal of misgovernment. The effort to do so gave striking evidence of the cowardice of assassins. Men whose very name had inspired terror, and whose appearance in the corridors of hotels or barrooms hushed into silence the free or merry expression of their patrons, now fled and hid away "like damned ghosts at the smell of day" from the popular uprising of the people. The event which precipitated the movement—the last and crowning act of this oligarchy—was the shooting of James King, of William, a banker and publisher of a paper dedicated to the exposure and denunciation of this ring of dishonest officials and assassins. It was done in broad daylight on Montgomery Street, the main thoroughfare of the city. Mr. King, of William County, Maryland, was a terse writer, a gentleman highly esteemed for integrity and devotion to the best interests of his adopted State. Many of the gang who had time and opportunity hid on steamers and sailing vessels to facilitate escape, but quite a number were arrested and taken to Fort Gunny for trial. One or two of the most prominent took refuge in the jail—a strong and well-appointed brick building—where, under the protection of their own hirelings in fancied security considered themselves safe. A deputation of the committee from the fort placed a cannon at proper distance from the entrance to the jail. With a watch in his hand, the captain of the squad gave the keepers ten minutes to open the doors and deliver the culprits. I well remember the excitement that increased in intensity as the allotted period diminished; the fuse lighted, and two minutes to spare; the door opened; the delivery was made, and the march to Fort Gunny began. A trial court had been organized at which the testimony was taken, verdict rendered, and judgment passed. From a beam projecting over an upper story window, used for hoisting merchandise, the convicted criminals were executed.

The means resorted to for the purification of the municipality were drastic, but the ensuing feeling of personal safety and confidence in a new administration appeared to be ample justification. Much has been said and written in defense and in condemnation of revolutionary methods for the reformation of government. It cannot but be apparent that when it is impossible to execute the virtuous purposes of government, the machinery having passed to notorious violators, who use it solely for vicious purpose, there seems nothing left for the votaries of order than to seize the reins with strong right arm and restore a status of justice that should be the pride and glory of all civilized people.

But what a paradox is presented in the disregard for law and life today in our common country, including much in our Southland! It is a sad commentary on the weakness and inconsistencies of human nature and often starts the inquiry in many honest minds, as a remedial agency, is a republican form of government the most conducive in securing the blessings of liberty of which protection to human life is the chief?

For the actual reverse of conditions that existed in California in those early days are present in others of our States today. All the machinery and ability for the just administration of the law are in the hands of those appointed mainly by the ballot of the intelligence and virtue of these States, who, if not participants, are quite as censurable for their "masterly inactivity" in having allowed thousands of the most defenceless to be lynched by hanging or burning at the stake. That there have been cases of assault on women by Negroes for which they have been lynched, it is needless to deny. That they have been lynched for threatening to do bodily harm to white men for actual assaults on the Negro wife and daughter is equally true. The first should be denounced and arrested (escape being impossible) and by forms of law suffer its extreme penalty. The other for the cause they were murdered should have the highest admiration and the most sincere plaudits from every honest man. Is it true that "he is a slave most base whose love of right is for himself and not for all the race," and that the measure you mete out to others—the same shall be your portion. All human history verifies these aphorisms; and that the perpetrators and silent abettors of this barbarism have sowed to the winds a dire penalty, already being reaped, is evidenced by disregard of race or color of the victim when mob law is in the ascendant. And further, as a salvo for their own acts, white men are allowing bad Negroes to lynch others of their kind without enforcing the law.

The Negro, apish in his affinity to his prototype in a "lynching bee," is beneath contempt.

Chapter 6

Early in the year 1858 gold was discovered on Fraser River, in the Hudson Bay Company's territory in the Northwest. This territory a few months later was organized as the Colony of British Columbia and absorbed; is now the western outlook of the Dominion of Canada. The discovery caused an immense rush of gold seekers, traders, and speculators from all parts of the world. In June of that year, with a large invoice of miners' outfits, consisting of flour, bacon, blankets, pick, shovels, etc., I took passage on steamship Republic for Victoria. The social atmosphere on steamers whose patrons are chiefly gold seekers is unlike that on its fellow, where many have jollity moderated by business cares, others reserved in lofty consciousness that they are on foreign pleasure bent. With the gold seeker, especially the "tenderfoot," there is an incessant social hilarity, a communion of feeling, an ardent anticipation that cannot be dormant, continually bubbling over. We had on board upward of seven hundred, comprising a variety of tongues and nations. The bustle and turmoil incident to getting off and being properly domiciled; the confusion of tongues and peculiarity of temperament resembled the Babel of old. Here the mercurial Son of France in search of a case of red wine, hot and impulsive, belching forth "sacres" with a velocity well sustained. The phlegmatic German stirred to excitability in quest of a "small cask of lager and large box of cheese;" John Chinaman "Hi yah'd" for one "bag lice all samee hab one Melican man," while a chivalric but seedy-looking Southerner, who seemed to have "seen better days," wished he "might be—if he didn't lay a pe-yor of boots thar whar that blanket whar." Not to be lost in the shuffle was a tall canting specimen of Yankee-dom perched on a water cask that "reckoned ther is right smart chance of folks on this 'ere ship," and "kalkerlate that that boat swinging thar war a good place to stow my fixin's in." The next day thorough system and efficiency was brought out of chaos and good humor prevailed.

Victoria, then the capital of British Columbia, is situated on the southern point of Vancouver's Island. On account of the salubrity of its climate and proximity to the spacious land-locked harbor of Esquimault it is delightful as a place of residence and well adapted to great mercantile and industrial possibilities. It was the headquarters of the Hudson Bay Company, a very old, wealthy, and influential English trading company.

Outside the company's fort, enclosing immense storehouses, there were but few houses. The nucleus of a town in the shape of a few blocks laid out, and chiefly on paper maps, was most that gave promise of the populous city of Victoria of the present. On my arrival my goods were sold at great advance on cost, an order for more sent by returning steamer. I had learned prior to starting that city lots could be bought for one hundred dollars each, and had come prepared to buy two or three at that price. A few days before my arrival what the authorities had designated as the "land office" had been subjected to a "Yankee rush," which had not only taken, and paid for all the lots mapped out, but came near appropriating books, benches, and window sashes; hence the office had to close down and haul off for repairs, and surveyed lots, and would not be open for business for ten days. Meanwhile those that were in at the first sale were still in, having real estate matters their own way. Steamers and sailing craft were constantly arriving, discharging their human freight, that needed food, houses, and outfits for the mines, giving an impetus to property of all kinds that was amazing for its rapidity. The next afternoon after the day of my arrival I had signed an agreement and paid one hundred dollars on account for a lot and one-story house for $3,000–$1,400 more in fifteen days, and the balance in six months. Upon the arrival of my goods ten days later I paid the second installment and took possession. Well, how came I to take a responsibility so far beyond my first intended investment? Just here I rise to remark: For effective purposes one must not be unduly sensitive or overmodest in writing autobiography—for, being the events and memoirs of his life, written by himself, the ever-present pronoun "I" dances in such lively attendance and in such profusion on the pages that whatever pride he may have in the events they chronicle is somewhat abashed at its repetition.

Addison truly says: "There is no passion which steals into the heart more imperceptible and covers itself under more disguises than pride." Still, if in such memoirs there be found landmarks of precept or example that will smooth the ruggedness of Youth's pathway, the success of its mission should disarm invidious criticism. For the great merit of history or biography is not alone the events they chronicle, but the value of the thought they inspire. Previous to purchasing the property I had calculated the costs of alteration and estimated the income. In twenty days, after an expenditure of $200 for improvements, I found myself receiving a rental of $500 per month from the property, besides a store for the firm.

Anyone without mechanical knowledge with time and opportunity to seek information from others may have done the same, but in this case there was neither time nor opportunity; it required quick perception and prompt action. The trade my mother insisted I should learn enabled me to do this. Get a trade, boys, if you have to live on bread and apples while attaining it. It is a good foundation to build higher. Don't crowd the waiters. If they are content, give them a chance. We received a warm welcome from the Governor and other officials of the colony, which was cheering. We had no complaint as to business patronage in the State of California, but there was ever present that spectre of oath denial and disfranchisement; the disheartening consciousness that while our existence was tolerated, we were powerless to appeal to law for the protection of life or property when assailed. British Columbia offered and gave protection to both, and equality of political privileges. I cannot describe with what joy we hailed the opportunity to enjoy that liberty under the "British lion" denied us beneath the pinions of the American Eagle. Three or four hundred colored men from California and other States, with their families, settled in Victoria, drawn thither by the two-fold inducement—gold discovery and the assurance of enjoying impartially the benefits of constitutional liberty. They built or bought homes and other property, and by industry and character vastly improved their condition and were the recipients of respect and esteem from the community.

An important step in a man's life is his marriage. It being the merging of dual lives, it is only by mutual self-abnegation that it can be made a source of contentment and happiness. In 1859, in consummation of promise and purpose, I returned to the United States and was married to Miss Maria A. Alexander, of Kentucky, educated at Oberlin College, Ohio. After visits to friends in Buffalo and my friend Frederick Douglass at Rochester, N. Y., thence to Philadelphia and New York City, where we took steamship for our long journey of 4,000 miles to our intended home at Victoria, Vancouver Island. I have had a model wife in all that the term implies, and she has had a husband migratory and uncertain. We have been blessed with five children, four of whom are living—Donald F., Horace E., Ida A., and Hattie A. Gibbs; Donald a machinist, Horace a printer by trade. Ida graduated as an A. B. from Oberlin College and is now teacher of English in the High School at Washington, D. C.; Hattie a graduate from the Conservatory of Music at Oberlin, Ohio, and was professor of music at the Eckstein-Norton

University at Cave Springs, Ky., and now musical director of public schools of Washington, D. C.

In passing through the States in 1859 an unrest was everywhere observable. The pulse-beat of the great national heart quickened at impending danger. The Supreme Court had made public the Dred Scott decision; John Brown had organized an insurrection; Stephen A. Douglass and Abraham Lincoln at the time were in exciting debate; William H. Seward was proclaiming the "irrepressible conflict." With other signs portentous, culminating in secession and events re-enacting history—for that the causes and events of which history is the record are being continuously re-enacted from a moral standpoint is of easy observation. History, as the narration of the actions of men, with attendant results, is but a repetition. Different minds and other hands may be the instruments, but the effects from any given course involving fundamental principles are the same. This was taught by philosophers 2,000 years ago, some insisting that not only was this repetition observable in the moral world, but that the physical world was repeated in detail—that every person, every blade of grass, all nature, animate and inanimate, reappeared upon the earth, engaged in the same pursuits, and fulfilling the same ends formerly accomplished.

However skeptical we may be as to this theory of the ancients, the student of modern history has accomplished little if he fails to be impressed with the important truth standing out on every page in letters of living light—that this great world of ours is governed by a system of moral and physical laws that are as unerring in the bestowal of rewards as certain in the infliction of penalties. The history of our own country is one that will ever be an exemplification of this pre-eminent truth. The protests of the victims of oppression in the old world resulted in a moral upheaval and the establishment by force of arms of a Republic in America. The Revolutionary Congress, of which, in adopting the Federal Constitution, closed with this solemn injunction: "Let it be remembered that it has been the pride and boast of America that the rights for which she contended were the rights of human nature." And it was reserved for the founders of this nation to establish in the words of an illustrious benefactor, "a Government of the people, for the people, and by the people"—a Government deriving all its powers from the consent of the governed, where freedom of opinion, whether relating to Church or State, was to have the widest scope and fullest expression consistent with private rights and public good—where the largest individuality could be developed and the patrician and plebeian meet on a common level and aspire to the highest honor within the gift of the people.

This was its character, this its mission. How it has sustained the character, how fulfilled the mission upon which it entered, the impartial historian has indited, every page of which is redolent with precept and example that point a moral.

With the inauguration of republican government in America the angel of freedom and the demon of slavery wrestled for the mastery. Tallyrand has beautifully and forcibly said: "The Lily and Thistle may grow together in harmonious proximity, but liberty and slavery delight in the separation." The pronounced policy of the best minds at the adoption of the Federal Constitution was to repress it as an institution inhuman in its character and fraught with mischief. Foretelling with accuracy of divine inspiration, Jefferson "trembled for his country" when he remembered that God was just and that "His justice would not sleep forever." Patrick Henry said "that a serious view of this subject gives a gloomy prospect to future times." So Mason and other patriots wrote and felt, fully impressed that the high, solid ground of right and justice had been left for the bogs and mire of expediency.

They died, leaving this heritage growing stronger and bolder in its assumption of power and permeating every artery of society. The cotton gin was invented and the demand for cotton vaulted into the van of the commerce of the country. Men, lured by the gains of slavery and corrupted by its contact, sought by infamous reasoning and vicious legislation to avert the criticism of men and the judgment of God. In the words of our immortal Douglass, "To bolster up and make tolerable what was intolerable; to make human what was inhuman; to make divine what was infernal." To make this giant wrong acceptable to the moral sense it was averred and enacted that slavery was right; that God himself had so predetermined in His wisdom; that the slave could be branded and sold on the auction block; that the babe could be ruthlessly taken from its mother and given away; that a family could be scattered by sale, to meet no more; that to teach a slave to read was punishable with death to the teacher. But why rehearse this dead past—this terrible night of suffering and gloom? Why not let its remembrance be effaced and forgotten in the glorious light of a happier day? I answer, Why?

All measure of value, all estimates of greatness, of joy or sorrow, of health or suffering, are relative; we judge by comparison, and if in recalling these former depths we temper unreasonable criticism of waning friendships, accelerate effort as we pass the mile-stones of achievement, and stimulate appreciation of liberty in the younger generation, the mention will not be fruitless.

But to the resume of this rapid statement of momentous events: Meanwhile, the slave, patient in his longings, prayed for deliverance. Truly has it been said by Elihu Burrit that "you may take a man and yoke him to your labor as you yoke the ox that worketh to live, and liveth to work; you may surround him with ignorance and cloud him over with artificial night. You may do this and all else that will degrade him as a man, without injuring his value as a slave; yet the idea that he was born to be free will survive it all. 'Tis allied to his hope of immortality—the ethereal part of his nature which oppression cannot reach. 'Tis the torch lit up in his soul by the omnipotent hand of Deity Himself." The true and tried hosts of freedom, represented and led by Garrison, Douglass, Lovejoy, Phillips, Garnet, Harriet Beecher Stowe, and Frances Ellen Harper, and others—few compared to the indifferent and avowed defenders of slavery, welcoming outrage and ostracism, by pen and on forum, from hilltop and valley, proclaimed emancipation as the right of the slave and the duty of the master. The many heroic efforts of the anti-slavery phalanx were not without effect, and determined resistance was made to the admission of more slave territory which was in accordance with the "Proviso" prohibiting slavery in the Northwest. Slavery controlled the Government from its commencement, hence its supporters looked with alarm upon an increasing determination to stay its progress.

California had been admitted as a free State, after a struggle the most severe. Its admission John C. Calhoun, the very able leader of the slave power, regarded as the death-knell of slavery, if the institution remained within the union and counseled secession. Washington, Jefferson, and Madison, in despair at the growth of slavery; Calhoun at that of freedom. But how could this march of moral progress and national greatness be arrested? Congress had, in 1787, enacted that all the territory not then States should forever be reserved to freedom. The slave power saw the "handwriting on the wall" surround it with a cordon of free States; increase their representatives in Congress advocating freedom, and slavery is doomed. The line cherished by the founders, the Gibraltar against which slavery had dashed its angry billows, must be blotted out, and over every rod of virgin soil it was to be admitted without let or hindrance.

Then came the dark days of compromise, the era of Northern fear of secession, and, finally, opinion crystallizing into legislation non-committal, viz: That States applying for admission should be admitted as free or slave States, as a majority of their inhabitants might determine. Then came the struggle for Kansas. Emigration societies were fitted out in the New England and Northern States to send free State men to locate who would vote to bring in Kansas as a free State. Similar organizations existed in the slave States for the opposite purpose.

It is not pleasant to dwell nor fitly portray the terrible ordeal through which the friends of freedom passed. In 1859 they succeeded; right and justice were triumphant, the beneficial results of which will reach remotest time. It was in this conflict that the heroism of John Brown developed. It was there he saw his kindred and his friends murdered, and there registered his vow to avenge their blood in the disenthralment of the slave. The compeers of this "grand old man" or people of the nation could have scarcely supposed that this man, hitherto obscure, was to be the instrument of retributive justice, to inaugurate a rebellion which was to culminate in the freedom of 4,000,000 slaves. John Brown, at the head of a few devoted men, at Harper's Ferry, struck the blow that echoed and re-echoed in booming gun and flashing sabre until, dying away in whispered cadence, was hushed in the joyousness of a free nation. John Brown was great because he was good, and good because he was great, with the bravery of a warrior and the tenderness of a child, loving liberty as a mother her first born, he scorned to compromise with slavery. Virginia demanded his blood and he gave it, making the spot on which he fell sacred for all time, upon which posterity will see a monument in commemoration of an effort, grand in its magnanimity, to which the devotees of liberty from every clime can repair to breathe anew an inspiration from its shrine—

> *"For whether on the gallows high*
> *Or in the battle's van,*
> *The noblest place for man to die*
> *Is where he dies for man."*

The slave power, defeated in Kansas, fearful of the result of the vote in other territories to determine their future status, found aid and comfort from Judge Taney, a Supreme Judge of the United States. Bancroft, the historian, has said: "In a great Republic an attempt to overthrow a State owes its strength to and from some branch of the Government." 'Tis said that this Chief Justice, without necessity or occasion, volunteered to come to the rescue of slavery, and, being the highest court known to the law, the edict was final, and no appeal could lie, save to the bar of humanity and history. Against the memory of the nation, against decisions and enactments, he announced that, slaves being property, owners could claim constitutional protection in the territories; that the Constitution upheld slavery against any act of a State Legislature, and even against Congress. Slavery, previous to 1850, was regulated by municipal law; the slave was held by virtue of the laws of the State of his location or of kindred slave States. When he escaped that jurisdiction he was free. By the decision of Judge Taney, instead of slavery being local, it was national and freedom outlawed; the slave could not only be reclaimed in any State, but slavery could be established wherever it sought habitation.

Black laws had been passed in Northern States and United States Commissioners appointed in these States searched for fugitives, where they had, in fancied security, resided for years, built homes, and reared families, seizing and remanding them back into slavery, causing an era of terror, family dismemberment, and flight, only to be remembered with sadness and horror. For had not the heartless dictum come from a Chief Justice of the United States—the "Jeffry of American jurisprudence," that it had been ruled that black men had no rights a white man was bound to respect?

The slave power, fortified with this declaration, resolved that if at the approaching election they did not *succeed* they would *secede*. Lincoln was elected, and the South, true to its resolve, prepared for the secession of its States. Pennsylvania is credited with having then made the last and meanest gift to the Presidency in the person of James Buchanan. History tells of a Nero who fiddled while Rome burned. The valedictory of this public functionary breathing aid and comfort to secession, was immediately followed by South Carolina firing on Fort Sumter, and Southern Senators advised their constituents to seize the arsenals and ports of the nation. Rebellion was a fact.

Chapter 7

Abraham Lincoln, the President-elect, was the legitimate outgrowth of American institutions; in him was presented choice fruit, the product of republican government. Born in a log cabin, of poor, uneducated parents, his only aids untiring industry, determination, and lofty purpose. Hewing out his steps on the rugged rocks of poverty, climbing the mountains of difficulty, and attaining the highest honor within the gift of the nation—"truly a self-made man, the Declaration of Independence," says a writer, "being his daily compendium of wisdom, the life of Washington his daily study, with something of Jefferson, Madison, and Clay." For the rest, from day to day, he lived the life of the American people; "walked in its light; reasoned with its reason; thought with its powers of thought, and felt the beatings of its mighty heart." In 1858 he came prominently forward as the rival of Stephen A. Douglass, and, with wealth of argument, terseness of logic, and enunciation of just principles, took front rank among sturdy Republicans, battling against the extension of human slavery, declaring that "the nation could not endure half free and half slave."

On the 4th of March, 1861, he took the oath of office and commenced his Administration. With confidence and doubt alternating, our interest as a race became intensified. We knew the South had rebelled; we were familiar with the pagan proverb "Those whom the gods would destroy they first made mad." We had watched the steady growth of Republicanism, when a tinge on the political horizon "no bigger than a man's hand," increase in magnitude and power and place its standard-bearer in the White House. But former Presidents had professed to hate slavery. President Fillmore had, yet signed the fugitive slave law; Pierce and Buchanan had both wielded the administrative arm in favor of slavery. We had seen Daniel Webster, Massachusetts' ablest jurist, and the most learned constitutional expounder—the man of whom it was said that "when he speaks God's own thunder can be seen pent up in his brow and God's own lightning flash from his eye"—a man sent by the best cultured of New England to represent the most advanced civilization of the century—we had seen this brilliant star of anti-slavery Massachusetts "pale his ineffectual fires" before the steady glare, the intolerance, blandishment, and corrupting influences of the slave power—and tell the nation they must compromise with slavery.

When Daniel O'Connell, Ireland's statesman and philanthropist, was approached in Parliament by West India planters with promises of support for measures for the relief of Ireland if he would vote in the interest of slavery in British colonies, he said: "'Tis true, gentlemen, that I represent a poor constituency—God only knows how poor; but may calamity and affliction overtake me if ever I, to help Ireland, vote to enslave the Negro." A noble utterance! Unlike the Northern representatives sent to Congress, who "bent the pliant, servile knee that thrift might follow fawning." What wonder our race was keenly alive to the situation? The hour had arrived—was the man there?

For Abraham Lincoln impartial history will answer "Nor memory lose, nor time impair" his nobility of character for humanity and patriotism that will ever ennoble and inspire. Mr. Lincoln was slow to believe that the rebellion would assume the proportions that it did, but he placed himself squarely on the issue in his inaugural address: "That he should, to the extent of his ability, take care that the laws of the nation be faithfully executed in all the States; that in doing it there would be no bloodshed unless it was forced upon the national authority." His patriotism and goodness welling up as he said: "We are not enemies, but friends, though we may have strained, it must not break our bonds of affection. The mystic chords of memory, stretching from every battlefield and hearthstone, will yet swell the chorus of the Union when again touched by the better angels of our nature."

"But the die was cast;
Ruthless rapine righteous hope defied."

The necessity for calling the nation to arms was imminent on the 15th of April, 1861; the call for 75,000 men rang like a trumpet blast, startling the most apathetic. The response from the Northern and portions of the Southern States was hearty and prompt. The battle at Bull Run dispelled the President's idea that the war was to be of short duration. Defeat followed defeat of the national forces; weeping and wailing went up from many firesides for husbands and sons who had laid down on Southern battlefields to rest. The great North, looking up for succor, saw the "national banner drooping from the flagstaff, heavy with blood," and typical of the stripes of the slave. For 200 years the incense of his prayers and tears had ascended. Now from every booming gun there seemed the voice of God, "Let my people go"—

> *"They see Him in watch fires*
> *Of a hundred circling camps;*
> *They read His righteous sentence*
> *By the dim and flaring lamps."*

The nation had come slowly but firmly up to the duty and necessity of emancipation. Mr. Lincoln, who was now in accord with Garrison, Phillips, Douglass, and their adherents, had counseled them to continue urging the people to this demand, now pressing as a military necessity. The 1st of January, 1863, being the maturity of the proclamation, lifted 4,000,000 of human beings from chattels to freemen, a grateful, praying people. Throughout the North and wherever possible in the South the colored people, on the night of December 31, assembled in their churches for thanksgiving. On their knees in silence—a silence intense with suppressed emotion—they awaited the stroke of the clock. It came, the thrice-welcomed harbinger of freedom, and as it tolled on, and on, the knell of slavery, pent-up joy could no longer be restrained. "Praise God, from whom all blessings flow," from a million voices, floated upward on midnight air. While some shouted "Hallelujah," others, with folded arms, stood mute and fixed as statuary, while "Tears of joy like summer raindrops pierced by sunbeams" fell.

When Robespierre and Danton disenthralled France, we learn that the guillotine bathed in blood was the emblem of their transition state, from serfs to freemen. With the Negro were the antithesis of anger, revenge, or despair, that of joy, gratitude, and hope, has been memory's most choice trio.

This master stroke of policy and justice came with telling effect upon the consciousness of the people. It was now in deed and in truth a war for the Union coeval with freedom; every patriot heart beat a responsive echo, and was stirred by a new inspiration to deeds of heroism. Now success followed success; Port Hudson, Vicksburg, Chattanooga, Gettysburg, and the Mississippi bowed in submission to the national power. The record of history affirms subsequent events that during the ensuing twelve months war measures more gigantic than had been witnessed in modern times were inaugurated; how the will of the people to subdue the rebellion crystallized as iron; that General

Grant, planting himself before Richmond, said he would "fight it out on that line if it took all summer," and General Sherman's memorable march fifty thousand strong from Atlanta to the sea. General Grant's campaign ended in the surrender of General Lee, and Peace, with its golden pinions, alighted on our national staff.

Abraham Lincoln was again elected President, the people seeming impressed with the wisdom of his quaint phrase that "it was best not to swap horses while crossing a stream." Through all the vicissitudes of his first term he justified the unbounded confidence of the nation, supporting with no laggard hand, cheering and inspiring the citizen soldier with noble example and kindly word. The reconstruction acts, legislation for the enrollment of the colored soldier, and every other measure of enfranchisement received his hearty approval, remarking at one time, with much feeling, that "I hope peace will come to stay, and there will be some black men that can remember that they helped mankind to this great consummation."

Did the colored troops redeem the promise made by their friends when their enlistment was determined? History records exhibitions of bravery and endurance which gave their survivors and descendants a claim as imperishable as eternal justice. Go back to the swamps of the Carolinas, the Savannahs of Florida, the jungles of Arkansas; or on the dark bosom of the Mississippi. Look where you may, the record of their rugged pathway still blossoms with deeds of noble daring, self-abnegation and a holy devotion to the central ideas of the war—the freedom of the slave, a necessity for the salvation of free government.

The reading of commanders' reports bring no blush of shame. At the terrific assault on Fort Hudson, General Banks reported they answered "every expectation; no troops could have been more daring." General Butler tells of his transformation from a war Democrat to a radical. Riding out at early morn to view the battlefield, where a few hours before shot and shell flew thick and fast, skillfully guiding his horse, that hoofs should not profane the sacred dead, he there saw in sad confusion where lay the white and black soldier, who had gone down together. The appeal, though mute, was irresistible. Stopping his horse and raising his hand in the cold, grey light to heaven, said: "May my tongue cleave to the roof of my mouth and my right hand forget its cunning if I ever cease to insist upon equal justice to the colored man." It was at the unequal fight at Milliken's Bend; it was at Forts Wagner and Pillow, at Petersburg and Richmond, the colored troops asked to be assigned the posts of danger, and there before the iron hail of the enemy's musketry "they fell forward as fits a man." In our memory and affections they deserve a fitting place "as those long loved, and but for a season gone."

Slavery, shorn of its power, nurtured revenge. On the 14th day of April, 1865, while sitting with his family at a public exhibition, Abraham Lincoln was assassinated, and the nation was in tears. Never was lamentation so widespread, nor grief so deep; the cabin of the lowly, the lordly mansion of wealth, the byways and highways, gave evidence of a people's sorrow. "Men moved about with clinched teeth and bowed-down heads; women bathed in tears and found relief, while little children asked their mothers why all the people looked so mournful," and we, as we came up out of Egypt, lifted up our voices and wept. Our friend was no more, but intrenched in the hearts of his countrymen as one who did much "to keep the jewel of liberty in the family of nations."

Since that eventful period the Negro has had a checkered career, passing through the reconstruction period, with its many lights and shadows, despite the assaults of prejudice and prescription by exclusion from most of the remunerative callings and avocations, partiality in sentencing him to the horrors of the chain-gang, lynching, and burning at the stake. Despite all these he has made progress—a progress often unfairly judged by the dominant race. Douglass has pithily said: "Judge us not from the heights on which you stand, but from the depths from whence we sprung." So, with a faith and hope undaunted, we scan our country horizon for the silver lining propitious of a happier day.

Regarding that crime of crimes, lynching by hanging and burning human beings, a barbarity unknown in the civilized world save in our country, it is cheering to observe an awakening of the moral sense evidenced by noble and manly utterance of leading journals, notably those of Arkansas; the Governor of Georgia, and other Southern Governors and statesmen, have spoken in derogation of this giant crime.

When others of like standing and State influence shall so pronounce, this hideous blot upon the national escutcheon will disappear. It is manly and necessary to protest when wronged. But a subject class or race does but little for their amelioration when content with its denouncement. Injustice can be more effectually arraigned by others than the victim; his mere proclamation, however distinct and unanswerable, will be slow of fruition. A measure of relief comes from the humane sympathies of the philanthropist, but the inherent attraction of forces (less sympathetic, perhaps, though indispensable) for his real uplifting and protection will be in the ratio of his morality, learning, and wealth. For vice is ever destructive; ignorance ever a victim, and poverty ever defenceless. Morality should be ever in the foreground of all effort, for mere learning or even wealth will not make a class of brave, honest men and useful citizens; there must be ever an intensity of purpose based upon convictions of truth, and "the inevitable oneness of physical and moral strength." St. Pierre de Couberton, an eminent French writer on education and training, has pertinently said: "Remember that from the cradle to the grave struggle is the essence of life, as it is the unavoidable aim, the real life bringer of all the sons of men. Existence is a fight, and has to be fought out; self-defence is a noble art, and must be practiced. Never seek a quarrel, but never shun one, and if it seeks you, be sure and fight to the last, as long as strength is given you to stand, guard your honesty of purpose, your good faith; beware of all false seeming, of all pretence, cultivate arduous tasks, aspire to what is difficult, and do persistently what is uncomfortable and unpleasant; love effort passionately, for without effort there can be no manliness; therefore acquire the habit of self-restraint, the habit of painful effort, physical pain, is a useful one." With such purpose the Negro should have neither servility, bitterness, nor regret, but "instinct with the life of the present rise with the impulse of the age."

Chapter 8

My election to the Common Council of the City of Victoria, Vancouver Island, in 1866, was my first entry to political life, followed by re-election for succeeding term.

The exercise of the franchise at the polls was by "viva voce," the voter proclaiming his vote by stating the name of the candidate for whom he voted in a distinct voice, which was audited on the rolls by clerks of both parties.

Alike all human contrivances, this mode of obtaining the popular will has its merits and demerits. For the former it has the impossibility of ballot-stuffing, for the by-stander can keep accurate tally; also the opportunity for the voter to display the courage of his conviction, which is ever manly and the purpose of a representative Commonwealth. On the other hand, it may fail to register the desire of the voter whose financial or other obligation may make it impolitic to thus openly antagonize the candidate he otherwise would with a secret ballot, "that falls as silently as snow-flakes fall upon the sod" and (should) "execute a freeman's will as lightning doth the will of God." This is its mission, the faithful execution of its fiat, the palladium of liberty for all the people. Opposition to the exercise of this right in a representative government is disintegrating by contention and suicidal in success. It has been, and still is, the cause of bitter struggle in our own country. Disregard of the ultimatum of constitutional majorities, the foundation of our system of government, as the cause of the civil war, the past and ever-occurring political corruption in the Northern and the chief factor in the race troubles in the Southern States, where the leaders in this disregard and unlawful action allow the honors and emoluments of office to shut out from their view the constitutional rights of others; and by the criminality of their conduct and subterfuge strive to make selfish might honest right.

That slavery was a poor school to fit men to assume the obligations and duties of an enlightened citizenship should be readily admitted; that its subjects in the Elysium of their joy and thankfulness to their deliverers from servitude to freedom, and in ignorance of the polity of government, should have been easy prey to the unscrupulous is within reason. Still the impartial historian will indite that, for all that dark and bloody night of reconstruction through which they passed, the record of their crime and peculation will "pale its ineffectual rays" before the blistering blasts of official corruption, murder, and lynching that has appalled Christendom since the government of these Southern States has been assumed by their wealth and intelligence. The abnormal conditions that prevailed during reconstruction naturally produced hostility to all who supported Federal authority, among whom the Negro, through force of circumstances, was prominent and most vulnerable for attack, suffered the most physically, and subsequently became easy prey for those who would profit by his disfranchisement.

The attempt to justify this and condone this refusal to allow the colored American exercise of civil and constitutional rights is based on caste, hatred, and alleged ignorance—conditions that are world-wide—and the measure of a people's Christianity and the efficiency of republican institutions can be accurately determined by the humanity and zeal displayed in their amelioration, not in the denial of the right, but zealous tuition for its proper exercise.

During the civil war the national conscience, hitherto sluggish, was awakened and great desire prevailed to award the race the full meed of civil and political rights, both as a measure of justice and recognition of their fealty and bravery in support of the national arm.

The Freedman's Bureau, Christian and other benevolent agencies were inaugurated to fit the freedman for the new obligations. Handicapped as he has been in many endeavors, his record has been inspiring. Four-fifths of the race for generations legally and persistently forbidden to learn to read or write; with labor unrequited, a conservative estimate, in 1898, little more than three decades from slavery, finds 340,000 of their children attending 26,300 schools and their property valuation $750,000,000, while in learned professions, journalism, and mercantile pursuits their ability and efficiency command the respect and praise of the potential race.

When the amendments were being considered, opinion differed as to the bestowal of the franchise; many favored only those who could read and write. The popularity of this phase of opinion was voiced in the following interview with Hon. Schuyler Colfax, afterward Vice President, who was at that time Speaker of the lower house of Congress, and was said to have the "Presidential bee in his bonnet." While "swinging around the circle" he touched at Victoria, and the British Colonist of July 29, 1865, made the following mention: "A committee consisting of Abner Francis and M. W. Gibbs called on Hon. Schuyler Colfax, Speaker of the House of Representatives of the United States, yesterday morning. On being introduced by the American Consul, Mr. Gibbs proceeded to say that they were happy to meet him and tender him on behalf of the colored residents of Victoria their esteem and regard. They were not unacquainted with the noble course he had pursued during the great struggle in behalf of human liberty in the land of their nativity. They had watched with intense interest the progress of the rebellion and rejoiced in the Federal success and sorrowed in its adversity. Now that victory had perched on the national standard—a standard we believe henceforth and forever consecrated to impartial liberty—they were filled with joy unspeakable. And he would allow them to say that it had afforded them the greatest pleasure to observe the alacrity with which the colored men of the nation offered and embraced the opportunity to manifest their devotion and bravery in support of the national cause.

"They had full confidence in the magnanimity of the American people that in the reconstruction of the seceded States they would grant the race who had proved their claim by the most indisputable heroism and fidelity, equality before the law, upon the ground of immutable justice and importance of national safety. Without trespassing further on his valuable time they would only tender him, as the distinguished Speaker of the popular house of Congress, as well as the sterling friend of freedom, their sincere respect and esteem.

"Mr. Colfax, in reply, said he was truly glad to see and meet the committee and felt honored by the interview.

"For himself he had ever been an enemy of slavery. From his earliest recollections he had ever used his influence against it to the extent of his power; but its abolition was environed by so many difficulties that it seemed to require the overruling hand of God to consummate its destruction. And he did not see how it could have been brought about so speedily but for those who desired to perpetuate it by raising rebellious hands against the nation. Now, with regard to the last sentiment expressed, concerning reconstruction, he would say that it was occupying the earnest attention of the best and purest minds of the nation. Most men were in favor of giving the ballot to colored men; the question was to what extent it should be granted. Very many good men were disposed to grant it indiscriminately to the ignorant as well as the more intelligent. For himself he was not, but among the other class. If colored men generally were as intelligent as the gentleman who had honored him with this interview—for he considered the speech he had just listened to among the best he had heard on the coast—there would be no trouble; but slavery had made that impossible. He knew that the President—decidedly an anti-slavery man—was not in favor of bestowing the franchise on all alike, while Charles Sumner and others favored it.

"The honorable gentleman closed his remarks by desiring the colored people not to consider the Administration inimical to their welfare, if in the adjustment the right of suffrage was not bestowed on all, for it was probable that reading and writing would be the qualification demanded. He paid a high tribute to the colored people of Washington, D. C., for their intelligence, moral worth, and industry, and said that it was probable that the problem of suffrage would be solved in the District of Columbia. After a desultory conversation on phases of national status succeeding the rebellion, both parties seeming well pleased with the meeting, the committee retired."

I did not then, nor do I now, agree with the views of that distinguished statesman. The benignity of the ballot lies in this: It was never devised for the protection of the strong, but as a guardian for the weak. It is not true that a sane man, although unlettered, has not a proper conception of his own interests and what will conserve them—what will protect them and give the best results for his labor. You may fool him some of the time, as you do the most astute, but he will be oftener found among those of whom Lincoln said "You could not fool all the time." William Lloyd Garrison, jr., "a worthy son of a noble sire," pointedly says: "Whoever laments the scope of suffrage and talks of disfranchising men on account of ignorance or poverty has as little comprehension of the meaning of self-government as a blind man has of the colors of the rainbow. I declare my belief that we are suffering not from a too extended ballot, but from one too limited and unrepresentative. We enunciate a principle of government, and then deny its practice. If experience has established anything, it is that the interest of one class is never safe in the hands of another. There is no class so poor or ignorant in a Republic that it does not know its own suffering and needs better than the wealthy and educated classes. By the rule of justice it has the same right precisely to give them legal expression. That expression is bound to come, and it is wisest for it to come through the ballot box than through mobs and violence born of a feeling of misery and despair."

James Russell Lowell has said: "The right to vote makes a safety valve of every voter, and the best way to teach a man to vote is to give him a chance to practice. It is cheaper, too, in the long run to lift men up than to hold them down. The ballot in their hands is less dangerous than a sense of wrong in their heads."

Chapter 9

Among the estimable friendships I made on the Pacific Coast forty years ago was Philip A. Bell, formerly of New York City, one of nature's noblemen, broad in his humanity and intellectually great as a journalist. As editor of The Elevator, a weekly newspaper still published in San Francisco, he made its pages brilliant with scintillations of elegance, wealth of learning, and vigor of advocacy. To his request for a correspondent I responded in a series of letters. I forbear to insert them here, as they describe the material and political status of British Columbia thirty-five years ago—being well aware that ancient history is not the most entertaining. But, as I read them I cannot but note, in the jollity of their introduction, the immature criticism, consciousness of human fallibility, broadening of conclusions, mellowed by hope for the future that seemed typical of a life career. Like the horse in "Sheridan's Ride," their beginning "was gay, with Sheridan fifty miles away;" but if they were helpful with a truth-axiom or a moiety of inspiration—as a view of colonial conduct of a nation, with which we were then and are now growing in affinity—the purpose was attained.

At first the affairs of British Columbia and Vancouver were administered by one Governor, the connection was but nominal; Vancouver Island had control by a representative Parliament of its own; the future seemed auspicious. Later they, feeling it "in fra dig" to divide the prestige of government, severed the connection. But Vancouver finding it a rather expensive luxury, and that the separation engendered strife and rivalry, terminating in hostile legislation, determined to permanently unite with British Columbia.

But alas, for political happiness. Many afterward sighed for former times, when Vancouver Island, proud beauty of the North, sat laving her feet in the genial waters of the Pacific, her lap verdant with beautiful foliage and delicious fruits; her head raised with peerless majesty to brilliant skies, while sunbeams playing upon a brow encircled by eternal snows reflected a sheen of glorious splendor; when, conscious of her immense wealth in coal, minerals, and fisheries, her delightful climate and geographical position, she bid for commercial supremacy. It is said of States, as of women, they are "fickle, coy and hard to please." For, changed and governed from England's Downing Street, "with all its red tape circumlocution," "Tile Barncal," incapacity, and "how-not-to-do-it" ability that attached to that venerable institution, its people were sorely perplexed.

During the discussion which the nature and inefficiency of the Government evoked several modes of relief from these embarrassments were warmly espoused, among them none more prominent than annexation to the United States. It was urged with much force that the great want of the country, immigration and responsible government, would find their fulfillment in such an alliance. All that seemed wanted was the "hour and the man." The man was considered present in Leonard McClure, editor of a local, and afterward on the editorial staff of the San Francisco Times. He was a man of rare ability, a terse writer, and with force of logic labored assiduously to promote annexation. But the "hour" was "non est." For while it was quite popular and freely discussed upon the forum and street, influential classes declined to commit themselves to the scheme, the primary step necessary before presentation to the respective Governments. Among the opposition to annexation, naturally, were the official class. These gentry being in no way responsible to the people, an element ever of influence, and believing that by such an alliance they would find their "occupation gone," gave it no quarter. Added to these was another possessed of the prestige and power that wealth confers—very conservative, timid, cautious, self-satisfied, and dreading innovations of popular rule, but especially republicanism. Amid these two classes, and sprinkled among the rank and file, was found a sentiment extremely patriotic, with those who saw nothing worth living for outside of the purview of the "tight little island."

There seems a destiny in the propriety of territory changing dominion. God seems to have given this beautiful earth, with its lands, to be utilized and a source of blessing, not to be locked by the promptings of avarice nor the clog of incapacity; that it should be occupied by those who, either by the accident of locality or superior ability, can make it the most efficient in development. There should be, and usually is, regard for acquired rights, save in the case of Africans, Indians, or other weak peoples, when cupidity and power hold sweet converse. Nor should we slightly estimate the feeling of loyalty to the land of birth and the hearths of our fathers, the impulse that nerves the arm to strike, and the soul to dare; that brings to our country's altar all that we have of life to repel the invader of our homes or the usurper of our liberties. That has given to the world a Washington, a Toussant, a Bozzaris—a loyalty that will ever stand with cloven helmet and crimson battle-ax in the van of civilization and progress. But, like other ennobling sentiments, it can be perverted, allowing it to permeate every view of government, finding its ultimatum in the conclusion that, if government is despotic or inefficient, it is to be endured and not removed. Such patriots are impressed with the conviction that the people were made for governments, and not governments for the people. A celebrated poet has said—

> "Our country's claim is fealty,
> I grant you so; but then
> Before man made us citizens
> Great Nature made us men."

Men with essential wonts and laudable aspirations, the attainment of which can be accelerated by the fostering love and enlightened zeal of a progressive government.

In 1859 at Esquimault, the naval station for British Columbia, I had a pleasant meeting with Lady Franklin, widow of Sir John Franklin, the Arctic explorer, who sailed in 1845 and was supposed to have perished in 1847. With a woman's devotion, after many years of absence, she was still in quest, hoping, from ship officer or seaman of her Majesty's service, some ray of light would yet penetrate the gloom which surrounded his "taking off" in that terra incognito of the North pole, whose attraction for the adventurer in search of scientific and geographical data in the mental world is akin to its magnetic attraction in the physical. To her no tidings came, but still lingered "hope, the balm and life-blood of the soul."

In 1868 the union of British Columbia with the Dominion of Canada was the political issue, absorbing all others. But the allurements of its grandeur and the magnitude of promised results were insufficient to allay opposition, ever encountered on proposal to change a constitutional polity by those at the time enjoying official honors or those who benefit through contracts or trade, and are emphatic in their protest; these, however, constitute an element that is unwittingly the safety valve of constitutional government. Wherever the people rule the public welfare is ever endangered whenever radical changes are to be introduced, unaccompanied with a vigorous opposition. A healthy opposition is the winnowing fan that separates the politician's chaff from the patriot's wheat, presenting the most desirable of the substantial element needed. At the convention in 1868 at Fort Yale, called by A. Decosmos, editor of

The British Colonist, and others, for the purpose of getting an expression of the people of British Columbia regarding union with the Dominion of Canada (and of which the writer was a delegate), the reduction of liabilities, the lessening of taxation, increase of revenue, restriction of expenditure, and the enlargement of the people's liberties were the goal, all of which have been attained since entrance to the Dominion, which has become a bright jewel in his Majesty's Crown, reflecting a civilization, liberal and progressive, of a loyal, happy people.

The "British American Act," which created the Dominion of Canada, differs from the Constitution of the United States in important particulars. It grants to the Dominional, as well as the provincial Legislatures the "want of confidence principle," by which an objectionable ministry can be immediately removed; at the same time centralizing the national authority as a guard against the heresy of "State rights" superiority. Among the terms stipulated, the Dominion was to assume the colonial debt of British Columbia, amounting to over two million dollars; the building of a road from the Atlantic to the Pacific within a stipulated time. The alliance, however, contained more advantage than the ephemeral assistance of making a road or the assumption of a debt, for with confederation came the abolition of the "one-man system of government" and in its place a responsible one, with freedom of action for enterprise, legislation to encourage development, and assist budding industries; the permanent establishment of schools, and the disbursement of revenue in accordance with popular will.

It is ever and ever true that "right is of no sex, and truth of no color." The liberal ideas, ever struggling for utterance and ascendancy under every form of government, are not the exclusive property of any community or nation, but the heritage of mankind, and their victories are ever inspiring. For, as the traveler sometimes ascends the hill to determine his bearings, refresh his vision, and invigorate himself for greater endeavors, so we, by sometimes looking beyond the sphere of our own local activities, obtain higher views of the breadth and magnitude of the principles we cherish, and perceive that freedom's battle is identical wherever waged, whether her sons fight to abolish the relics of feudalism or to possess the ballot, the reflex influence of their example is mutually beneficial.

But of the Dominion of Canada, who shall write its "rise, decline, and fall?" Springing into existence in a day, with a population of 4,000,000 people—a number larger than that possessed by the United States when they commenced their great career—its promise is pregnant with benign probabilities. May it be the fruition of hope that the banner of the Dominion and the flag of our Republic, locked and interlocked, may go forward in generous rivalry to bless mankind.

The most rapid instrumentalities in the development of a new country are the finding and prospecting for mineral deposits. The discovery of large deposits of gold in the quartz and alluvial area of British Columbia in 1858 was the incipiency of the growth and prosperity it now enjoys. But although the search for the precious is alluring, the mining of the grosser metals and minerals, such as iron, lead, coal, and others, are much more reliable for substantial results.

The only mine of importance in British Columbia previous to 1867 was at Naniamo, where there was a large output of bituminous coal. In that year anthracite was discovered by Indians building fire on a broken vein that ran from Mt. Seymour, on Queen Charlotte Island, in the North Pacific. It was a high grade of coal, and on account of its density and burning without flame, was the most valuable for smelting and domestic purposes. A company had been formed at Victoria which had spent $60,000 prospecting for an enduring and paying vein, and thereafter prepared for development by advertising for tenders to build railroad and wharfs for shipping. Being a large shareholder in the company, I resigned as a director and bid. It was not the lowest, but I was awarded the contract. The Hudson Bay Co. steamship Otter, having been chartered January, 1869, with fifty men, comprising surveyor, carpenters, blacksmiths, and laborers, with timber, rails, provisions, and other necessaries for the work I embarked at Victoria. Queen Charlotte Island was at that time almost a "terra incognito," sparsely inhabited solely by scattered tribes of Indians on the coast lines, which were only occasionally visited by her Majesty's ships for discovery and capture of small craft engaged in the whisky trade.

Passing through the Straits of Georgia, stopping at Fort Simpson, and then to Queen Charlotte Island, entering the mouth of Skidegate River, a few miles up, we reached the company's quarters, consisting of several wooden buildings for residence, stores, shops, etc. At the mouth and along the river were several Indian settlements, comprising huts, the sides of which were of rough riven planks, with roof of leaves of a tough, fibrous nature. At the crest was an opening for the escape of smoke from fires built on the ground in the center of the enclosure. As the ship passed slowly up the river we were hailed by the shouting of the

Indians, who ran to the river side, got into their canoes and followed in great numbers until we anchored. They then swarmed around and over the ship, saluting the ship's company as "King George's men," for such the English are known and called by them. They were peaceful and docile, lending ready hands to our landing and afterward to the cargo. I was surprised, while standing on the ship, to hear my name called by an Indian in a canoe at the side, coupled with encomiums of the native variety, quite flattering. It proved to be one who had been a domestic in my family at Victoria. He gave me kind welcome, not to be ignored, remembering that I was in "the enemy's country," so to speak. Besides, such a reception was so much the more desirable, as I was dependent upon native labor for excavating and transportation of heavy material along the line of the road. While their work was not despatched with celerity of trained labor, still, as is general with labor, they earned all they got. "One touch of nature makes the whole world kin." I found many apt, some stupid; honesty and dishonesty in usual quantities, with craft peculiar to savage life.

Their mode of stealing by stages was peculiar. The thing coveted was first hid nearby; if no inquiry was made for a period deemed sufficiently long the change of ownership became complete and its removal to their own hut followed, to be disposed of when opportunity offered. If you had a particle of evidence and made a positive accusation, with the threat of "King George's man-of-war," it was likely to be forthcoming by being placed secretly nearby its proper place. But through it we see the oneness of human frailty, whether in the watered stock of the corporation or that of its humble servitor the milkman, there is kinship. To get something for nothing is the "ignis fatuus" ever in the lead. My experience during a year's stay on the island, and constant intercourse with the natives, impressed me more and more with the conviction that we are all mainly the creatures of environments; yet through all the strata and fiber of human nature there is a chord that beats responsive to kindness—a "language that the dumb can speak, and that the deaf can understand."

The English mode of dealing with semi-civilized dependents is vastly different from ours. While vigorously administering the law for proper government, protection of life, and suppression of debauchery by unscrupulous traders, they inspired respect for the laws and the love of their patrons. Uprisings and massacres among Indians in her Majesty's dominions are seldom, if ever, to be chronicled. Many of our Indian wars will remain a blot on the page of impartial history, superinduced, as they were, by wanton murder or the covet of lands held by them by sacred treaties, which should have been as sacredly inviolate. Followed by decimation of tribes by toleration of the whisky trade and the conveyance of loathsome disease. The climate of the island was much more pleasant than expected. The warm ocean currents on the Pacific temper the atmosphere, rendering it more genial than the same degree of latitude on the Atlantic. A few inches of snow, a thin coat of ice on the river, were the usual attendants of winter. But more frequently our camp was overhung by heavy clouds, broken by Mt. Seymour, precipitating much rain.

After being domiciled we proceeded with the resident superintendent to view the company's property, comprising several thousand acres. Rising in altitude, and on different levels, as we approached Mt. Seymour, croppings of coal were quite frequent, the broken and scattered veins evidencing volcanic disturbance. The vein most promising was several hundred feet above the level of the sea, and our intended wharf survey was made, which showed heavy cuttings and blasting to obtain grade for the road. The work was pushed with all the vigor the isolated locality and climatic conditions allowed. Rain almost incessant was a great impediment, as well as were the occasional strikes of the Indian labor, which was never for more wages, but for more time. The coal from the croppings which had been at first obtained for testing, had been carried by them in bags, giving them in the "coin of the realm" so many pieces of tobacco for each bag delivered on the ship. There was plenty of time lying around on those trips, and they took it. On the advent of the new era they complained that "King George men" took all the time and gave them none, so they frequently quit to go in quest. The nativity of my skilled labor was a piece of national patchwork—a composite of the canny Scotch, the persistent and witty Irish, the conservative but indomitable English, the effervescent French, the phlegmatic German, and the irascible Italian. I found this variety beneficial, for the usual national and race bias was sufficiently in evidence to preclude a combination to retard the work. I had three Americans, that were neither white nor colored; they were born black; one of them—Tambry, the cook—will ever have my grateful remembrance for his fatherly kindness and attention during an illness.

The conditions there were such that threw many of my men off their feet. Women and liquor had much the "right of way." I was more than ever impressed with the belief that there was nothing so conclusive to a worthy manhood as self-restraint, both morally and physically, and the more vicious and unrestraining the environment the greater the achievement. Miners had been at work placing many tons of coal at the mouth of the mine during the making of the road, the grade of which was of two elevations, one from the mine a third of the distance, terminating at a chute, from which the coal fell to cars on the lower level, and from thence to the wharf. After the completion of the road and its acceptance by the superintendent and the storage of a cargo of coal on the wharf, the steamer Otter arrived, was loaded, and despatched to San Francisco, being the first cargo of anthracite coal ever unearthed on the Pacific seaboard. The superintendent, having notified the directors at Victoria of his intention to return, they had appointed me to assume the office. I was so engaged, preparing for the next shipment on the steamer.

Chapter 10

My sojourn on the island was not without its vicissitudes and dangers, and one of the latter I shall ever remember—one mingled, as it was, with antics of Neptune, that capricious god of the ocean, and resignation to what seemed to promise my end with all sublime things. The stock of oil brought for lubricating cars and machinery having been exhausted, I started a beautiful morning in a canoe with three Indians for their settlement at the mouth of Skidegate River for a temporary supply. After a few hours' paddling, gliding down the river serenely, the wind suddenly arose, increasing in force as we approached the mouth in the gulf. The high walls of the river sides afforded no opportunity to land. The storm continued to increase in violence, bringing billows of rough sea from the ocean, our canoe dancing like a feather, one moment on a high crest by its skyward leap, and in the next to an abyss deep, with walls of sea on either side, shutting out a view of the horizon, while I, breathless with anxious hope, waited for the succeeding wave to again lift the frail bark. The better to preserve the equilibrium of the canoe—a conveyance treacherous at the best—wrapped in a blanket in the bottom of the canoe I laid, looking into the faces of the Indians, contorted by fright, and listened to their peculiar and mournful death wail, "while the gale whistled aloft his tempest tune."

I afterward learned that they had a superstition based upon the loss of many of their tribe under like conditions, that escape was impossible. The alarm and distrust in men, aquatic from birth, in their own waters was to me appalling. I seemed to have "looked death in the face"—and what a rush of recollections that had been long forgotten, of actions good and bad, the latter seeming the most, hurried, serried, but distinct through my excited brain; then a thought, bringing a calm content, that "To every man upon this earth death cometh soon or late;" and with a fervent resignation of myself to God and to what I believed to be inevitable; then a lull in the wind, and, after many attempts, we were able to cross the mouth of the river to the other side—the place of destination.

In 1869 I left Queen Charlotte Island and returned to Victoria; settled my business preparatory to joining my family, then at Oberlin, Ohio. It was not without a measure of regret that I anticipated my departure. There I had lived more than a decade; where the geniality of the climate was excelled only by the graciousness of the people;

there unreservedly the fraternal grasp of brotherhood; there I had received social and political recognition; there my domestic ties had been intensified by the birth of my children, a warp and woof of consciousness that time cannot obliterate. Then regret modified, as love of home and country asserted itself.

> *"Breathes there a man with soul so dead*
> *Who never to himself hath said:*
> *'This is my native land'—*
> *Whose heart has not within him burned*
> *As homeward footsteps he has turned*
> *From wandering on a foreign strand?"*

En route my feelings were peculiar. A decade had passed, fraught with momentous results in the history of the nation. I had left California disfranchised and my oath denied in a "court of justice" (?); left my country to all appearances enveloped in a moral gloom so dense as to shut out the light of promise for a better civil and political status. The star of hope glimmered but feebly above the horizon of contumely and oppression, prophetic of the destruction of slavery and the enfranchisement of the freedman. I was returning, and on touch of my country's soil to have a new baptism through the all-pervading genius of universal liberty. I had left politically ignoble; I was returning panoplied with the nobility of an American citizen. Hitherto regarded as a pariah, I had neither rejoiced at its achievement nor sorrowed for its adversity; now every patriotic pulse beat quicker and heart throb warmer, on realization that my country gave constitutional guarantee for the common enjoyment of political and civil liberty, equality before the law—inspiring a dignity of manhood, of self-reliance and opportunity for elevation hitherto unknown.

Then doubt, alternating, would present the immense problems awaiting popular solution. Born in the seething cauldron of civil war, they had been met in the arena of fervid Congressional debate and political conflict. The amendments to the Constitution had been passed, but was their inscription a record of the crystallization of public sentiment? Subsequent events have fully shown that only to the magnanimity and justice of the American people and the fruition of time can they be commended. Not to believe that these problems will be rightfully solved is to doubt not only the efficacy of the basic principles of our Government, but the divinity of truth and justice. To these rounds of hope's ladder, while eager in obtaining wisdom, the Negro should cling with tenacity, with faith "a higher faculty than reason" unconquerable.

Having resolved to locate in some part of the South for the purpose of practicing law, I had while in Victoria read the English Common Law, the basis of our country's jurisprudence, under Mr. Ring, an English barrister. Soon after my arrival in Oberlin, Ohio, where my family, four years before, had preceded me, I entered the law department of an Oberlin business college, and after graduation proceeded South, the first time since emancipation. In an early chapter I described my first contact with and impressions of slavery, when a lad; then the hopelessness of abject servitude and consciousness of unrequited toil had its impress on the brow of the laborer. Now cheerfulness, a spirit of industry, enterprise, and fraternal feeling replaced the stagnant humdrum of slavery. Nor was progress observable only among the freedmen. Many evidences of kindness and sympathy were shown and expressed by former owners for the moral and mental advancement of their former bondsmen, which, to a great degree, unfortunately, was counterbalanced by violence and persecution.

My brother, Jonathan C. Gibbs, was then Secretary of State of Florida, with Governor Hart as executive. He had had the benefit of a collegiate education, having graduated at Dartmouth, New Haven, and had for some years filled the pulpit as a Presbyterian minister. The stress of reconstruction and obvious necessity for ability in secular matters induced him to enter official life. Naturally indomitable, he more than fulfilled the expectations of his friends and supporters by rare ability as a thinker and speaker, with unflinching fidelity to his party principles. I found him at Tallahassee, the capital, in a well-appointed residence, but his sleeping place in the attic contracted, and, as I perceived, considerable of an arsenal. He said that for better vantage it had been his resting place for several months, as his life had been threatened by the "Ku Klux," that band of midnight assassins whose deeds of blood and carnage darken so many pages of our national history, and was the constant terror of white and black adherents to the national Government's policy of enfranchisement. He was hopeful of better conditions in Florida, and introduced me to Governor Hart. Both urged me to locate in the State, promising me their support. I highly appreciated the affection of the one and the proffered friendship of the other. But the feeling paramount was that my brother had "won his spurs" by assiduity and fidelity through the scathing and fiery ordeal of those troublesome times; that it would ill become me to profit or serenely rest beneath the laurels he had won. It was the last interview or sight of my brother. Subsequently after a three hours' speech, he went to his office and suddenly died of apoplexy.

I continued my tour of observation, and, having been appointed a delegate from Ohio to a national convention to be held in Charleston, South Carolina, I attended. It was the first assembly of the kind at which I had been present since emancipation. I had hitherto met many conventions of colored men having for their object the amelioration of oppressive conditions. This gathering was unlike any similar meeting. The deliberations of the convention presented a combination of a strong intellectual grasp of present needs and their solution, with much uninformed groping and strife for prominence, features of procedure I have observed not confined to Negro assemblies.

The majority were unlettered, but earnest in their mental toiling for protection to life and equality before the law. Hitherto the purpose had been to make earnest appeals to the law-making power for such legislation as would abolish slavery and award equal justice—the first supported by the national conscience, but mainly as a military necessity, was a "fait accompli;" the other had been legislatively awarded, but for its realization much more was necessary than its simple identification on the statute books of a nation, when public sentiment is law. More than a third of a century has now passed, enabling a view more dispassionate and accurate of the conditions surrounding the freedmen directly after emancipation and the instrumentalities designed for fitting him for citizenship.

It is not surprising, neither is he blameworthy, if in the incipiency of joy for freedom bestowed he could not properly estimate the factors necessary to form an homogenous citizenship. The ways for two centuries had been divergent paths. The dominant claiming and exercising, as an heirloom, every civil and political right; the subordinate, with knowledge the most meager of their application or limits, by compulsion was made to concede the claim. Neither is it singular that participation in the exercise of these rights by the freedman should have created a determined opposition in a majority of the former, who claimed their fitness to rule as the embodiment of the wealth and intelligence (which are generally the ruling factors world-wide), and would have at an early date derived a just "power from the consent of the governed," did not history record the unnecessary and inhuman means resorted to to extort it, the obliquity of which can be erased only by according him the rights of an American citizen. Mutual hostility, opposition on the one hand to the assumption and exercise of these rights, and consequent distrust by the freedman, often fostered by unscrupulous leaders, have been alike detrimental to both classes, but especially so to the Negro, for his constant need in the Southland is the cordial friendship and helping hand of "his brother in white." He deserves it for his century of unrequited labor in peace and in war for fidelity to the tender ties committed to his care. Anti-revolutionist in his nature, he will continue to merit it and possibly save the industrial life in the South in the coming conflict of capital and labor.

That, as a class, they are in antagonism to the prevailing political sentiment is the legitimate result of the manner of their emancipation and a commendable gratitude and kinship for the party through which they obtained their freedom. But Gibbon, in his "Decline and Fall of Rome," has said that "gratitude is expensive," and so the Negro has found it, and is beginning to echo the sentiment and would gladly hail conditions and opportunity where he could, after thirty-five years of blood and fidelity, be less partisan and more fraternal politically, conscious his united affiliation with his early alliance, and consequent ostracism of the opposition has given him a "hard road to travel." Commendable as has been his devotion, he finds commendation a limited currency and not negotiable for the protection and benefits that should accompany the paladium of citizenship. While his treatment by the Democratic party has made a continuous political relation compulsory, it is unfortunate; for the political affinity of no other class of American citizens is judged by the accident of birth. It is detrimental to the voter whose proclivity is thereby determined. Wherever the Negro vote, in the estimation of any party, is an uncertain quantity, its value as a factor will have increased, consolidated, and in numbers controlling, it has been considered a menace and vigorously eliminated.

This view has to an extent an auxiliary in certain Republican circles, where it is avowed that the party could get in the South a large accession of hitherto Democratic voters, giving it a commanding influence, but for its colored contingent, which is averred to be repellant. There may be difference of opinion as to the merit of such conclusions and the fitness of their rehearsal "to the marines;" but none as to the measure of welcome of those that hold them. However, given that they are correct. Self-respect and a desire to help the old party can go hand in hand, and when possible in a manly way, room should be made for such anticipated accession.

There is another phase of present conditions that deserves, and I have no doubt has claimed, attention. It is the emphatic trend of the national leaders of the party to conciliate the hitherto discordant elements in the South in the interest of national harmony, an object lesson of which was presented by the late President on his Southern tour. But few years have elapsed since no man seeking a renomination on the Republican ticket would have put on and worn a Confederate badge. This President McKinley did, receiving the indiscriminate applause and the concurrence of his own party. Such an act, which is not only allowable, but commendable, would formerly have been political suicide. This being a movement in the house of his political alliance, it is up to the Negro to consider which is his best interest, should the olive branch of political friendship be extended by those from whom he receives his chief support. Under like conditions, his white brother would have no hesitancy.

There is yet another phase which indicates the Negro in jeopardy on industrial lines. A few years hence the South will have ceased to be chiefly agricultural. Mills for cotton, iron, and other factories will have dotted hilltop and valley, and with them will come the Northern operative with his exclusive "unions" and trade prejudice, shutting the doors of mills and foundries against him. To meet this scramble for favor from the wealth and intelligence of the Southland—the ruling factors— he should avail himself of every appliance for fostering harmony and co-operation along all the lines of contact. In slavery and in his subsequent journey in freedom he has suffered much. But what nation or people have escaped that ordeal who have made mark in the world's history? There is now prospective unfriendly legislation in several Southern States; also the lowest of the whites, as they deem occasion may require, go, often undisturbed, on shooting and lynching expeditions.

The problem that continues to force itself for solution is, How the innocent are to receive immunity from these outrages or a fair trial, when accused of crime. These being under the purview of State sovereignty, the Federal arm is not only powerless, but there exists no Northern sentiment favoring drastic means for their correction. Hence it is evident that relief can only come from those who fashion the sentiment that crystallizes into law. But with the bitter is mingled the sweet; much of his advancement along educational and material lines is due to the liberality of the white people of the South, who, it has been computed, have contributed one hundred millions of dollars since emancipation by taxes and donations for his education, and there are many evidences that the best thought of the South is in line with Negro employment and his educational advancement in the belief that the more general the intelligence the greater the State's progress, morally and materially. This conviction was emphatically expressed by an overwhelming negative vote in the Arkansas Legislature recently, where a measure was introduced to abandon him to his own taxable resources for education. The ratio of his moral and material product will be the measure of his gratitude for this great boon. For, after all, many of "our great dangers are not from without."

General ——, a leading Democrat of this State, and an unmistakable friend of the negro, referring to the above evidence of good feeling, said he did not see why I, and other reputed leaders, in view of such evidences of friendship, did not induce our people to be fraternal politically. I replied that the effort had once been made, but that the Democratic party, intrenched as it was in large majorities in the South, "by ways that are dark and tricks that are vain," its leaders say they "do not need, neither do they solicit, the colored vote; but if they choose, they may so vote." He said that certainly had a ringing sound of independence and was uninviting as an announcement—an independence, however, that will not forever outlive the vagaries of sound, for it is not unlikely that he will not only vote the ticket, but be earnestly solicited to do so. "For it will happen, during the whirligig of time and action, in my party as well as others, that there will be a change of policies, new issues, local dissatisfaction, friction, contemplated antagonism and the political arithmetic sounded. But I cannot but believe that the clannishness of the Negro has been the boomerang that has knocked him out of much sympathy, being impractical as a political factor and out of harmony with the material policies of the Southern people."

I replied I had thought the highest ideal of patriotism was adherence to measures materially as well as politically that were for the benefit of the whole people.

He said: "I know your party preach that they have a monopoly of wisdom; but the fact is the wisest statesmen of the world are divided in opinion as to the benefits claimed for the leading policies of your party. But how do they benefit you, as a dependent class? Your immediate need is employment and good educational facilities. You should be less sentimental and more practical. You may honestly believe in a protective tariff, having for its object the protection of the American working-man, but does it help you when you know that the doors of mills, foundries, and manufactories are shut against you? As to the currency, you are at a disadvantage when you attempt to antagonize the financial views of your employers.

"It reminds me of an incident," he continued, "in my native town in Virginia, not long after reconstruction. There had been a drought and short crop, succeeded by a pretty hard winter. My father, whose politics, you may well judge, I being 'a chip of the old block,' without soliciting money or favor, threw open his cellar, wherein was stowed many bushels of sweet potatoes; invited all the destitute to come. It is needless to say they came. In the spring Tobey, the Negro minister of the Baptist Church—a man illiterate, but with much native sense—after morning service, said: 'Brethren, there's gwine to be a 'lection here next week, and I wants you all to vote in de light dat God has gin you to see de light, but I spects to vote wid de taters.' Now, this may seem ludicrous, but Tobey, in that act, was a fit representative of the white man in politics—for every class of American citizens except the Negro divide their vote and put it where to them personally it will do the most good."

"Much," I replied, "that you have said is undoubtedly true. But can you wonder at the Negro's cohesion? Is it not a fact that his is the only class of citizens that your party deny equal participation in the franchise, and unjustly discriminate against in the application of the laws? Where better could a change of conduct which you would admire and he so happily embrace, be inaugurated than within your own political household; where could nobility of character be more grandly displayed than by the abolition of these vicious hindrances to the uplifting of the weak and lowly?"

"Be that as it may," he replied, "your race is not in a condition to make friends by opposing the prevailing local policies of their environments."

I have narrated this interview for the reason that it is a fitting type of the views of friends of the Negro of the South who somehow fail to see the difficulty in his fraternizing with them in the midst of so much political persecution and bodily outrage. I referred in the above interview to an effort of colored leaders to assimilate with Southern politics.

Chapter 11

In 1876 (twenty-five years ago) I was President of a National Convention held at Nashville, Tenn, and of which H. V. Redfield, an able correspondent of the "Cincinnati Commercial," made the following unduly flattering mention: "Mifflin W. Gibbs, of Arkansas, was selected as President. It may be interesting to know that Gibbs is strongly in favor of Bristoe, now an aspirant for the Presidency. He will likely be a delegate from Arkansas to the National Republican Convention at Cincinnati. He is a lawyer, one of the foremost of his race in Arkansas. He is rather slender and a genteel-looking man, with something in his features that denotes superiority" ("Though poor in thanks," Redfield, yet I thank thee.) "His speech upon taking the chair, was another event. It was the third good speech of the day and calculated to leave the believers of internal inferiority in something of a muddle.

"He made a manly plea for equal rights for his race. All they wanted was an equal chance in the battle of life. They did not desire to hinder any man for exercising his political rights as he saw fit, and all they claimed was liberty of thought and action for themselves. He was sorry there was occasion for a convention of black men to consider black men's status. The fact alone was evidence that the race had not been accorded right and justice. Of the treatment of his race in Arkansas he had little to complain of, but spoke bitterly of the murders at Vicksburg, Miss. He gave the Republican party, as administered at Washington, several blows under the chin. He complained of bad treatment of colored men by that party, notwithstanding all its professions. He made the bold declaration that all the whites of the South need do to get their votes was to promise equal and exact justice and stand to it. All they wanted was their rights as American citizens and would go into the party that would secure them. He said the question primarily demanding the attention of the convention were educational and political, and he hoped the proceedings would be so orderly as to convince the whites present that we were capable of self-control. His speech had a highly independent flavor and the particular independent passages were applauded by whites and blacks alike."

While the call for the convention was not distinctly political, that feature of the proceedings was the most pronounced. For at that early day, through an experience the most bitter, the lesson had been learned that politics was not the panacea, but that our affiliation with the Republican party was the main offence. Hence a disposition to fraternize with Southern politicians for race protection and opportunity had many adherents, and voiced by Governor Pinchback and other prominent leaders in the South, who, while preferring to maintain their fealty to the Republican party, were willing to sacrifice that allegiance if they could secure protection and improve conditions for the race. Had the leaders of Southern opinion met these overtures, even part of the way, much of the friction and turbulence of subsequent years would have been avoided. But that there will be a breaking up of the political solidarity of the South, not on sentimental but on material lines, at no distant day all signs promise, and be its status what it may, the Negro will benefit by commingling with the respective parties in political fellowship. Laying down the "old grudge" at the door of opportunity and entering, should the premises be habitable, he could "report progress and ask leave to sit again."

It has been alleged to the discredit of the Negro that he too soon forgets an injury. Nevertheless as a virtue it should redound to his credit. He is swift to forgive and, if necessary, apologize for the shortcomings of his adversary. But human nature seldom appreciates forgiveness, preceded as it is by censure, the subject of which usually repels, and another melancholy phase is often apparent, for the pricks of conscience for those we have wronged, we seek solace by hating. There are in both parties a fraction of saints, who, notwithstanding his immense contribution by unrequited labor to the wealth of the nation whilst a slave; his fidelity and bravery in every war of the Republic, have for him neither care nor regard; denounce him as an incapable and a bad legacy. He should, nevertheless, be patient, diligent, and hopeful, with appreciation for his friends and for his enemies a consciousness expressed in the Irishman's toast to the Englishman—

> "Here's to you, as good as you are;
> And here's to me, as bad as I am;
> But as good as you are,
> And as bad as I am,
> I'm as good as you are,
> As bad as I am."

Very ill considered is the opinion held and advocated by some, that he should defer or eschew politics—who say: "Let the Negro be deprived of this right of citizenship until he learns how to exercise it with wisdom and discretion." As well say to the boy, Do not go into the water until you learn to swim! The highest type of civilization is the evolution of mistakes. While education, business, and skilled labor should have the right of way and be primarily cherished, his right to vote and persistent desire to exercise it should never be abandoned, for he will yet enjoy its fullest fruition all over this, our God-blessed land.

Among the delegates I met at the South Carolina convention in 1871 were the Hon. William H. Grey, H. B. Robinson, and J. H. Johnson, of Arkansas, prominent planters and leaders in that State. I was much impressed with the eloquence of Grey, and the practical ideas advanced by Robinson, the one charmed, the other convinced. Learning that I sought a desirable place to locate in the South, they were enthusiastic in describing the advantages held out by the State of Arkansas. The comparative infancy of its development, its golden prospects, and fraternal amenities. Crossing the Arkansas River in a ferry-boat, in May, 1871, I arrived in Little Rock a stranger to every inhabitant. It was on a Sunday morning. The air refreshing, the sun not yet fervent, a cloudless sky canopied the city; the carol of the canary and mocking bird from treetop and cage was all that entered a peaceful, restful quiet that bespoke a well-governed city. The chiming church bells that soon after summoned worshipers seemed to bid me welcome. The high and humble, in their best attire, wended their way to the respective places of worship.

Little Rock at that date, not unlike most Western cities in their infancy, and bid for immigration, was extensively laid out, but thinly populated, having less than 12,000 inhabitants. From river front to Twelfth Street, on the south, and to Chester on the west, it was but sparsely settled. The streets were unimproved, but the gradual rise from river front gave a natural drainage. Residences and gardens of the more prominent, on the outskirts, gave token of culture and refinement. The nom de plume "City of Roses" seemed fittingly bestowed, for with trellis or encircling with shady bower, the stately doorway of the wealthy, or the cabin of the lowly could be seen the rose, the honeysuckle, or other verdure of perfume and beauty, imparting a grateful fragrance, while "every prospect pleases." My first impressions have not been lessened by lapse of time; generous nature has enabled human appliance to make Little Rock an ideal city.

As knowledge of the local status of a State, as well as common law, must precede admission to the bar, I applied and was kindly permitted to enter the law office of Benjamin & Barnes, at that time the only building on the square now occupied by the post office and the Allis Block. In this for preparatory reading I was very fortunate. I not only found an extensive law library, but the kindness and special interest shown by Sidney M. Barnes was of incalculable benefit. Mr. Barnes was an able jurist, one of nature's noblemen, genial, generous, and patriotic. A wealthy slaveholder in Kentucky, when the note of civil war was sounded, called together his slaves, gave them their freedom, and at an early date had them enrolled in the Federal army, and went forth himself to fight for the Union. James K. Barnes, his son, now a prominent citizen of Fort Smith, and the able United States Attorney for the Western district of Arkansas, and whose fellowship and kindness has extended through all my political career in Arkansas, is "a worthy son of a noble sire," having courage of conviction and eloquence in their enunciation. Among the young men then practicing law was Lloyd G. Wheeler, a graduate from a law school in Chicago, popular and an able lawyer, with considerable practice. In 1872 we joined, under the firm name of Wheeler & Gibbs, opening an office in the Old Bank Building, corner Center and Markam Streets.

It is not without considerable trepidation that an infant limb of the law shies his castor into the ring, puts up his shingle announcing that A, B, or C is an "Attorney and Counsellor at Law." His cerebral column stiffens as, from day to day, he meets members of the bar, who congratulate him upon his advent, and feels his importance as he waits from day to day for the visit of his first client, but collapses when he arrives and with ghostly dread salutes him and prepares to listen with a disturbed sense of an awful responsibility he is about to undertake. For, side by side with his client's statements there seem to appear in stately majesty all the adjuncts of the law: First, the inquisitive glance of the judge, like a judicial searchlight, scans him as he rises to defend Mr. Only Borrow, charged with larceny. Will he be able to think on his feet at the bar as he did in his chair in his office? Will he succeed or fail in stating his case, with eye and ear of every veteran of the bar intent on his first utterance? How about the jury, that unknown quantity of capricious predilections? Will they give him attention, or will their eyes find a more congenial resting place? Unbidden, the panorama insists on prominence. He attempts the most nonchalant air, tells Mr. B.

to proceed and state his case. This was not the first time that he had been requested to perform this incipient step of the law's demand, and he does it with such astuteness and flippancy, and how he had been wronged and persecuted by the plaintiff, that tears, unbidden, are ready to glisten in your eyes. Injured innocence and your sworn duty to your profession inspire courage and induce you to take his case. Later on the tyro will have learned that it was highly probable that Mr. B. would not have called on him but for the fact that he was not only out of cash, but out of credit with able and experienced practitioners.

At the time of my examination for entry to the bar by the committee, of which William G. Whipple was one, I was instructed that the most important acquisition for a member of the bar was ability to secure his fee. Having noted all the points of defence for his honesty, the last, but not the least matter to be considered was the fee, resulting in an exchange of promises and his departure. When the case was called, for reasons not divulged, the plaintiff failed to appear. Mr. Borrow was acquitted; I won my case and am still wooing my fee. The study of the law is not solely of advantage to those who intend adopting it as a profession, for its fundamental principles are interwoven with the best needs of mankind in all his undertakings, making it of value to the preacher or laymen, the merchant or politician. For the young man intending the pursuit of the latter it is quite indispensable. The condition in the South for a quarter of a century giving opportunity for colored men to engage in the professions has not been neglected. In each of the States there are physicians and lawyers practicing with more or less success. With equality of standing as to culture, ability and devotion, the doctor has had the advantage for a growing and lucrative practice. This can be accounted for partly on account of the private administrations of the one and the public career of the other. The physicians has seldom contact with his professional brother in white and escapes much of the difficulty that lies in wait for the colored disciple of Blackstone.

During my practice I found the judges eminently fair in summing up the evidence produced, noting the points and impartially charging the jurors, who were also fair when plaintiff and defendant were of the same race, but who, alas, too often, when the case had been argued by, or the issue was between the representatives of the two races, bowed to the prevailing bias in their verdict. Bishop, in his introduction to his "Criminal Law," has fittingly said: "The responsibilities which devolve on judicial tribunals are admitted. But a judge sitting in court is under no higher obligation to cast aside personal motives and his likes and dislikes of the parties litigant, and to spurn the bribe if proffered than any other official person acting under a jurisdiction to enforce laws not judicial. Happy will be the day when public virtue exists otherwise than in name." It often happens with cases commanding liberal fees and where the litigant has high regard for the legal learning and ability of the colored lawyer, yet conscious of this hindrance to a successful issue of his case, very naturally goes elsewhere for legal assistance. Hence, as an advocate not having inducement for continued research and opportunity for application of the more intricate elements of the law, confined to petty cases with corresponding fee, he is handicapped in his effort to attain eminence as a jurist. It has been said that great men create circumstances. But circumstances unavoidably produce great men. Henry Drummond is quoted as saying: "No matter what its possibilities may be, no matter what seeds of thought or virtue lie latent in its breast, until the appropriate environment presents itself, the correspondence is denied, the development discouraged, the most splendid possibilities of life remain unrealized, and thought and virtue, genius and art, are dead."

It should be the solemn and persistent duty of the race to contend for every right the Magna Charta of the Republic has granted them, but it might assuage the pang of deprivation and stimulate opportunity did he fully know the stages of savagery, slavery, and oceans of blood through which the Anglo-Saxon passed to attain the exalted position he now occupies. Much of the jurisprudence we now have responding to and crystallizing the best needs of humanity were garnered in this sanguine and checkered career. It is said that the law is a jealous mistress, demanding intense and entire devotion and unceasing wooing to succeed in winning her favor, or profiting by her decrees. Yet, for student or layman, the study is instructive and ennobling. It is an epitome of ages of human conduct, the products, the yearnings, and strivings of the human heart, as higher conceptions of man's relation to his fellow found echo or inscription in either the common or written law. Locality, nationality, race, sex, religion, or social manner may differ, but the accord of desire for civil liberty—the "torch lit up in the soul by the omnipotent hand of Deity itself"—is ever the same. Constitutional law "was not attained by sudden flight," but it is the product of reform, with success and restraint alternating through generations. It is the ripeness of a thousand years of ever-recurring tillage, blushing its scarlet rays of blood and conquest ante-dating historic "Runny Meade."

It is well to occasionally have such reminiscent thought; it makes us less pessimistic and gives life to strive and spirit and hope. We cannot unmake human nature, but can certainly improve conditions by self-denial, earnest thought, and wise action.

Chapter 12

Previous to my resolve to settle in the South I had read and learned much of politics and politicians; the first as being environed by abnormal conditions unstable and disquieting—the class that had established and controlled the economy of the Southern States; had been deposed in the wage of sanguinary battle on many well contested fields—deposed by an opponent equally brave, and of unlimited resources; defeated, but unsubdued in the strength of conviction in the rightfulness of their cause. A submission of the hand but not of the heart. New constitutions granting all born beneath the flag equality of citizenship and laws in unison adopted, and new officers alien to local feeling were the executors.

It is unnecessary here to remark that if a succession of love feasts had been anticipated, they had been indefinitely postponed.

For the officers of the new system were by their whilom predecessors ordered to go "nor stand upon the order of their going," the bullet at times conveying the order. Assassinations, lynchings, and reprisals by both parties to the feud were of daily occurrence. The future for life, liberty, and pursuit of happiness in busy city or sylvan grove, was not alluring. My subsequent career makes it necessary for me to arise to explain. Taking at the time a calm survey of the situation, an addition to the column of martyrs seemed to me unnecessary. I believed in the principles of the Republican party and as a private I was willing to vote, work, and be slightly crippled; but had not reached the bleeding and dying point. With such conclusions I resolved to come, and confine myself to the pursuit of my profession and give politics a "terrible letting alone." Oh, if abandoned resolutions were a marketable commodity, what emporium sufficiently capacious and who competent to classify!

The organization of the Republican party of Arkansas was on the eve of disruption. Its headquarters were in the building and over the law office of Benjamin & Barnes, with whom I was reading. Violent disputes as to party policy, leadership, and the distribution of the plums of office were of frequent occurrence. I very distinctly remember the day when the climax was reached and "the parting of the ways" determined. The adherents of Senator Clayton and the State administration on the one part, and Joseph Brooks and his followers on the other, coming down the stairs—some with compressed lip and flashing eye, others as petulant as the children who say: "I don't want to play in your yard; I don't like you any more." It was the beginning of the overt act that extinguished Republican rule in Arkansas. The factions led by Powell Clayton and Joseph Brooks, respectively, were known as the "Minstrels" and "Brindle Tails."

Incongruity, being the prevailing force, possibly accounted for the contrary character of the names, for there was little euphony in the minstrelsy of the one or a monopoly of brindle appearance in the other, for each faction's contingent, were about equally spotted with the sons of Ham. My friends, Benjamin & Barnes, were prominent as Brindles, and I, being to an extent a novice in the politics of the State, in a position to hear much of the wickedness of the Minstrels and but little of the "piper's lay" in his own behalf, fidelity to my friends, appalled at the alleged infamy of the other fellows, susceptible to encomiums which flattered ambition, I became a Brindle, and an active politician minus a lawyer.

In 1873 I was appointed County Attorney for Pulaski, and after a few months' service resigned to assume the office of Municipal Judge of the City of Little Rock, to which I had been elected. I highly appreciated this, as exceedingly complimentary from a population of 16,000, a large majority of which were not of my race. I entered upon and performed the duties of the office until some time after the culmination of the Brooks and Baxter war in the State. It having been announced that I was the first of my race elected to such an office in the United States, it was not without trepidation that I assumed the duties that the confidence of my fellow citizens had imposed upon me for the novelty of such an administration attracted attention.

A judge who has to deal with and inflict penalties for violation of law consequent upon the frailties and vices of mankind encounters much to soften or harden his humanity, which may have remained normal but for such contact. His sworn duty to administer the law as he finds it often conflicts with a sense of justice implanted in the human soul, of which the law, imperfect man has devised is often the imperfect vehicle for his guidance; but nevertheless to which his allegiance must be paramount, even when attempting to temper justice with mercy.

Nowhere is so plainly presented as many of the various lights and shadows of human character. Love and faithlessness, sincerity and deceit, nobility and dishonor, kindness and ingratitude, morality and vice—all the virtues and their antitheses take their place at the bar of the court of justice and await the verdict, while truth and deception strive for conquest; an honest son of toil arrested in a den of infamy whither he has been decoyed and his week's earnings filched; his wife in tears before you; the clash of prejudice when the parties litigant were of opposite races; the favorable expectation of the rich, prominent, and influential when confronted by the poor and lowly; humble and conscientious innocence appalled when rigid law would mulct them in fine and imprisonment; the high and the haughty incensed at discharge of the obscure and indigent. In cases slight, where the justice of leniency was apparent and yet the mandates of the law had to be enforced, I would pronounce the penalty and suspend the fine during good behavior. But if the culprit returned, mercy was absent.

An incident in relation to the suspension of the fine will show that I did to others as I would have others do to me: A member of the court was at times irritable and vexatious. During a session there was a misunderstanding, which, upon adjournment, growing in intensity, resulted in my committing an assault. The chasm, however, was soon bridged with mutual pledges. Nevertheless I requested the chief of police to have charge entered upon docket, to come up at next session of court, whereupon the judge, after expressing regret that the law had been violated, fined Citizen Gibbs and suspended the fine during good behavior, and, as the citizen was not again arraigned, it may be presumed that his conduct was reasonably good, however doubtful may be the presumption.

I was fortunate in having the confidence of the community, always an important adjunct to the bench, for it is not always that the executor of the law has to deal with the humble of no repute. An old resident, wealthy and prominent, was arrested and was to appear before me for trial. During the interim it was several times suggested to me in a friendly way that I had better give the case a letting alone by dismissal, as it would probably be personally dangerous to enforce the law, as he was known to be impulsive and at times violent. I heard the case, which had aggravated features, together with resisting and assaulting an officer, and imposed the highest penalty provided by law. Those who had thought that such action would give offence little knew the man. It being the last case on the docket for the day, descending from the bench and passing, I saluted him, which he pleasantly returned, without a murmur as to the justice of the fine. Subsequently, on several occasions, he placed me under obligations to him for favors. Personally, insignificant as I may have been to him, he recognized in me for the time being a custodian of the majesty of the law, which he knew he had violated. When it shall happen as a rule and not as the exception that men will esteem, applaud and sustain the honest administration of the law, irrespective of the administrator, a great step will have been taken toward a better conservation of constitutional liberty. In Arkansas the political cauldron continued to boil. In Powell Clayton were strongly marked the elements of leadership, fidelity to friends, oratorical power, honesty of purpose, courage of conviction, with unflinching determination to enforce them. The late Joseph Brooks, an ex-minister of the Methodist Church, and who secularized as a politician, was an orator to be reckoned with. Sincere, scathing, and impressive, his following was large and devoted. Senator Clayton, the present Ambassador to Mexico, has outlived the political bitterness that so long assailed him, and was lately guest of reception and banquet given him and largely attended by Democrats, chiefly his political opponents.

The divided Republicans held their State convention in 1872. The Clayton faction (the Minstrels) had for their nominee Elisha Baxter, a North Carolinian by birth, and hence to the Southern manor born. This, is was premised, would bring strength to the ticket. Joseph Brooks was the nominee of the Brindle wing of the party, and a battle royal was on. Although a minority of Democrats respectable in number joined the Brooks faction, the majority stood off with wish for "plague on both your houses," and awaited the issue. It was in my first of twenty-eight years of recurrent canvassing. Many districts of the State at that time being destitute of contact by railroads, made wagon and buggy travel a necessity.

After nominations were made for the various State officers in convention, appointments were made and printed notices posted and read at church and schoolhouse neighborhoods, that there would be "speaking" at stated points.

The speakers, with teams and literature and other ammunition of political warfare known and "spiritually" relished by the faithful, would start at early morn from their respective headquarters on a tour of one or two hundred miles, filling ten or twenty appointments. Good judgment was necessary in the personal and peculiar fitness of the advocate. For he that could by historic illustration and gems of logic carry conviction in a cultured city would be "wasting his sweetness on the desert air" in the rural surroundings of the cabins of the lowly. I have heard a point most crudely stated, followed by an apposite illustrative anecdote, by a plantation orator silence the more profuse cultured and eloquent opponent.

As he was still at his lesson on the duties and responsibilities of citizenship, it was a study worthy the pencil of a Hogarth to watch the play of lineament of feature, while gleaning high ideals of citizenship and civil liberty amid the clash of debate of political opponents; cheerful acquiescence, cloudy doubt, hilarious belief, intricate perplexity, and want of comprehension by turns impressed the countenance. But trustful in the sheet anchor of liberty, they were worthy students, who strove to merit the great benignity. Canvassing was not without its humorous phases during the perilous times of reconstruction. The meetings, often in the woods adjoining church or schoolhouse, were generally at a late hour, the men having to care for their stock, get supper, and come often several miles; hence it was not unusual for proceedings to be at their height at midnight. I was at such a gathering in the lower part of the State, where Jack Agery, a noted plantation orator, was holding forth, denouncing the Democracy and rallying the faithful. He was a man of great natural ability and bristling with pithy anecdote. From a rude platform half a dozen candles flickered a weird and unsteady glare. Agery as a spellbinder was at his best, when a hushed whisper, growing into a general alarm, announced that members of the Ku Klux, an organization noted for the assassination of Republicans, were coming. Agery, a born leader, in commanding tones, told the meeting to be seated and do as he bid them. The Ku Klux, disguised and pistol belted, very soon appeared, but not before Agery had given out, and they were singing with fervor that good old hymn "Amazing Grace, How Sweet It Sounds to Save a Wretch Like Me." The visitors stood till the verse was ended, when Agery, self-controlled, called on Brother Primus to next lead in prayer.

Brother P. was soon hammering the bench and calling on the Lord to come on His "white horse, and to come this very minute." "Oh," said the chief of the night riders, "this is only a nigger prayer meeting. Come, let us go." Scouts were sent out and kept out to see that "distance lent enchantment to the view," and the political feature of the meeting was resumed.

The Negro is not without many of the prominent characteristics of the successful politician. He is aggressive, conservative, and astute, as occasion demands. Of the latter trait Hon. John Allen, ex-member of Congress from Mississippi, and said to have been the prince of story tellers, at his own expense gives this amusing incident. It was on the occasion of the Carmack-Patterson contested election case. In beginning his speech he called attention to Mr. Patterson's remarks.

"Did any of you," he said, "ever hear anyone pronounce a more beautiful eulogy on himself than that just pronounced by Josiah Patterson? In listening to it I was reminded of what my friend Jake Cummings once said about me. It was in the great campaign of 1884. The Cleveland-Hendricks-Allen Club at Tupelo had a meeting, and Mr. Taylor and Mr. Anderson spoke to the club that night. As I chanced to be at home from my campaigning, I attended the club meeting. After the regular speakers I was called for and submitted some remarks about myself and my campaign. After I had spoken the crowd called for Jake Cummings, a long, black, slick old Negro carpenter, who lives in Tupelo. Jake's speech ran about this way: 'Well, gentlemen, it's gettin' kinder late now. I don't know as it's necessary for me to say anything. You's heerd Mister Taylor and Mister Allen on the general politics of the day. They's dun told you what sort of man Blaine is, and what sort of a man Cleveland is. It don't look to me like no honest man ought to have trouble in picking out the fittinest man of them two. And then you's heerd Mister Allen on hisself, and he has ricommended hisself so much higher than any the rest of us kin ricommend him it ain't worth while for me to say nuthin' about him.'"

Chapter 13

There is at present a lowering cloud on prospect of righteous rule in many of the Southern States, but the relative rights and responsibilities of equitable government, enunciated from desk in church, schoolhouse, or from stump in grove by the Republicans during and since reconstruction, have been an education to the poor whites, hitherto ignorant and in complete political thraldom to the landed class, and to the freedman a new gospel, whose conception was necessarily limited to his rights as a newly-fledged citizen. Nevertheless, they were the live kernels of equality before the law, that still "have their silent undergrowth," inducing a manhood and patriotism that is now and will more and more blossom with national blessing. Friends regretfully and foes despairingly sometimes speak of the tardiness of his progress. He will compare favorably, however, for all history records that it is slowly, through the crucible of physical and mental toiling, that races pass to an elevated status. For of serfs he was not the least in his appreciation of liberty.

Sir Walter Scott, in his note on English history during the reign of George III, of the "colliers and salters, who were not Negroes," says: "The persons engaged in these occupations were at the time bondsmen, and in case they left the ground of the farms to which they belonged, and as pertaining to which their services were bought and sold, they were liable to be brought back by a summary process. The existence of this species of slavery being thought irreconcilable with the spirit of liberty, the colliers and salters were declared free, and put on the same footing with other servants by the act of George III. But they were so far from desiring or prizing the blessing conferred on them that they esteemed the interest taken in their freedom to be a mere decree on the part of the proprietors to get rid of what they called "head or harigold money" payable to them when a female of their number, by bearing a child, made an addition to the live stock of their master's property."

If the fitness for liberty is the measure of persecution sustained in an effort for its enjoyment, of that disciplinary process the freedmen have not been deprived, for ever since his maiden attempt to exercise the right of an American citizen he has encountered intense opposition and physical outrage, all of which has been met by non-resistance and manly appeal to the American conscience for protection; first from the "Ku Klux band" of murderers, and subsequently against the vicious practices to deprive him of his political rights, should establish his claim. Nevertheless, after a third of a century of successful endeavor, educationally and materially, efforts are being made in Southern States for his disfranchisement and the curtailment of his education. On this attempt George C. Lorimer, a noted divine and writer, in a late article in "The Watchman," under the head of "The Educational Solution of Race Problems," has this to say:

> "But may it not be that this reactionary movement rather expresses a fear of education than a serious doubt of its power? We must remember that conditions are peculiar in the South, and, in some quarters, there exists a not unnatural apprehension that Negro supremacy may prevail. To avert this political catastrophe, extraordinary measures have been adopted. To the difficulties that beset the Southern people we cannot be indifferent, and neither should we assume that we would act very differently, were we similarly situated. But we think, in view of all the circumstances, that their position on this subject exposes them to the suspicion that it is the success of education they fear, and not its failure. This apparent misgiving reasonably awakens distrust in the soundness of their contention."

It is assumed by many who oppose the educational solution that inferior races are unassimilable in their nature to the higher civilization. Proof is sought for in the alleged decadence or disappearance of the Turanian people of Europe, the natives of South America, and the West India Islands. But what is this civilization that is so fatal in its operation? What do we mean by the term? What is that exalted something before which African and Asiatic must perish? Does it consist in armies, machinery, saloons, breweries, railways, steamboats, and certain commercial methods that are fatal to truth and honesty. Baron Russell, Lord Chief Justice of England, included none of these in his conception of its character. He is recorded as saying: "It's true, signs are thoughts for the poor and suffering, chivalrous regard and respect for women, the frank recognition of human brotherhood, irrespective of race or color, or nation or religion; the narrowing of the domain of mere force as a governing factor in the world, the love of ordered freedom, abhorrence of what is mean and cruel and vile, ceaseless devotion to the claims of justice. Civilization in its true, its highest sense, must make for peace."

Previous to the National Convention which nominated General Grant for a second term, there had been held a conference of colored leaders, who assembled at New Orleans to elicit opinion and divine the probable course of the colored delegates at that convention. It was there I first met that faithful, able, and invincible champion of the race, Governor P. B. S. Pinchback and Captain James Lewis, my fellow-member of the "Old Guard," who, true in peace as war, never surrendered. The conference, though not great numerically, was strong in its mental calibre and representative character, with Douglas, Langston, Cuney, and others who have since passed to the great beyond. The colored office holders at Washington under Grant were much in evidence and naturally eager for his endorsement.

There was much discussion, and while an ardent advocate for Brooks, I could not follow his supporters—the Brindle wing of the party in my State—in their choice of Horace Greely for President. My slogan in the State canvass had been Grant for President and Brooks for Governor. The wisdom of the conference determined upon a non-committal policy. It was thought unwise, in our peculiar condition, to hasten to proclaim in advance of the gathered wisdom of such an august body as a National Convention. Hence, the conference concluded by setting forth by resolutions, grievances, and a reaffirmation of fealty to the Republican party.

The result of the State election in Arkansas in 1872 was that Brooks got the votes and Baxter the office, whereupon a contest was inaugurated, terminating in civil war. The Baxter, or Minstrel, wing of the party, with the view of spiking the guns of the Brindles, had, in their overtures to the Democrats during the campaign and in their platform at the nominating convention declared in favor of enfranchising the Confederates that took part in the war against the Union. Baxter's movement in that direction and his appointment of Democrats to office created discontent in both wings of the Republican party, leading to their union and determined steps for his removal and the seating of Brooks, who, both factions now declared, was elected. The doctrine of estoppel "cutting no figure" with the Baxter contingent. A writ of ouster was obtained from Judge Vicoff, of the Circuit Court, which Sheriff Oliver, accompanied by Joseph Brooks, J. L. Hodges, General Catterson, and one or two others, including the writer, proceeding to the State House and made service.

No notice of such action having preceded, Governor Baxter was ill-prepared for the announcement. After a short parley with his private secretary, General McCanany, escorted by the Sheriff and General Catterson down the stairway, they were met by Hon. J. N. Smithea, the able editor of the "Arkansas Gazette." Leaving the building, they went direct to the Antony House, on East Markam Street. Word was sent to A. H. Garland, U. B. Rose, R. C. Newton, and other prominent Democrats, who soon joined him in consultation. Governor Baxter immediately notified President Grant of the situation and sent instructions to the custodian of State arms at the U. S. Arsenal to honor none but his order for delivery. Joseph Brooks was sworn in, and the two Governors made immediate preparations for siege and defence. Main Street south from the river to the boundary line of the city was the dividing line of the two factions. Governor Baxter to the east on Markam Street, and Governor Brooks, at the Antony House, to west; at the State House established their respective quarters.

A condition of unrest had pervaded the State for several months preceding this event, and when the slogan of war was sounded the respective adherents by hundreds from all over the State hastened to the capital. On the morning following the "coup d'etat" a report reached the State House that a company of colored men, commanded by Gen. King White, from Pine Bluff, had arrived and was quartered on Rock Street. On the assumption that the men were misinformed as to the merits of the quarrel, it was proposed that they be interviewed. To do that was to cross the line and enter the enemy's territory. It was not unlike the query of the rats in the fable, Who shall bell the cat? I was solicited, and, learning I had friends in the company, consented to go. Going south on Center Street to cross the line by a circuitous route, I reached Rock Street, and nearly the rendezvous. But the "best laid plans of men and mice oft gang a glee." The emissary had been discovered and reported. Approaching me at a rapid rate, mounted on a charger which seemed to me the largest, with an artillery of pistols peeping from holsters, rode General George L. Bashman, of the Baxter forces. Reining up his steed he said, not unkindly: "Judge Gibbs, I am instructed to order you to leave the lines immediately, or subject yourself to arrest." As formerly intimated, and not unlike Artemus Ward, I was willing that all my wife's relatives might participate in the glories and mishaps of war. Hence I bowed a submissive acquiescence and returned. I appreciated the amity expressed in the manner and delivery of the order—an amity of which

I have been the recipient from my political opponents during the thirty years of my domicile in Arkansas.

General Rose, who held command at the Arsenal, and had received instructions from Washington to keep peace pending a settlement of the controversy, with a detail of soldiers, had erected a barricade opposite the City Hall on Markam Street and placed a piece of artillery on Louisiana Street, pointing to the river. In the afternoon of their arrival, General White's troops, headed by a brass band, marched on Markam Street to the Antony House. While so doing a report became current that they were preparing to attack the State House. General Rose attempted to investigate and, with his orderly, rode rapidly on Markam Street, across Main, toward the Antony House. At the moment a shot, increasing into volleys, from combatants on either side, who primarily were the aggressors was never known. It resulted in several casualties. Colonel Shall was killed in the Antony House, and others within the precincts of the City Hall and Metropolitan Hotel. Markam Street suddenly assumed a Sunday-like appearance, the Brooksites seeking safety in the State House and the Baxterites in the Antony. The feet of General White's troops fought bravely. Three hours later it was announced that they had made the fifty miles to Pine Bluff without a break, windless, but happy. Each faction was deficient in arms to equip their adherents. A company of cadets from St. John's College had been placed at the service of Baxter.

At the State University at Fayettville were stored rifles and ammunition, the property of the State. Thither Col. A. S. Fowler, of the Brooks forces, proceeded, and, with courage and diplomacy, succeeded in obtaining and placing a supply on a flat boat, and commenced his trip down the river. Information of this movement having reached the Antony House, the river steamer Hallie, with a detachment of Baxter forces, was dispatched up the river to intercept, and succeeded in passing the State House without interference. The circuitous character of the river enabled a company from the State House, by quick march, to overhaul it at a bend of the river, a fusillade of whose rifle shots killed the captain, wounded several others, and disabled the steamer, which was captured and brought back to the State House. A restless quiet then ensued, occasionally broken by random shots.

In the meantime Governor Baxter had called an extraordinary session of his legislative adherents, vacancies of recalcitrant Republicans filled, the Brooks government denounced, and an appeal to the President for support. All the records and appurtenances of the Secretary of

State's office, including the great seal of the State, were in possession of Brooks at the State House. Information that a duplicate had been made in St. Louis and was en route to the Antony House was received, whereupon General D. P. Upham made application for a search warrant to intercept it, a copy of which is as follows:

I, D. P. Upham, do solemnly swear that one Elisha Baxter and his co-conspirators have ordered and caused to be made, as I am informed, a counterfeit of the great seal of the State of Arkansas, and that the same is now or soon will be in the express office of the city of Little Rock, as I am informed, and that the same is intended for the purpose of defrauding, counterfeiting, and forging the great seal of the State of Arkansas by the paid Elisha Baxter and his co-conspirators, and to use the same for illegal and fraudulent purposes, against the peace and dignity of the State of Arkansas, and I ask that a search warrant may issue forthwith, according to law, to search for and seize said counterfeit seal, wherever or in whomsoever possession it may be found.

(Signed.) D. P. Upham

Subscribed and sworn to before me this
1st day of May, 1874. M. W. Gibbs,
City Judge

The warrant was duly served and return made, with the seal. Baxter, having now ignored the men who placed him in power, called around him as supporters and advisers the brain and strength of the Democratic party. Meanwhile each party had representatives in Washington, urging their claims for recognition. As a party, the Republicans were at a disadvantage. When Brooks, being elected, was contesting Baxter's right to the Governorship, Baxter was supported by the leading and most prominent republicans of the State, who swore "by all the gods at once" that he and not Brooks was elected; but now they swore at once at all opposing gods, who said that Baxter was.

A committee of Brooks men, of whom the writer was one, was sent to Washington to present the claims and conditions to the President. When the train, en route, stopped at Alexandria a gentleman came hurriedly in and, accosting another, said: "What do you think? Grant has recognized Baxter." I did not learn the thought or hear the response, being possessed immediately by a feeling not unlike the boy whose "piece of bread and butter falls with the butter side down." We pursued our way to Washington to find the report true. We called at the White House several times, but the engagements of the President prevented an interview. Late of an afternoon, sitting in my room on I Street, I saw the President approaching slowly and alone. I put on my hat, and was soon with him, and, with becoming salute, addressed him. General Grant, who was ever accessible to the most humble, attentively listened, as we walked, to my brief statement of our case. He replied that his sympathies were with us, for he believed that Brooks was elected; but that his Attorney General had given an opinion that the people, through the expression of their last Legislature, had endorsed Baxter, and that he must acquiesce.

That this avowal was sincere was shown by a subsequent message to Congress on the subject, condemning the process by which the Democracy had vaulted into power. When the dispatch from Washington recognizing Baxter was received at the Antony House the faithful, while making the welkin ring, made immediate preparations to take undisturbed possession of the State House. The march of Governor Baxter and his adherents to the capital was made, as imposing as had his former exclusion been humiliating. A band playing inspiring music not unlike "See, the Conquering Hero Comes," and stepping to the air came an array, led by General King White, on horseback, with flags flying, animated and exhilarated with all the pomp and circumstance of a victorious legion, entered and occupied the building which Brooks and his following, defeated and depressed, had vacated, in obedience to the President's mandate. The prospect for their rehabilitation seemed shadowy, but, with that hope said "to spring eternal in the human breast," they had resolved to carry their contest to Congress.

It may be properly said of Joseph Brooks, as of Charles II, "His fault—and no statesman can have a worse one—was that he never saw things as they really were. He had imagination and logic, but he was an idealist, and a theorizer, in which there might have been good if only his theories and ideals had not been out of relation with the hard duties of a day of storm."

There was opportunity for him to have secured the approval of the Poland Committee. But the tenacity of his ideal of no concession allowed it to pass.

Chapter 14

In 1874 a constitutional convention was called and a new constitution adopted. At the State convention of the Democratic party for the nomination of State officers Baxter was the favorite for re-election as Governor, and probably would have been the choice, had not the more astute politicians put the United States senatorial "bee in his bonnet," which induced a letter, fervid and patriotic, declining the nomination. Baxter was confiding and honest, but not an adept in the wily ways of the politician. Augustus H. Garland was elected Governor, and in the United States senatorial race Baxter was "left at the stand." It was then, as it oft happens, that—

> *"God and the soldier all men adore,*
> *In time of war, and not before.*
> *When the war is over and all things righted,*
> *God is forgot, and the soldier slighted."*

Augustus H. Garland was a Senator in the Confederate Congress in 1861, succeeding Baxter as Governor, then United States Senator from Arkansas, and subsequently a member of President Cleveland's Cabinet, evidencing in every position that it was a selection "fit to be made" not only for his ability and attainments as a statesman, but for rugged honesty of purpose and broad humanity as a man. Taking the reins of government at the zenith of a successful revolution, when violence sought gratification, desire rampant for prosecution and persecution, Governor Garland, by a conservative policy, soothed the one and discouraged the other—a policy early announced in his first proclamation, an extract of which is as follows: "Should there be any indictments in the courts for past political offences, I would suggest and advise their dismissal. Let people of all parties, races and colors come and be welcomed to our State and encouraged to bring her up to a position of true greatness." His friendship I highly esteemed, and, learning of his demise, could not but submit the following token:

Tamatave, Madagascar,
April 17, 1899

Editor Little Rock Gazette
    Sitting in the Consulate, way down on the banks of
the Indian Ocean, the Gazette comes to me laden with

expressions of sorrow on the passing of my friend, ex-United States Attorney General A. H. Garland. Truly, 'a great man has fallen.' In him the nation has lost an eminent statesman and Arkansas a most distinguished citizen, celebrated for his intellectuality and valued services to the Commonwealth. I said 'my friend,' and I reiterate, in no platform sense of that term. Twenty-five year ago I was municipal judge of the city, at the time when the conflict for party ascendancy was most intense. When passion struggled for the mastery, as Governor, he was in reality to me a friend. During his residence at the capital I have never visited Washington without seeking and as promptly receiving his kindly greeting. On several occasions his services, eagerly given, were most helpful. He was not only mentally eminent, but morally great.

Ever approachable, he was a manly man, with courage of conviction, and, while urging them with a zeal born of honest belief, had the inestimable faculty of winning adherents by strength of presentation, blended with suavity of manner. He was conspicuous in this, that his broad soul expanded with tender and affectionate regard for the poor and humble. Reserved in manner, magnanimous and catholic in a spirit that embraced the 'world as his country, and all mankind as his countrymen.' So in the archives of memory I make haste to lay this small tribute to a departed friend, who still seems as 'one long loved and but for a season gone.'

I was present, but not a delegate, at the convention that nominated General Grant for a second term, at the Academy of Music, in Philadelphia, in 1872.

The proceedings, reported and published, of a National Convention are always interesting, but lose much of the impression and force of actuality with which an auditor and spectator is affected. The gayety and magnetism of numbers, the scintillations of brain in special advocacy, followed by tumultuous accord. The intensity, the anxiety depicted, while results far-reaching and momentous are pending, furnish a scene vivid and striking that cannot be pictured. Here is being formed the policy of a party which is to be subjected to the winnowing fan of acute and honest criticism, and by denunciation by opposite parties, striving to obtain the administration of the Government, the fiat of which and the selection of the standard-bearer constitute the claim for the suffrage of the people. They are the preparatory cornerstones of self-government, fashioned and waiting for the verdict of the nation.

Committees on platform and resolutions are generally composed of the radical and conservative elements of a party, so that, while the canvass is up and on, it shall have steered between "the rocks of too much danger and pale fear" and reached the port of victory. Experience during the period since last it met may have had much to do with silence or brief mention of the heretofore darling shibboleth with which they were wont to inspire the faithful, rally the laggards, or capture converts. "Consistency, thou art a jewel" that dazzles, confuses, but doth not bewilder the ordinary politician, who can allow a former policy noiseless and forsaken to sink into the maelstrom of neglected and unrequited love. Prolific in schemes is the procedure of a minority party, not the least is the selection of a standard-bearer, who has been the most sparse and reticent in utterance, hence a record the least assailable, that extracts from his opponents the exclamation of one in Holy Writ, "Oh, that mine enemy had written a book."

Among the men who made mark at the convention above referred to was Oliver P. Morton, of Indiana, styled the "War Governor," for the patriotism and alacrity which he summoned his State in response to the national call, caught up and followed by every loyal State during the Civil War. A confirmed invalid, with lower limbs paralyzed, with massive head and inspired brain, assisted by two servants to a chair to the front of the platform, he made the speech of the convention. Another novel incident was the occupation of the platform of a National Convention by Afro-Americans. The Late Hon. William H. Gray, the faithful and eloquent leader of the colored Republicans of Arkansas, and the late Hon. R. B. Elliott, Congressman from South Carolina, were invited to speak.

A few of their well-chosen words in exordium were as follows:

Mr. Gray said: "Gentlemen of the Convention: For the first time, perhaps, in the history of the American people, there stands before you in a National Convention assembled, a representative of that oppressed race that has lived among you for two hundred and fifty years; who, by the magnanimity of this great nation, lifted by the power of God and the hands of man from the degradation of slavery to the proud position of an American citizen."

Mr. Elliott said: "Gentlemen of the Convention: It is with great appreciation of the compliment paid my State that I rise to respond to your invitation to address you. I stand here, gentlemen of the convention, together with my colleagues from the several States, as an illustration of an accomplished fact of American emancipation, not only as an illustration of the management of the American people, but as a living example of the justice of the American people."

The speeches of which the foregoing are but a part of their introduction, expressive of gratitude and fidelity, a conception of the needs of the hour, delivered with an eloquence that charmed, elicited hearty response, the Academy echoing and re-echoing with the plaudits of the vast assembly. At each National Convention of the Republican party representatives of the race have shown not alone oratorical power, but an intelligent grasp of the political situation. At this period of General Grant's nomination, the nation's heart still jubilant with the success of the Federal arms; its conscience awakened by the dread penalty paid by contributions from every loyal hearthstone for the subjugation of slavery, was now eager and active in providing that the Negro who had been faithful in peace and heroic in war, should enjoy the rights of an American citizen. It was history repeating itself, for in England's history we read that it was Henry at Ajincourt who said: "Who this day sheds his blood with me today shall be my brother; were he ne'er so vile, today shall gentle his condition." For the Civil War, as it matured, became no ordinary case of political contention; the soul of its suppression sprang from the most sacred impulses in the mind of man. It was response to the self-retort of Cain that came echoing down the ages, "Am I my brother's keeper?" Answer came in shot and shell.

But as time receded from these historic epochs, engrossed more and more in national development, mercantile aspirations, internal improvements, rivalry of parties, self-aggrandizement—in short, all the agencies and factors inseparable from human nature that influence on material lines, have effaced much of the general solicitude that formerly existed. This decadence of purpose is not unnatural; a wardship is a duty, and should not be a continuous necessity, its greatest blessing a consciousness that its ideals and purposes have been assimilated by its wards, and lifted higher in humanity's scale. Too much dependence is as hurtful as entire neglect. The more persistent the call for the forces within the greater the response from the assistants without. The lethargy or neglect to give the Negro protection in the exercise of his constitutional rights is developing a spirit of self-help and intensity of purpose, to find and adopt a course and measures remedial that may be practical and efficient; to ignore the sentimentality of politics and subordinate them to conditions irrespective of party. He has found that "the mills of the gods grind slowly;" that the political lever needs for its fulcrum a foundation as solidly material as equitably sentimental.

Proclaim brotherhood, justice, and equal rights ever so much, men will nod acquiescence with a mental reservation of "but," significant of "Who are you? What can you do, or what have you done?" It is your current life's answer to these interrogatives that most interest people in this material world in your behalf. Only as we increase in commercial pursuits, ownership of property, and the higher elements of production through skilled labor will our political barometer rise. Upon these we should anchor our hopes, assured that higher education, with its "classic graces, will follow in their proper places."

Of the latter a humorous writer, in answer to the question from the president of an Eastern college, "Is there any good reason why our sons should not study the dead languages?" said: "While our sons are not on speaking terms with many live languages, it ill becomes them to go fooling around the dead and dying. I do not think it necessary that our sons should study these defunct tongues. A language that did not have strength enough to pull through and crawled off somewhere and died, doesn't seem worth studying. I will go further, and say I do not see why our sons should spend valuable time over invalid languages that aren't feeling very well. Let us not, professor, either one of us, send our sons into the hospital to lug out languages on a stretcher just to study them. No; let us bring up our sons to shun all diseased and disabled languages, even if it can't be proved that a language comes under either of those heads; if it has been missing since the last engagement, it is just as well not to have our sons chasing around after it with a detective, trying to catch and pore over it. You may look at it differently, professor. Our paths in the great realm of education of youth may lie far apart; but it is my heartfelt wish that I may never live to see a son of mine ride right past healthy athletic languages and then stand up in the stirrups and begin to whoop and try to lariat some poor old language going around on a crutch, carrying half of its alphabet in a sling. If two-thirds of the words of a language are flat on their back, taking quinine, trying to get up an appetite, let us teach our sons that they cannot hope to derive benefit from its study."

But Lord Rosebery, ex-Premier of England, in a late address before the University of Glasgow on "Questions of Empire," in the following, on action and learning, takes a serious view:

"There was a time, long years ago, when the spheres of action and learning were separate and distinct; when laymen dealt hard blows and left letters to the priesthood. That was to some extent the case when our oldest universities were founded. But the separation daily narrows. It has been said that the true university of our days is a collection of books. What if a future philosopher shall say that the best university is a workshop? And yet the latter definition bids fair to be the sounder of the two. The training of our schools and colleges must daily become more and more the training for action, for practical purpose. The question will be asked of the product of our educational system: Here is a young fellow of twenty; he has passed the best years of acquisition and impression; he has cost so much; what is his value? For what, in all the manifold activities of the world, is he fit? And if the answer be not satisfactory, if the product be only a sort of learned mummy, the system will be condemned. Are there not thousands of lads today plodding away at the ancient classics, and who, at the first possible moment, will cast them into space, never to reopen them? Think of the wasted time that that implies; not all wasted, perhaps, for something may be gained in power of application; but entirely wasted so far as available knowledge is concerned."

And in keeping with this line of thought, the "Washington Post," of Washington, D. C., in a recent issue, makes the following pertinent and truthful mention:

"Almost without exception, the colleges and universities are beginning another year with unusually large classes. Many of these institutions report the largest number of matriculates in their history. The aggregate attendance is unquestionably greater by thousands than that of any previous year. This is due in part to the prevalence of business prosperity and in part to the steadily increasing approbation of higher education for women, while the natural increase of population is also something of a factor. The 'Cleveland Leader,' speaking of the reports of large classes of freshmen all over the country, says:

"'That appears to be the best and most conclusive reply which the American people can make to those gentlemen of wealth and prominence who, like Mr. Schwab, of the Steel Trust, discourage higher education as preparation for the life of the business world. It is the solidest kind of evidence that the old love of knowledge for its own sake and the old faith in the beneficial effects of college training upon the youth of a country having such a government and social organization as this Republic has developed remain as strong as ever.'"

To which the Post replies:

"That is somewhat hasty and a probably erroneous conclusion. The "higher education" which Mr. Schwab discourages, the old-time classical course, has not grown in popular favor. The reverse is true. The demand for a more practical education in this utilitarian age has compelled the colleges and universities to make radical changes in their curriculum. The number of students who elect to take the old-time course is smaller in proportion to the population and wealth of this country than it ever was. Science, both pure and applied, takes a far more prominent place in collegiate studies than it formerly occupied. Many of the leading institutions of learning have introduced a commercial department. Everywhere the practical, the business idea is becoming dominant.

"While no intelligent man questions the value of classical studies or disputes the proposition that a knowledge of the classics is indispensable to a thorough understanding of our own language, the area of practical study has become so vast, by reason of new discoveries in science and the arts, that a choice between the two is compulsory to young persons who have their own fortunes to make. The old-time course of mathematics and classics furnishes splendid mental discipline, with much knowledge that may or may not put its possessor on the road to success in business. But the time required for that course, if followed by a three or four years' term of practical study, sets a young man so far along in life that he has a hopeless race with younger men who dispensed with the classical and went in zealously for the practical.

"The change from the old to the new lines of education is even more marked in the common schools than in the colleges and universities. The practical begins in the free kindergarten and runs with more or less directness through all the grades. Millions are expended upon industrial training. The business high schools are a great feature of the free school system. All this is comparatively new. It has come because of the necessities of an industrial age.

"'Knowledge for its own sake' is becoming more and more a luxury, in which the sons and daughters of the rich indulge, while the representatives of families that are merely well to do feel that they must acquire knowledge for practical uses. And this tendency is likely to continue, for, as we have said, the field of the practical is expanding. Take, for example, electricity and its uses. All that was known of this subject in the time of our grandfathers could be learned in a few days or weeks. To be an up-to-date electrical scientist and practical electrician in 1901 means that years have been devoted to hard work."

The crude notion held by some, that in far-off climes, to the American Negro unknown, who, with small capital and limited education; with an inherited mental inertia that is being dispelled and can only be eradicated by contact with superior environment, that there awaits him peace, plenty, and equality, is an ignis fatuus the most delusive. Peace is the exhaustion of strife, and is only secure in her triumphs in being in instant readiness for war; equality a myth, and plenty the accumulation of weary toil.

With travel somewhat extensive and diversified; residence in tropical latitudes of Negro origin, I have a decided conviction, despite the crucial test to which he has been subjected in the past and the present disadvantages under which he labors, nowhere is the promise along all the lines of opportunity brighter for the American Negro than here in the land of his nativity. For he needs the inspiriting dash, push, and invincible determination of the Anglo-Saxon (having sufficient of his deviltry) to make him a factor acknowledged and respected. But the fruit of advantage will not drop as ripe fruit from the tree; it can be gotten only by watchful, patient tillage, and frugal garnering. Ignorance and wastefulness among the industrious but uneducated poor render them incapable to cope with the shrewd and unprincipled. The rivalry to excel in outward appearance and social amenities beyond the usual moderate means on the part of the educated is a drawback to any people, but one disastrous to the Negro in his march through arduous toil and restricted conditions to financial independence.

Chapter 15

At the Arkansas State election in 1876 I was selected as Presidential elector, receiving the highest vote on the Republican ticket. The national election of that year was followed by the memorable canvass of the contested vote for Rutherford B. Hayes, which was ultimately settled by a commission appointed under the Compromise Bill, which was passed by Congress in January, 1877, Florida, Louisiana, and South Carolina declaring for Hayes. That the compromise was the result of an agreement that the United States troops should by withdrawn from Southern soil cannot be doubted, and for so doing he was bitterly criticised and denounced by many of his party, resulting, as it did, in the transfer of those States in the South from Republican, by continuous and unblushing disfranchisement, to Democratic rule.

President Hayes, not unlike many of historic fame, may have been "born before his time;" that his action in removing U. S. troops was immature, a continuation and increase of intimidation and violence abundantly proved. At what period of their remaining on Southern soil would have been a fitting time for removal, is an enigma hard to elucidate. Their retention ultimately rested with the sentiment and judgment of the nation. In the South the menace of their presence was galling and increasing in intensity. The North was daily growing averse to the bivouac of troops over a people who swore that they were on terms of "peace with all the world and the rest of mankind." Would compulsion soften animosity? Hayes was undoubtedly honest and sincere, but not of that class of epoch-making men who anchor on the right, await and buffet the advancing storm. Conciliation coyed as gently as loving dove his mate, while within easy reach glistened the jewel "President" of a fraternized Republic.

There are possibly men who would have spurned the enchantress. But an array of figures and ability to enumerate would not be sorely taxed in finding the number. I was among those at that period who saw the inutility of depending on physical force to extract justice and lawful methods from an unwilling constituency; that the reaction from a forced compulsion in the moral world was as evident and unfailing under the conditions as from compression in the physical. I was hopeful of good results, and so expressed myself in an interview with the President. He replied that he was "sincere in his policy, and should adhere to it unless it seemed impracticable that the policy of force and musket had been tried in the South and had failed and public sentiment now demanded a change." We had and have the change, and it would have been a bright jewel in the autonomy of many of the Southern States had it been more liberal and righteous.

History, as a record of the lower to a higher status of civilization increases in intensity and value as it records superior conditions, and the degree of unrest and earnestness of appeal for the abrogation of oppression is indicative of the appreciation and fitness for the rights of citizenship.

It should be remembered that as it became men dowered with the proud title of American Citizen, the Negro has not been remiss in stating his grievances and appealing for justice. To have done less would have banished sympathy and invited contempt. In Arkansas and some other Southern States there is a growing demand for the forms of law and the maintenance of order, and, while not attaining the zenith of accomplishment, it will be observable when contrasted with the lawlessness depicted in the following resolutions of a convention of colored men held in Little Rock August 29, 1883. They contain views and convictions I there presented, the equity of which 'tis fondly hoped have not been lost by lapse of time:

"Be it resolved, That this convention of colored men of the State of Arkansas have still to complain that violence and injustice to their race still exists to an alarming extent. In most cases the perpetrators go unwhipped of justice. That when they are arraigned the law is administered with such laxity and partiality that the escape of the criminal is both easy and possible. In no instance is the penalty of the law enforced against a white man for the murder of a Negro, however palpable the case may be; whilst in most instances the bare accusation of a Negro committing a homicide upon a white man is sufficient for law, with all its forms, to be ruthlessly set aside and the doctrine of lynch, swift and certain to be enforced.

"Case after case is chronicled by the press of Negroes hung by infuriated mobs without trial to determine their guilt or innocence. The farcical proceedings at law in their inefficiency of prosecution, the selection and manipulation of jurors, and the character of public sentiment have had painful illustration in several cases, and but recently of Johnson, the colored man murdered in this, the capital county of the State. The homicide of this man, a servant at a picnic, of a Christian society of white people, and in their presence, without provocation, was universally admitted. Notwithstanding, a jury of twelve men, with almost indecent haste, finds the murderer not guilty. A verdict fit to shock the sense of every friend of right and justice. Robinson, a white man, for killing a colored man because his victim asked for the return of money loaned, received but two years in the penitentiary. Burril Lindsey, a colored farmer, who had homesteaded land in Van Buren County and had commenced cultivation, was waited upon and told he must leave; that they would have no "niggers" in the settlement. They came back at midnight and broke down his door. One of the mob, lying dead on the threshold was Burril Lindsey's response. The press of our city—to their honor be it noted—said he did the proper thing. Respectable men in the neighborhood who knew Lindsey said the same. But yet, after being harrassed by threats and legal persecution for months, a jury found him guilty of an assault with intent to kill, and six years in the penitentiary at hard labor is the penalty for defending his home.

"Homicide has no local habitation; it is the accident of every community, in every nation, and the justice and impartiality with which the law is administered is the measure of their humanity and civilization. But here we have the spectacle of the press, pulpit, and rostrum of the State, with exceptions scarcely to be noted, either entirely dumb or a mere passing allusion, more often in commendation than censure. We are positive in our confidence that those, and only those who expose and denounce and lay bare this conduct, and thereby create a sentiment that will lessen this evil, are the only true friends to the State's moral as well as its material progress. That the attempt to deny and evade responsibility does not meet the issue in the minds of thoughtful men, who believe that no life is safe where the humblest is unprotected.

"We insist that value of the colored brother as a tiller of the soil, the increasing thrift and economy conceded in securing homes and taxable property, their favorable comparison (by fair judgment) with any other classes as to their moral and law-abiding character, should at least merit justice in the courts, and we ask for him consideration and fair settlement for labor. For where could superiority and nobility of character be better displayed than by generous treatment to the former bondsmen. That the better element of the Democratic party do not favor this lawlessness we are continually assured. But the ugly fact stands out in bold relief that they are unable or unwilling, with forces of wealth and intelligence, to create a healthier sentiment. To them, and just men everywhere, we appeal to assist in bringing the moral power of denunciation against this great wrong, that impartial justice shall be the law for every citizen of the Commonwealth; and that the president and secretary be empowered to sign a petition in behalf and as the earnest request of this convention for presentation to his Excellency the Governor, asking executive clemency in the pardon of Burril Lindsey, now incarcerated in the penitentiary, under a sentence of six years."

The Governor was graciously pleased to pardon him, but for personal safety he was compelled to abandon his homestead and leave the State.

For some time a general unrest among the colored people on account of violence had permeated the South, and thousands of the most substantial planters had already settled in Kansas, Indiana, and other Western States to enjoy legal protection hitherto denied them. Upon the question of Negro emigration the white South were divided. The planters and leading politicians were adverse. The planter for the reason that he could not supplant him by more efficient and tractable labor; the politician for fear of reducing Congressional representation, each regardless of the conditions creating his discontent. A minority respectable in numbers and prominent for standing, approved of his removal, alleging that the movement would be mutually beneficial, that it would induce white immigration, relieve the congested overproduction of the staples of the Southern States, introduce a higher class of industries, and simplify the so-called problem by removing the bugbear of Negro domination by means unobjectionable.

Of this class of opinion the "Nashville American," of the State of Tennessee, was a fair exponent. In its issue of May 9, 1879, it had this to say: "We rather rejoiced at a movement which will bring about a better understanding and teach both races a lesson they ought to learn. To the Negro it is simply a question as to whether he will be better off there or here. If there, he ought to go; if here, he ought to stay; and this simple economic proposition will settle it."

This, the sentiment of the best Southern thought, encountered an adverse which, while unwilling to grant the Negro the right of an American citizen, maltreated and imprisoned immigrant agents; desiring his retention in a specious of serfdom. Such being the conditions existing at the time of the meeting of the Nashville Conference in 1879, induced it by resolution to request Senator Windom, Chairman of the National

Executive Committee, to appoint a committee to visit the Western States to ascertain what inducement they offered for immigration.

In pursuance whereof I received the following, containing words of wisdom warranting their insertion here:

United States Senate,
Washington, D. C.,
Jan. 10, 1879

My Dear Sir

In compliance with the resolution of the Nashville Convention requesting me, as Chairman of the National Executive Committee, to appoint a committee of three to visit Western States and Territories and report, not later than the 1st of November, upon the health, climate, and productions of said States and Territories, I have the honor to designate you as one of the number of said committee. In doing so I may add that the duty involves great labor and responsibility on your part and requires the exercise of that sound discretion for which you are noted among your friends. The exodus of the colored people involves the greatest consequences to themselves and should only be undertaken after the most careful inquiry and preparation. If judiciously guided and regulated, I am thoroughly convinced that it will result in great good. If not so regulated, it may cause incalculable suffering to the colored race, and work great injury to the industrial interest of the South. If the Negro can have fair treatment as a citizen and a man in his present home, he will probably not care to remove. If he cannot obtain such treatment there, it is his right and duty to secure it by every means in his power, and no one has the right to say he may not change his residence at his own will and pleasure.

Your proposed inquiry will contribute much to inform and control the action of those who may desire to emigrate and your discretion gives the best assurance that no rash action will be advisable. I regret the committee has no funds at command to pay your necessary traveling expenses.

Hon. James P. Rapier, Member of Congress, of Montgomery, Alabama, I have also designated as a member of said committee, but I am not sufficiently advised to name the third member.

Very respectfully yours,
(Signed.) WM. WINDOM,
Chairman

Mifflin W. Gibbs, Little Rock, Ark.

It often happens that distance lends enchantment to the view; that while contending with hardship, disappointment, and earnest toil, we are apt to imagine that at some far locality, amid new surroundings, there abides a reign of contentment and happiness, where labor has its highest rewards and where there is a minimum of those trials inseparable from human existence. The gratification of this migratory impulse has in many instances proved disastrous, the yielding to which should be only indulged after every possible effort has been made to remove local obstacles by uprightness, softening animosities, and by industry accumulate wealth. But emigrants have been illustrious as nation builders, their indomitable spirit blessing mankind and leaving impress on the scroll of time. The bump on the head of the Negro that the phrenologists call "inhabitiveness" is very prominent; he is not naturally migratory—"content to bear the ills he has, than fly to those he knows not of." Hence there appeared reason, if not entire "method in his madness."

In all movements of like character there are always conflicting rumors and reports as to success or failure of the benefit or loss of the venture, and this was no exception. Colored immigrants to the number of 10,000 had left the South during a brief period, and the wildest rumors circulated as to reception and success of these forerunners, and, as bad news is ever alert, much was heard that was discouraging and demanded investigation; hence the action of the Nashville Conference referred to. In pursuance of our appointment, J. T. Rapier and myself, in August, 1879, went to Topeka, Kan., and from there, chiefly by wagon travel, visited different colonies of the immigrants. Kansas had received seven or eight thousand. At Topeka we found nearly 100 at immigrant camp receiving rations, some sick, others looking for work; the balance had settled on lands or had found work as laborers. At Dunlop we found a colony of 300 families settled upon 20,000 acres of land. In Wabunsee County 230 families had settled on their land, while in Lawrence and other counties hundreds had found work. Mechanics receiving $2 to $2.25 per day and farm hands $13 to $15 per month and board. We found women in great demand for house servants from $6 to $8 per month.

In our interviews with the colonists we found the list and nature of their grievances were the same as have impelled men in all ages to endeavor to better their condition, and should five or ten thousand, for a period, annually leave the South and settle in Western States and Territories, the effect would be mutually beneficial to whites and blacks alike. In Emporia we found the colony in a very prosperous state. Out of 120 families one-half owned their houses and land on which they lived. We remained twenty days in Kansas and had not opportunity to visit Indiana and other States that had received immigrants. But the information we received, with few exceptions, was similar to that of those visited. There had been suffering and destitution in some localities during the past winter; that was to be expected, as many had come wholly unprepared and without that push and ready adaptation to the status of a new country.

We made an extended report to Senator Windom, which contained data as to the success and prosperity of the many and advice to the moneyless to avoid the suffering which might lie in wait.

Chapter 16

In 1877 I was appointed by the President Register of the United States Land Office for the Little Rock District of Arkansas. The State was blessed with a valuable patrimony, by having at the time of its admission into the Union an extensive area of agricultural, besides thousands of acres of swamp, school and other lands, under State control and disposition. The United States Government had reserved many millions of acres, which under its homestead law became available for applicants for 40, 80, or 160 acres. No economy of the Government has been more fruitful in substantial blessing upon the industrious poor than throwing open these lands for entrance and ownership of homes by the payment of a nominal fee for recording and proof of actual settlement thereon.

The renowned and lamented Robert J. Ingersoll, once, while extolling the benignity and patriotic effect of the homestead law, said: "Who do you suppose would take up arms to defend a boarding house?" The opportunity to enjoy the ownership of a home strongly appeals, not alone to our avarice, but to the instincts of our nature. For here is located the citadel of our hopes and fears, our joys and griefs; here congregated are ties the most sacred, and a love devoted. It is the ever-burning light, the steady heat-giving impulse, and inspiration to deeds of domestic utility or of noble daring. For its protection the heart leaps and the arm strikes. Hence, for domestic felicity, or national autonomy, the home is an experience, and for liberty a conservator. Having these convictions during my 12 years' service in the Land Office as Register and afterwards as Receiver of Public Moneys, I was earnest in my endeavor to have the poor of all classes enter these lands. On the political stump at every election, while having as my mission the political ascendancy of my party, I always felt it a duty to dwell impressively upon that theme. Upon asking all those living on their own lands to hold up their hands, the gleam of pride on the countenances of many of my colored auditors as, standing tiptoe, with hands at arms' length, was shared by me, and a stimulus to the luke-warm, for on subsequent visits I would find an increase of holdings.

For the Negro ownership of land and home is not only an important factor, in his domestic life, for as taxpayer, there is a mutuality of interest between himself and other members of the body politic, business and

MIFFLIN WISTAR GIBBS

trade seek him, it impels reverence for the law, and protection of the public peace. His own liability to outrage becomes small. His character for credit increases in the ratio of his holdings, and while manhood suffrage is the professed but often disavowed legacy for all born beneath the flag, his rights of citizenship are more often accorded.

While in the Land Service of the United States there were many examples of heroic conduct by colored settlers worthy of the highest praise. Many of them, emigrants from other Southern States, seeking better conditions, and arriving with barely sufficient to pay entrance fee, and nothing to sustain them in their fight with nature to clear their heavily-wooded land and fit it for cultivation. Hiring to others for brief spells, as necessity compelled them, to obtain small stocks of food and tools, five years after entrance, when they proved up their holdings and got their deeds, found them in comfortable log or frame houses of two or more rooms; sheds, with a cow, calves, swine, and poultry, and ten or more acres under cultivation, according to the number and availability of labor in their families. And, best of all, better than the mere knowledge of success, themselves crowned with that pride of great achievement ever and only the result of rigid self-denial and incessant toil.

In the National Republican Convention held at Chicago, June, 1880, was a contest that will be ever memorable as pertaining to a third term for the Presidency.

Landing at San Francisco, September, 1879, from his tour of two years around the world, and the honored guest of the crowned heads of Europe, General Grant's travel through the States was a continued ovation. On his arrival at Little Rock, Ark., citizens from all over the State hastened to do him honor, culminating with a banquet at the Capitol Hotel. The gathering was democratic in the best sense of that word, political lines were erased, Republicans and Democrats vieing with each other in giving the distinguished man a fitting reception. Nor were social lines adhered to, the writer being a guest and responding to the toast "The Possibilities of American Citizenship."

At the Arkansas Republican State Convention in 1880 I was elected a delegate to the National Convention of June 2 of that year. As a memento I highly prize my bronze medal proclaiming me as one of the historic "306" that never surrendered—compact and erect, "with every gun shotted and every banner flying," went down with General Grant in an unsuccessful effort to nominate him for a third term. It was there that Roscoe Conkling made the nominating speech in behalf of the General that will live in history, stirring the hearts of the immense audience to a climax of patriotic fervor. When he said, "Should you ask from whence he comes, the answer it shall be, He comes from Appomattox and the famous apple tree."

The fiat of the Convention was an illustration of the ephemeral character of cotemporary popular acclaim. Ambitious rivalry, the anticipations of envy, the bitterness of disappointed office seekers during two former Administrations, the honest belief of the timid that a third term for one soever trustworthy presaged and paved the way to an imperial monarchy; the mistakes unavoidable from misplaced confidence, happening in the career of all men and inseparable in the administration of government—all these elements, although incongruous in their nature and make-up, when they conspire are a formidable factor, and as such accomplished his defeat. Though dead, Ulysses Grant still lives on; the attributes of his personal nobility as a man, his patriotism as a citizen of the Republic, his ability and clear perspective as a statesman, his genius as a warrior, his magnanimity and kindness to a chivalrous, heroic but fallen foe, will ever typify his greatness in civic virtues and valiant deeds.

The manner of General Grant's defeat was peculiar. The name of James A. Garfield, the successful nominee, and in political parlance the "dark horse" (undoubtedly foreplanned but kept in the shade), was suddenly sprung upon the Convention and amid a whirlwind of excitement quickly received adherents from the opposition which increased in volume at each successive balloting, until the climax was reached that gave General Garfield the coveted prize. For some time there was much bitterness, and interchange of compliments more emphatic than polite. Within the party charges of infidelity to promises were rife. But the second sober thought of a wise conservatism, which is ever evidence and measure of a people's civilization, tempered strife and assuaged the pangs of disappointment. He was handsomely supported and elected, and on the 4th of March, 1881, was inaugurated as President, amid acclaim, with promise of a successful Administration. But upon what a slender thread do human plans rely! Scarcely had five months elapsed when President Garfield was assassinated by Charles Guiteau, a man of no repute, and emblems of sorrow drooped throughout the nation. This national calamity necessitated the second inauguration of a President during the year 1881. The then Vice-President, Chester A. Arthur, was duly installed September 30 of that year. His execution of the duties of that high office, assumed under conditions intricate and most trying, disarmed criticism by its wisdom and ability.

When a prospective candidate for re-election in 1884 the press of New York, having solicited expressions of fitness from delegates to the last National Convention, I was pleased with the opportunity to make this small contribution.

Little Rock, Ark.
Aug. 1, 1884

Dear Sir

"I but voice the sentiment of the country when I say that I consider the Administration of President Arthur has been signalized by its justice, eminent statesmanship and wise discretion."

Such was the tenor of mention, but much more pronounced, by men of the party, and Mr. Arthur's nomination previous to the assembling of the next Presidential Convention seemed a foregone conclusion.

Nothing I can write will fittingly describe the personnel of James G. Blaine, who was to be the prime feature of the Convention on nomination day. As a man in the field of statesmanship and in intensity of devotion, he was more idolized than any since his prototype, Henry Clay. With political erudition was blended an eloquence inspiring and fascinating; a nobility of character often displayed as the champion of the weak; a disputant adept in all the mazes of analysis, denunciation, or sarcasm, he had created antipathy as bitter as his affections were unyielding. While Speaker of the House, with his counterpart in eloquence, Roscoe Conkling, he had many tilts. One of the most noted and probably far-reaching in impeding his Presidential aspirations, was his defense of General Fry, whom Conkling sought to have impeached, but who was successfully vindicated and afterwards promoted by the War Department. During the struggle Conkling hurled a javelin of taunt and invective, incisive, but thought to be unjust, inducing a response said to have been terrific in its onslaught, confounding the speaker and raising excitement in the House to the highest pitch. I transcribe an epitome of the speech, which will be seen to have bristled with galling ridicule: "As to the gentleman's cruel sarcasm, I hope he will not be too severe. The contempt of that large-minded gentleman is so wilting, his haughty disdain, his grandiloquent swell, his majestic supereminent, overpowering turkey-gobbler strut, has been so crushing to myself and all the members of this House that I know it was an act of the greatest temerity for me to enter upon a controversy with him." Then, quoting ironically a newspaper comparison of Mr. Conkling and Henry Winter Davis, ascribing qualities held by them in common, he proceeded: "The resemblance is great, and it has given his strut additional pomposity. The resemblance is great, it is striking— Hyperion to a satyr; Thersites to Hercules; mud to marble; dunghill to diamond; a singed cat to a Bengal tiger; a whining puppy to a roaring lion. Shade of the mighty Davis, forgive the almost profanation of that jocose satire!"

But James G. Blaine, that master of diplomacy and magnetic fame, with an astute following inspired and wild with gilded promises; the nominating speech of Robert J. Ingersoll, prince of orators, lauding the nominee as "like a mailed warrior, like a plumed knight"—all these forces contributed to turn the tide from Arthur and give him the nomination. I was one of a lonely three of the Arkansas delegation that stood by the State's instructions and voted for Arthur, nine of the delegation voting for Blaine. For obeying the State and not the after conclusion of the delegation, in my next race for a delegate I was "left at the stand."

My failure reminded me of the boy—a humble imitator of the great George Washington—who hacked to death a choice tree. When asked who did it, jolly, gushing and truthful, said, "I did it, pap." The old man seized and gathered him, stopping the whipping occasionally to get breath and wipe off the perspiration, would remark: "And had der imperdence to confess it." The boy, when finally released, between sobs sought solace by saying, "I will never tell the truth again as long as I live." I did not conclude that one should be false to an implied promise with instructions received, but I was impressed with the conviction that it is unwise to trammel a delegation with decisive instructions. A general expression of the feeling or bias of the State Convention is proper, but so much can happen during the interim to change conditions that ultimate action should be largely left to the judgment and integrity of the delegation.

The manner of choosing a President is entirely different from that designed by the founders of the republic. The selection of candidates by an organized party was not anticipated. It was intended that men of high character should be chosen by the citizens of each State as electors, and they should select the men they deemed most fit to be President, and the selection thereafter ratified by the vote of the people. An elector now is but the mouthpiece of his party; no matter what may be his individual judgment, he dare not disregard its fiat. The result of the national election was the defeat of Mr. Blaine and the election of the Democratic candidate, Grover Cleveland. Mr. Cleveland had an independent personality and the courage of his convictions. Affable and cordial in his intercourse with Afro-Americans, and to those of his political household was prodigal in the bestowal of appointments. The effect of this was that many colored men, leaders of thought and race action, not seeing an increase of oppression, so freely predicted in the event of a Democratic President, advocated a division of the colored vote, with a view of harmonizing feeling and mutual benefit. A welcoming of that approach in the South may be deferred, but will yet be solicited, despite its present disloyalty to the fourteenth and fifteenth amendments to the Constitution.

Chapter 17

The closing decade of the past century was conspicuous for exhibitions of products of nature and skill intended to stimulate a country's consumption, but mainly to increase exportation; for a nation, not unlike an individual, that buys more than its resources warrant, bankruptcy is inevitable. Hence the industrial struggle of all progressive nations to produce more than they consume, export the residue and thereby add to the national wealth.

The United States not only excels in the magnitude of natural productions, but in skill in manufacturing articles. The vast stretch of agricultural lands for natural products, superiority of mechanical appliance, and the expertness of American workmen herald the supremacy of the United States for quantity, quality and celerity. For Yankee ingenuity has not only invented a needed article, but has invented a "thing to make the thing."

National and State expositions for the extension of American commerce and development of State undertakings have been marked features of American enterprise, creating a national fraternity, and stimulating domestic industries. While the financial motive is ever in the forefront and the impetus that gives it "a habitation and a name," the moral effect is the reflex influence of contact, the interchange of fraternal amenities that ripen and become helpful for the world's peace, progress and civilization. At the present time Consuls of our Government inform the State Department that agents of American manufacturers of steel, electric apparatus, city railroads and improvements in machinery are in evidence in Europe to an extent hitherto unknown. The directors of the World's Exposition held at New Orleans, La., in 1884, gave a pressing invitation to Afro-Americans to furnish exhibits of their production from farm, shop and home. The late B. K. Bruce, having been created Chief Director, appointed commissioners for the various States to solicit and obtain the best specimens of handicraft in their respective localities for "The Department of Colored Exhibits," and to which the following refers:

Washington, D. C., Aug. 13, 1884.
Hon. M. W. Gibbs,
Little Rock, Ark.

Dear Sir

By virtue of authority vested in me as Chief Director of the Department of Colored Exhibits of the World's Exposition, I have nominated you for Honorary Commissioner for the State of Arkansas. It is unnecessary for me at this time to make any suggestions relative to the importance of managing this business in a manner that will reflect credit on all immediately concerned and our people in general further than to say that my heart is thoroughly in the work. I will communicate with you from time to time, after being advised of your acceptance, giving necessary information and instructions.

Hoping that you will undertake the fulfillment of the trust, I am,

Very respectfully and truly yours,
B. K. BRUCE
Chief Director

I therefore accepted, and proceeded to canvass my State urging the great opportunity offered to show our progress in industry and culture, on the fields of nature or within the realms of art. The movement was a novel one, and the leading colored men and women in the different sections of the State had much to do to awaken the interest that resulted in a very commendable showing.

One of the specialties of these expositions was what was designated as "Emancipation Day," or colored people's day, for the two-fold purpose of directing the attention of the general public to race advancement, and inducing a larger attendance of the class directly concerned, and thereby stimulate race pride for greater achievements. With some of our brethren this appointment of a particular day seemed derogatory to their claim of recognition and equality of citizenship, and evoked considerable discussion. In this I thought some of us were unduly sensitive. Where intention can be ascertained it should largely govern our estimate of human action. This exposition was not only open each and every day to our people, but we were constantly invited, and the few who attended were most cordially treated and our exhibits were properly placed without distinction.

The directors of the exposition were gentlemen known to be most liberal in their dealings with us, and regretted the small attendance, remarking that aside from our patronage, the exhibits would be beneficial as object lessons, educating and inspiring, and proposed a day—"Colored-People's Day." It was not unlike in design and effect "Emancipation Day" at the Minneapolis Exposition, where noted colored leaders from various States attended and spoke, and were not impressed that it was derogatory to the race.

We have a deal of "gush" about recognition. A demand for recognition presupposes a rightful claim based upon an inherent interest—deportment, special fitness, or legal right. In politics we rightfully claim recognition in the ratio of our numerical contribution to the body politic, and from public carriers, for the reason of performance of our part of the contract.

In our demand for a more extended recognition on these material lines, we should first remember that our contributions are generally meager, and that these exhibitions are quite the product of the business ventures and expenditure of our "brother in white," and then brace up and thank Providence that excessive modesty will never "strike in" and kill the Negro. We have the men, the money and the ability to do much, very much more, on many business lines that are now almost exclusively followed by our more prosperous fellow-citizens. No man in our country need beg for recognition; he can compel it if he labors assiduously and takes advantage of opportunity. It can be truly said of Little Rock that the press and leading citizens have been more just and liberal to her colored citizens than any other Southern city. I well remember when her institutions relating to commerce, literature, professions, Board of Trade, Real Estate Exchange, bar and lyceum were open to us, whilst two-thirds of their members were our political opponents. These required but a moderate yearly outlay, repaying, largely, in the amount of information received. Scarcely any availed themselves of these opportunities. If for any reason we do not wish to profit by these overtures, when these trees bear let us not insist upon receiving the choicest of the fruit.

At an indignation mass meeting some time ago a good brother reached the climax of the grievance and then exclaimed:

"How long, O Lord, are we to bear these discriminations?"

"For some time longer," I answered, and then said: "All things considered, we are making progress, and will continue in the ratio we obtain education and wealth, and come forward in the incipiency of public enterprises with our money and practical knowledge from the best possible sources; and, although race identity still exists, the antagonisms and much of the prejudice of which we now complain will be buried under higher activities and greater enterprises—when we have more bank and railroad stock, fewer high-sounding societies, such as "The Seventeen Stars of the Consolidation," "The Rising, Persevering Free Sons of Joshua"; more landlords and fewer tenants, more owners of plantations and fewer share-workers, more merchants and fewer dudes, more piety and less religion, more economy and less wastefulness, more confidence and less envy. I simply rise to submit these as irresistible claims to a higher recognition." I succeeded in making my escape, for which I was thankful.

Chapter 18

Previous to the exposition at New Orleans in 1885, Mr. Henry Brown, of Oberlin, Ohio, visited the Southern States to obtain information as to the views and desire of leading colored men regarding the establishment of "Schools of Trade" in the South where the race could become proficient in all the mechanical arts. He came at the suggestion of philanthropic men of capital in Northern States, who thought by such special means colored men and women could have an opportunity to equip themselves with handicraft, denied them by the trades unions and other influences in the country.

On his presentation of the project in Little Rock, it being so completely in line with my view of a factor so important for the uplifting of the race to a higher manhood and financial standing, I eagerly co-operated. It was determined to take advantage of the attraction of the exposition at New Orleans, issue a call for a conference at that point, and thereby have a representative gathering to obtain their views. I therefore proposed, had printed and issued the following:

CALL FOR A CONFERENCE ON "SCHOOLS OF TRADE."

"Emancipated, turned loose, poor, ignorant and houseless, continually surrounded by difficulties and embarrassments sufficient to appall and retard, by commendable effort on their part, sustained by the generous aid of philanthropists friendly to education, our race in the South has made gratifying advance, mentally and morally. But with this progress of mind and morals, we are confronted with the need of opportunity to qualify ourselves for those activities and industries necessary to make a people prosperous and happy. Our great want now is 'cunning hands' to accompany cultured brains. After obtaining the benefit of our public schools our boys should be fitted for some useful and profitable means of livelihood. The restrictions engendered by trades unions, and the obstacles of race prejudice concur to make it impossible for them to obtain trades in the workshops of the country. Therefore, we need industrial schools where our youth can qualify in the various mechanical pursuits and thereby ennoble themselves, and add value to the State. For the establishment of these "schools of trade" we require a united effort and should make earnest appeal to the philanthropy of the nation.

"In view of this vital necessity the undersigned do hereby call a conference, without distinction, of delegates appointed by mass meetings in cities and counties; presiding officers of colleges, principals of schools, bishops, and leading ministers; editors and publishers friendly to the movement are also invited to meet at New Orleans, La., January 15, 1885, for expression on this subject. Signed,

"M. W. Gibbs, Little Rock, Ark.; Hon. J. C. Napier, Nashville, Tenn.; A. De Pose, New Orleans, La.; Hon. J. C. Clousen, Charleston, S. C.; Rev. B. F. Tanner, Philadelphia, Pa.; Joseph Carey, Galveston, Tex.; H. C. Smith, Cleveland, Ohio; W. G. Simmons, Louisville, Ky.; Peter H. Clark, Cincinnati, Ohio; Hon. B. K. Bruce, Washington, D. C.; P. A. Bell, San Francisco, Cal.; J. W. Cromwell, Washington, D. C.; J. Henri Herbert, Trenton, N. J.; Hon. Henry Demas, New Orleans, La.; Rev. E. Lee, Jacksonville, Fla.; W. H. Russell, Indianapolis, Ind.; F. L. Barnett, Chicago, Ill.; A. H. Grimke, Boston, Mass.; E. N. Overall, Omaha, Neb.; H. M. Turner, Atlanta, Ga.; Hon. James Lewis, New Orleans, La.; John S. Leary, Fayettville, N. C.; Hon. Fred Douglass, Washington, D. C.; T. Thomas Fortune, New York; Rev. M. Van Horn, Newport, R. I.; Lloyd G. Wheeler, Chicago, Ill.; J. W. Birney, La Crosse, Wis.; M. M. McLeod, Jackson, Miss.; George T. Downing, Newport, R. I.; D. Augustus Straker, Columbia, S. C.; Hon. P. B. S. Pinchback, New Orleans, La.; Peter Joseph, Mobile, Ala.; H. O. Wagner, Denver, Colo.; Hon. W. A. Pledger, Atlanta, Ga.; H. Fitzbutler, Louisville, Ky.; J. L. Walker, Atchison, Kan.; E. P. Wade, St. Paul, Minn.; F. G. Barbadoes, Washington, D. C."

As a duty, mingled with pleasure, by this humble means I reproduce a record of the names of men who in the last century were intent upon every occasion to promote the welfare of the race, many of whom were conspicuous in their battle for justice and the betterment of their fellow man, thus fitting themselves for harmonies of a higher clime, have now "quiet sleep within the grave," while with the residue "life's shadows are meeting" and will ere long "be lost to sight," with, let us hope, their memory only dimmed by greater activity and deeper consecration by their successors for the ideals they cherished. Ever loyal, we should not—

"Rob the dead of their sweet heritage,
Their myrrh, their wine, their sheet of lead and trophies buried"—

but—

"Go get them where they got them, when alive,
And as resolutely dig or dive."

With the departed was Hon. B. K. Bruce, who, living to manhood under the blighting influences of slavery, by honesty, native ability and persevering study, placed his name in the forefront, leaving his career as a model. With an astuteness of perception for the retention of friends, he had suavity of manner for the palliation of foes; with diligence and faithfulness winning a constituency that honored him with a seat in the United States Senate.

The conference called at New Orleans, La., to promote industrial education, above referred to, failed to be fruitful. Members of different religious organizations, without suggestion that their particular sect would furnish a modicum of the large expenditure necessary to the establishment of such "schools of trade," strove to have the movement inaugurated, and launched under some particular denominational control.

Mr. Brown, whose only object in desiring to have a conference, was to elicit an expression from leading colored men, an earnest desire for such "schools of trade," and helpful suggestions, looked on the needless strife with amazement and regret, and finally determined, as unity of purpose and a proper conception of what was needed were so sadly lacking, to abandon such an instrumentality to favor his purpose.

It can be properly noted here that among the many helpful signs of race advancement not the least is a broader fraternalization of our religious bodies, an increasing tolerance, indicative of greater intelligence, the product of a more widely discriminated educated ministry. Our churches, being our largest organizations numerically (and greatest of moral educators), having the ear of the masses, their opportunity and growing disposition to unite for the material as well as the spiritual progress of our people, cannot be too highly commended.

Industrial fairs, promulgated and held by the colored people in different Southern States, have been exceedingly beneficial and cannot be too often repeated. Several have occurred at Pine Bluff, Ark., on the extensive race and fair grounds owned by Mr. Wiley Jones, who, with Dr. J. H. Smith, Ferdinand Havis and other prominent colored men of the State, by executive ability, tact and judgment made them a success.

The following notice is from a correspondent of the Arkansas Gazette:

Pine Bluff, Ark.
Oct. 21, 1886

"This, the third day, of the fair was sunny and bright, and the hearts of the management were correspondingly light. Even before the gates were open a long array of teams were seeking admission. The executive officers were early at their posts and no time was lost in beginning the exercises of the day. President J. H. Smith won golden opinions by the pleasant yet firm manner he performed his duties. This morning the Capital Guards were formally received by the Colored Industrial Association.

"Judge Gibbs, of Little Rock, delivered the welcome address, which was a very eloquent and scholarly effort.

"He first praised the directors of the fair for their wonderful success, and said it argues well for the future of the colored people in that they have had extended such cordial support; that nations were influential in the ratio of their agricultural and mechanical development, and that the array of production here made proclaimed in hopeful tones that 'we are coming.'

"He recognized in the formation of the Capital Guards a hopeful omen. Drill develops precision and accuracy, aside from physical development; discipline is invaluable in inculcating the idea of subordination, without which no constitutional government can long exist. Even if they never come within the reach of fiery shot and shell, they would be benefited, and if war's stern summons swept over the land, he felt confident that no more ready response would be made by any class than by the Negro."

Captain Thompson responded in behalf of his company, and alluded to the whole-souled hospitality that had been bestowed upon them by the authorities of the fair and the citizens generally. The Press Association had by their speeches proclaimed that the "pen was mightier than the sword," which he denied; "that the independence of this country from the thraldom of England was won by Washington's sword, and that Lincoln's pen only became effective after the sword had paved the way. It was a recognized arbiter in the disputes of nations, although the pen could render secure what the sword had won." The Captain put his company through several evolutions that were very creditably performed.

In affairs of this character the comingling of the substantial and best element of the white race, their liberal subscriptions and fraternal endeavor, give impetus and valuable assistance, emphasizing the fact along the lines of a higher industrial advancement that they are in hearty sympathy. We cannot too often have these object evidences of our progress. They speak loud and convincing far beyond oral announcement the most eloquent. It stimulates the farmer to extra exertion and more careful measures for increase of quality and quantity of his crop; it inspires the artisan and mechanic for his best handiwork, and welcomes articles the product of our cultured and refined women from the realms of the home. We need this continued stimulus, shut out as we are from most of the higher industries, the incentive born of contact, and which promotes rivalry, to us is denied; hence our inspiration must be inborn and unceasing.

In the economy of God and nature, His handiwork, prominent is "the survival of the fittest." The fittest survive because they excel. Whether within the student's study or the mechanic's bench, it is excellence that counts and heralds its own superiority. If we desire not only the best personal success, but to be helpful to the race, it is not enough for one to be known as doctor, lawyer, mechanic, or planter; but it is upon what round of the ladder of science mechanics or agriculture he stands. Is he above mediocrity; does he excel? The affirmative answer to this is the heroic offspring of self-denial and unceasing mental toil.

A feature of attraction at these fairs has been the drill and martial bearing of our military companies, for while jubilant in the "pride and pomp and circumstance of glorious war," the measure of praise for precision of manouver of the soldier is only excelled by commendation for his bravery in action. The colored citizen took quiet pride and much interest in these companies and were saddened when many were commanded by the State authorities to disband. The motives which conspired and demanded their dissolution were not commendable, but ungrateful, for the Negro soldier in every war of the Republic has been valorous, loyal, and self-denying, and has abundantly earned a reputation for discipline and obedience to every military requirement.

The organization of these companies, furnished with State arms, authorized and under the patronage of the government of many of the Southern States, created an "esprit d'corps," a fellowship and worthy ambition conducive to harmony and the general welfare.

Political friction, no doubt, had much to do with their displacement. But now the Democracy, so long in power, with majorities in many of these States almost cumbersome, could well afford to allow and patronize these conservators for peace and efficient protectors in war, who are ever ready to say, as Jehu to Jonahab, "Is thy heart right, as my heart is with thine heart? If it be, give me thine hand."

Previous to a Presidential campaign I attended a meeting of leading colored Republicans at New Orleans, La. It was not called as a strictly political conference in the interest of any particular candidate, but to exchange views and hear suggestions relating to pending legislation in Mississippi and South Carolina for curtailing, if not abolishing Negro suffrage in those States. Although the political condition of the Negro was then and continues to be of such moment that at no intelligent gathering will it fail to "bob up" and demand a hearing, and this was no exception. While the claims of Reed, Morton, Allison, Harrison, and McKinley were freely discussed, the suffrage was the leading topic.

Prominent among the attendants were T. T. Fortune, of New York; N. W. Cuney and E. J. Scott, of Texas; W. A. Pledger and H. E. Johnson, of Georgia; P. B. S. Pinchback, James Lewis, and J. Madison Vance, of Louisiana; Stevens, of Alabama; Stevens, of Louisville, Ky.; E. Fortune, of Florida; C. W. Anderson, of New York, and others.

The late N. W. Cuney, of Texas, was a man of commanding presence, forceful and emphatic as a speaker; honest, tireless and self-sacrificing. His sterling qualities as a leader of men grows brighter as time recedes from his demise.

Fearless in enunciation, the timid thought him impractical. But there is ever this concerning unpopular truth: When it induces honest thought that burns to be spoken, you can depend it is not confined to a single possessor; it has habitation in many hearts. But he alone is the "leader of leaders," who, with Eolian harp or trumpet call summons its worshipers. Among matters discussed was the charge that Negro delegations were a marketable commodity, with no convictions as to national policy, no regard for manly probity, and were ever at the beck of the highest purchaser in the political market. Such a sweeping charge is most unjust; but, if granted, the admission cuts deeply in the opposite direction, requiring no analysis to discover the preponderance of venality. It may happen between the receiver of stolen goods and the thief that impulse to steal is sometimes weakened by uncertainty of market. The Negro delegate has no market to seek; the market is jammed under his nose at every turn by immaculate white men, often entrusted with large sums to be placed "where it will do the most good," report to those interested the purchase of Negro votes, when such was not the fact. Satisfied they had placed it where it would do them the most good, by allowing it to rest in their pockets, this was not only hard on the Negro, but mean to charge him up with it, then not let him have it. To say there were no colored men susceptible to such advances would be as idle as to say there were no white men thereby influenced; but in either case let us hope it was the exception and not the rule.

Conferences for statement and appeal for removing harsh conditions are historic, ante-dating and creating constitutional government; for, implanted in the hearts is a consciousness of right, however much selfish hate may shut out recognition, or avarice stifle its egress, and the measure of accord granted just claims of the petitioner is the moral and Christian status of a commonwealth.

It may be noted here that the character of accord given the Negro in his now severe battle for justice and equality before the law by the Christian churches and other organizations is of a peculiar kind. While the benefactions for moral and Christian education is to him indispensable, it is not the kind most prominent and effectually practiced by the Divine Master to dissipate wrong. He forbids the cry of peace when there is no peace. He was aggressive and distinct. The peculiarity of accord can be accounted for in this, that it is so much easier for the well-to-do Christian to donate to the Negro than by word or pen to denounce the wrongs to which he is subject. Wrong smiles complacently at any mode save direct attack. It is not in silent acquiescence, but on the forum of agitation and denouncement, that reform finds lodgment, so sadly needed in many of the States where he is the victim of lawlessness and murder, his ballot suppressed, and denied representation. The partiality and indecent haste with which he is tried and almost invariably sent to the penitentiary, where as convict he receives the most barbarous treatment. As a people no one denies that they are law-abiding; as laborers in all the avenues of industry in which they are capable they are faithful and honest: as patriots at the incipiency and duration of the Government they have been faithful and brave. If, then, in the roll of patriots, citizens and producers, they have maintained character for fidelity, deportment and industry, surely they can rightly claim and demand as citizens of the Republic protection from outrage, justice in the courts and in every way equality before the law. They ask for nothing more, and would be unworthy to be content with any less.

The cry of "Negro domination," like the "baseless fabric of a vision," has as little foundation. The problem to be solved is not what is or shall be the status of the colored man born beneath the flag, but whether the forces of Christian civilization, the genius and spirit of our Government, impartiality in the execution of law, without let or hindrance, are equal to the performance of their missions, or are only "sounding brass and tinkling cymbals." That is the problem for our white fellow-citizens to solve. That which most troubles the Negro is has the nation sufficient Christianity and regard for justice to allow these forces to prevail? The assumption that citizens of a common country cannot live together in amity is false, denying as it does that lawful citizenship is the panoply and bulwark of him who attains it, that should vindicate and shield him, whether he be high or low, at home or abroad, whenever or wherever his civil rights are invaded.

Chapter 19

Never in the history of conventions was there recorded such evidence of unswerving fidelity by an equal number to the nominee of their choice as that shown at the National Convention in 1880, when General Grant's name was before the assembly. Ordinarily when a leader is nominated for ballot his supporter's are faithful as long as his prospects are inviting, but at the first evidence of decadence no flock of partridges scamper more readily to find cover. For years his birthday has been celebrated by a reunion of the 306 who, from the first to the last of sounding of the 36th ballot, stood with ranks solidly closed and courage undaunted. At such a reunion at Philadelphia, in 1893, eighty were present, and with speech, reminiscence and good cheer "a feast of reason and a flow of soul," time sped "till the wee sma' hours." Of the colored delegates, Mr. Ferdinand Havis and the writer were present.

Mr. Havis, of Arkansas, "to the manor born," deserves more than mere mention as the representative of a class in the South.

He is a gentleman of fine qualities of head and heart. As a member of the Arkansas Legislature in 1873 and Clerk of Jefferson County for many years, he has by honesty as an official and courtesy of manner made an unimpeachable record, and was only dethroned "by fraud and force and iron will." During his leadership of Jefferson County, where three-quarters of all voters are colored, he was ever conservative and regardful of the views and business interests of the numerically weak but financially strong minority of Democrats, and by supporting a compromise ticket that gave most prominence to the minority sought to preserve harmony. But the efforts of such men have proved unavailing to stem the tide of political usurpation, now rampant at many places in the South.

The greatest menace to representative government is not solely the disfranchisement of the Negro, for according with the eternal verities there cannot be a continued disregard for the ballot in his hand and protection for his life, and respect for them in the person of the white man. Under the genius of our Government the rights of claim and exercise are linked and interlinked.

This truth stands out in bold relief on historic page, and should the future historian record the dismemberment of the Republic, he will indite its decay from the commencement of the violation of this basic principle of civil government, his being but another link in the evidence that rapidity of material, without equality of moral, advancement is ever attended with national decline.

Meanwhile, it is the duty (which is ever the highest policy) of the Negro to be patriotic in his devotion to his country, manly in his appeals for justice, and wise by discarding, by word or action, the fomenting of strife; ever on the alert to close the breach by increase of intelligence, moral worth and financial progress, and thus in great measure dissipate ignorance, vice and poverty, the abolition of which can be assisted, but not dispelled, save by a spirit of self-sacrifice on his part, subjecting his lower nature to the control of the higher. With such effort, united to a faith in God and the American conscience, he will yet soften ascerbities, dispel hindrance, and stem the tide.

Philanthropy may assist a man to his feet, but cannot keep him there unaided by self-effort and an unconquerable will power to stand; while relinquishing no part of his claim upon his white brother as recompense for more than a century of unrequited labor, if with an equal chance for work, education and legal protection, he cannot not only stand, but advance, exertion in his behalf is "love's labor lost," he having no rights worthy of respect.

But in no fair mind can there exist doubt as to his advancement. A people nine-tenths of whom 40 years ago did not legally own themselves or property, now having 140,000 farms, homes and industries worth $800,000,000; a people who, for a century previous to emancipation, were by law forbidden to learn to read or write, now have 3,000,000 children in 27,000 schools, and have reduced their illiteracy 45 per cent., have school and church property to the amount of $50,000,000, contributing themselves thereto $20,000,000; have written 300 books; have over 250 newspapers issued each week. His comparative success as merchant, mechanic or other line of industry which he is permitted to enter, speaks for itself, and finally, with per capita valuation of $75. Yet, in face of such statistical evidence, there are not wanting the Tillmans, Morgans, Burke Cockrans and other seers of a Montgomery convention, who, because the Negro, trammeled, as he is, does not keep step with the immense strides of the dominant class in their wondrous achievement, the product of a thousand years of struggle and culture, unblushingly allege that he is relapsing into barbarism, and with an ingratitude akin to crime, are oblivious to the fact that a large measure of the intellectual and material status of the nation and the cultured ability they so balefully use to retard him, are the product of a century of his unrequited labor.

The feeling that the results of the civil war have been beneficent, harmonizing theory and practice in the autonomy of the nation is manifest and conceded. The growing unity of the people of our country who 40 years ago were engaged in fraternal strife, should be a source of pleasure and welcomed by every patriotic heart; for, while bitterness can be assuaged, and laudable effort made to conform to new conditions, still convictions formed and baptized in the fiery ordeal of war, blood and material loss require fortitude, generosity and patriotism to soften their asperity, and much kindly intercourse to promote the general welfare. The increased desire in this direction is evidenced at each recurring "Decoration Day," when the Blue and the Gray harmoniously intermingle, recalling memories and incidents of the internal strife. The soldiers of each vieing in reciprocity, as with "a union of hearts and a union of hands" with fragrant flowers they bedeck historic sod.

But will the nation remember that after all that can be said or written, of heroic circumstance of war, or in praise of its participants, all these bereft of humanity and justice to the weak, fail to constitute an enduring State, for eternal and immutable is the decree that "righteousness exalteth a nation." Relative to this intermingling of former foes, whatever our estimate of the results of human action may be, we cannot unerringly divine impurity of motive; hence respect for honest conviction must be the prelude to that unity of patriotism which is ever the safeguard to the integrity of a nation.

The spirit that impelled contributions for the erection of the Confederate monuments in different sections of our country from donors, irrespective of former affiliation, has been benign in its influence. In 1897 the Hon J. N. Smithea instituted a movement for such a memorial in Little Rock, Ark., stipulating that responses should be limited to one dollar. Impressed that our race should not be indifferent to such an appeal, I transmitted the following:

J. N. Smithea, Editor "Gazette,"
Little Rock, Ark.

I notice your effort to erect a monument to the Confederate dead. A third of a century has elapsed since the civil war. Conviction in the minds of the participants on either side as to who was right and who was wrong is as firmly fixed as the eternal hills. Given, that a view of events leading up to that fraternal strife, the bravery of the one or heroic conduct of the other from standpoints necessarily different will never find mutual ground for justification, it seems the mission of patriotism and national unity to give the hand of welcome to every effort that will unite us in all that will promote the common glory of the Republic. As one of the representatives of a race, especially in this southland, I cheerfully subscribe my dollar to the fund, feeling that the Negro should joyfully hail every effort to soften animosities which are the outgrowth of a struggle in which, unwittingly, he was so important a factor.

No one should be more anxious to cement the friendly and good offices of our more-favored fellow-citizens, from whom we are receiving the largest share of our educational and material assistance, so greatly needed to bring us up to the full measure of a noble citizenship. By the providence of God we are here, and are here to stay. We are producers of wealth and the conservators of peace. Therefore, encourage us by the exercise of justice and magnanimity, that we can say to you, as Ruth to Naomi in Holy Writ: "Entreat me not to leave thee, or to return from following after thee, for whither thou goest I will go; and where thou lodgest I will lodge; thy people shall be my people, and thy God my God; where thou diest will I die, and there will I be buried; the Lord do so to me and more also, if aught but death part thee and me."

Very truly yours, etc.

Monuments are the mute mile stones, the connecting links between a finished effort, and an inspiration for continued struggle. But monuments are not created after the death of those they commemorate, although they may seem to be; they are but memorials of the structure already built, the solidity of whose base and symmetry of whose lines were projected and fashioned by intensity of conviction and the unswerving courage of their prototypes in ameliorating conditions while they lived. Bereft of this, "monuments themselves memorials need."

Having administered the office of Register of United States land by appointments from Presidents Hayes and Arthur, my last service in the Interior Department was under an appointment from President Harrison, who, in 1889, placed me as Receiver of Public Moneys at Little Rock, Ark., Land District. It was during this term that the Department ordered and appointed Special Commissioners to conduct the sale of unsold lots on the Hot Springs Reservation at auction. As one of the Commissioners and Receiver of Public Moneys, I was required and gave a qualified bond for $100,000 for the faithful performance of the trust, and with Register Raleigh proceeded and discharged the duties thereto. Harrison's term ended a career of twelve years in the land office. If in retrospective moments amid the many beneficent things you might have done, but left undone, you catch here and there glimpses of unselfish ambition or benefit you have conferred, it does much to abate regret, for the recollection to me is a source of pleasure that during those terms by personal convass and unofficial publication I contributed in inducing thousands of immigrants and others to homestead the virgin soil of Arkansas, who have now good homes, comprising 40, 80 or 160 acres of land, besides assisting them in establishing schools for their children.

Chapter 20

In October, 1897, by telegrams from my friends, Nathaniel McKay and Dr. Purvis, of Washington, D. C., I was informed that I had been appointed United States Consul for the island of Madagascar.

It was a surprise; for, while truth compels the admission that I was not averse to "being taken in and done for," Madagascar had not come within my purview; its distance had not "lent enchantment to the view." I gave it some thought, but could not perceive that I had been so annoyingly persistent to merit a response from the President, not unlike that given by Mr. Blaine to one Mr. Tite Barnacle, who was willing to compromise on a foreign appointment. "Certainly," was the reply; the "foreigner the better." I concluded, however, that the bard may have been right when he wrote "There is a destiny that shapes our ends," for it often happens that what a man desires is just what he ought not to have; and whether what he gets is to be beneficial depends largely upon its use.

I was summoned to Washington, and after a conference received my commission, returned to Little Rock to prepare for departure to my post, "10,000 miles away."

I received a warm greeting and a "jolly send-off" at a banquet given me on Christmas eve by many friends. To name a few of the devoted would be invidious to the many. It will suffice to say I felt grateful and touched by the many expressions, which added testimony to their valued appreciation. Arriving at New York I was met by Mr. W. H. Hunt, who had applied and been highly commended for the position of clerk to the consulate, and who, after a year's faithful service, in pursuance of my recommendation, was appointed Vice-Consul, and is now Consul.

This, my appointment as Consul to Tamatave, severs a decade's connection as "Secretary of the Republican State Central Committee," and especially with its Chairman, Mr. Henry Cooper, who, indefatigable as a worker, genial, but positive in his convictions, has managed the machinery of the party with but little friction. The remembrance of the partiality, honors and kindness of which I have been a recipient from members of the party, irrespective of "race or previous condition," will be ever bright and cheery.

On January, 1, 1898, we embarked on the French steamship Champagne, and arrived at Havre on the 9th, and took train for Paris. The cars either for comfort or retirement in no way equal ours, eight in a compartment, sitting omnibus fashion, face to face. We rolled on to the Capital, passing many fine villas, the product of French architecture. Everywhere one is impressed with the national peculiarities—the houses, the streets, modes of conveyance and transportation. Compactness, neatness, order and precision pervades their every undertaking; but for celerity and despatch of business they were painful to encounter or behold, for it ill accords with the American mode. A ride of four hours and we reach Paris. At the depot the baggage is placed on long tables awaiting examination by custom-house officers. Mine was passed without. Took cab for "Hotel de Binda," exquisitely furnished and centrally located, having easy access to places of note.

This being the most disagreeable time of year, a fire in the rooms was necessary, for outside everywhere was a damp, penetrating air, remaining here 15 days with the sight of the sun but once.

The next day after my arrival I called on the American Ambassador, Mr. Porter, in relation to my exequator, to be issued by the French Government. It is a recognition of status, and a formal permit from one nation to another to allow their respective Consuls to exercise the duties appertaining thereto and a guarantee of protection in their performance. Had a very cordial reception from Mr. J. R. Gowdy, our Consul at Paris. Visited the Paris office of the New York Herald, where many files of American and European papers can be perused. A visit to the "Louvre" is a joy for the layman, as for the connoisseur, galleries a mile or more in length hung with paintings grand in imagery and beauty of old masters, French and Italian, centuries old. Many showed the silent, slow and impressive steps of age. But "you may break, you may scatter the vase if you will, the scent of the roses will linger there still," for on shrunken canvas or from luster dimmed was imperial tone of materialized conception "not born to die."

Among the guests of the hotel were two gentlemen, one an American capitalist, the other a German merchant from Berlin, the latter speaking French like a native. We became pleasant companions, and concluded on Sunday evening to go to the "Follies Bergere"—in American parlance a variety theater.

Ten minutes' drive brought us to a very large building, lighted as if by sunlight, where a hundred finely-dressed men and women crowded for entrance. Outside of what we term pit and dress circle is a partition, three or four feet high, dividing them from a promenade ten or fifteen feet wide. You can stand or sit in this promenade, and see the performance. Our friends suggested this plan, as we could see and hear more of Parisian peculiarities. Here many very beautiful women promenaded. They had evidently been touched by artists, for their make-up was superb. But I could not but think of the refrain of a song we have all heard, "Oh, but what a difference in the morning." They had sweet, pretty sayings, clothed in all the softness of modulation and earnestness of gesture of the French people. My American friend, like myself, was Frenchless, and as a consequence invulnerable. The appearance of the occupants of the front row of seats very forcibly reminded me of a similar locality at the Capital Theater in the City of Roses, on similar occasions, where many of my old friends with gaze intent loved to congregate. The performance was spectacular and acrobatic, with usual evolutions, with more "abandon" and very artistic. Passing through the cafe, where hundreds of finely-dressed men and women were sitting at tables quietly talking, smoking and drinking wine or coffee, we passed to the street.

There is much to delight in a walk through the Tulleries and "Palace de la Concord." These public squares have an acreage of several hundred, and are adorned with flowing fountains and marvelous statuary. Passing through the Tulleries brings you to the "Dome de Invalids," in which is Napoleon's tomb. The building and dome is of the most exquisite architecture. Upon entry everywhere your gaze is confronted by stately columns of Italian marble arches, statuary, flags of many varieties, captured by Napoleon from his enemies on many battlefields, besides other trophies of war.

As you look down a circular pit twenty feet deep and forty feet wide, enclosed by a balustrade of Italian marble, you see the sarcophagus, in which is inclosed all that was mortal of the great Napoleon. The mosaic pavement at the bottom of the pit represents a wreath of laurels; on it rests the sarcophagus, consisting of a single block, highly polished, of reddish brown granite, fourteen feet high, thirteen long and seven wide, brought from Finland at a cost of $25,000. Above rises a lofty dome 160 feet high, divided into two sections, one of twelve compartments, each containing a figure of one of the twelve apostles; the other representing St. Louis offering to Christ the sword with which to vanquish his enemies.

While in Paris I visited Mrs. Mason, widow of James Mason, deceased. Mr. Mason was formerly a member of the Arkansas Senate and Sheriff of Chicot County. It will be remembered by old residents that the death of Mason's father, an old bachelor and rich planter, who died intestate, caused a suit at law of great interest and importance. It was an exciting trial, as many thousands of dollars were at stake in the issue. The fatherly care he had ever evinced for the education of his children (James having been educated in France and Martha at a Northern college); the solicitude and unfailing recognition, the many instances of which he had designated them as direct heirs, and other evidence, collateral and convincing, were availing. They received a jury award.

An appeal to the Supreme Court of the United States was taken, which dragged its weary way for a number of years, but resulted in confirming the decision of the lower court. Mrs. Mason was for many years, through the patronage and kindness of Senator Garland and other members of Congress from Arkansas, a clerk in the Land Office at Washington. I found Mrs. Mason living in well-appointed apartments with her daughter, an artistic painter of some note, with studio adjoining, where I was shown many beautiful productions of her brush. I was conversant with many instances in the North where Southern planters had brought their colored families to be educated, purchasing and giving them property for settlement and sustenance, especially that their girls might escape the environments which undoubtedly awaited them at the South. These were in fine and valuable contradistinction to many cases similarly related, where they were sold on the auction block to the highest bidder. But in all candor it cannot but be supposed that in many instances the sale of the planter's own flesh and blood was involuntary. High living, neglect of the comparative relation of resource and expenditure, gambling for big stakes on steamboat and at Northern watering places, brought the evil day with attending results to the "chattel" subject to the baneful caprice of unrestrained liberty.

On the 23d of January, 1898, I was taking my leave of Paris to meet my steamer at Marseilles for a 20-day voyage for Madagascar. My stay at the hotel had been pleasant, and I supposed had received all necessary attention from the servants that occasion demanded; but in character it had been individual. Now it was united, for in doorway and on staircase they were (like Tennyson's cannon) servants "to the right of me and servants to the left of me," smiling and gracious. One, of whom I had no recollection of having previously seen, approached me with an obeisance decidedly French to remind me that he was the "baggage man" and attended to it when I arrived. I replied, "You are not the man who took up my baggage." "No," he said; "I am the man who looked after the man who watched the man who did take it up." "Oh!" I said;

and then remembering that he and I had much in common, his English and my French being twins, I conceded his claim, "tipped" others that impeded my exit, and made hasty retreat.

Leaving Paris at 2:30 P. M., at 2 in the morning we reached Lyons, stopping 25 minutes for coffee and refreshments, which reached a long-felt want, arriving at Hotel de Louvre et de la Paix, at Marseilles, three hours later. Paris is prolific in names of its hotels, but this was commensurate in luxury and first class in every particular, very large, the finest in Marseilles and said to be unsurpassed in France. It is approached by a hall-way fifty feet long from Rue Canebrian (the street), which leads you into an oval-shaped court 100 by 200 feet. Around this court in niches are finely-sculptured statuary, paintings and choice flowers in porcelain vases. Out of this court you are conducted into the hotel proper. Spacious stairways of Italian marble, the tread of which covered with Turkish carpets, leads you to the interior. The court in the inner center of the hotel rises to a height of five or six stories, and is covered by parti-colored glass, which emits a soft and pleasing tint on all below. The dining room was "a thing of beauty," and the menu "a joy forever." The adornments of the room would well befit a palace. Oh, that I had the tongue of an orator or the pen of a ready writer, to fitly describe! Took breakfast and then a stroll along the principal streets of the city and the wharves of the Mediterranean. The city resembled a bee hive; the houses and streets are literally crowded with men and women of all nationalities and costumes.

Wending our way to "Notre Dame," a magnificent church on a hill, one thousand feet above the level of the city, entirely overlooking it, while the Mediterranean lies sparkling in the distance directly below. On the top of the dome of this edifice is a figure encased in gold, representing "Holy Mary" with the Christ in her arms. A gallery surrounds the church, from which the view is grand and imposing. Ascent and descent can be made by an elevator.

On the 25th of January we embarked on board our ship, the "Pie Ho," and found state room comfortable for the longest voyage of our travel. The view as we pass out of the harbor of Marseilles is quite picturesque, with its quaint old buildings, mountainous surroundings, its medley of ships, soldiers and sailors of every nation, differing in uniform and costume. Here, as I suppose it is everywhere where love and friendship dwell, hundreds had assembled at docks and quays and other points of vantage to waive hands and handkerchiefs of a loving farewell. I thought of my dear daughter on the wharf at New York and her anxious gaze until we were lost in the distance. This ship, the "Pie Ho," of a French line, is said to be old, but staunch, comfortable and giving good service; but a failure in that particular the want of which retards the success of many people of whom it could be truthfully said by Christian and moralist that they were good and reliable. The "Pie Ho" is not swift, but if she retains the commendation that oft accompanies slowness, that of being sure, we should be content. But age has its limits, and happy should all be who safely and honorably round up the voyage of life.

We are now in full view of Mount Strombol in the Mediterranean, a volcano in full blast, emitting fire and clouds of smoke. Yesterday we entered the Ionian Sea; today we have land on either side, Sicily on our right and Italy on our left, with a good view of its coast lines; cities, towns, cultivated fields and trains in motion. At 2 P. M. January 30 we see Dermot Lighthouse, and at 3 reach Port Said. The Khedive's dominion, a Government and business point, with many consular residences. It was the first sight of the "old flag" since leaving Marseilles. It is a new baptism of patriotism for one to see the national banner so far from home, and impromptu he sings, "long may it wave," for "with all thy faults I love thee still."

We anchored out in the bay, and with small boats went ashore. Port Said is quite cosmopolitan both in its business and residence features. Nearly every nationality has its representative in trade, but numerically the unspeakable Turk is very much in evidence. On landing one of the guards, numerous and whose charges are fixed by law, took us in charge to show us the city. The streets generally were unimproved and irregular, both in architecture and location. Through several dingy and untidy streets he led us to the public park, which made considerable pretension to order and neatness. The turban, the wrap, the sandals and other Oriental costumes, which made up the dress, were not more varied than the complexion of the people, but their features were generally fine-cut. A marble bust of De Lesseps, the contractor of the Suez Canal, which we shall soon enter, has a prominent place.

Through several streets, monotonous for disorder and uncleanliness, we reached the "Mosque," the Mahomedan place of worship. In the minaret high up on the tower stood an officer awaiting the hour to lower the flag as a signal to all Musselmen that they could eat, the day being one of their fast days. In all the streets through which we passed could be seen groups of the faithful with anxious look toward the minaret to catch the first downward movement of the flag. It came at last, and with it the shouting and running of the crowds to booths and stands for eating purposes that lined the sidewalks. We approached the "Mosque" with all the solemnity possible for hypocritical heretics to assume, and were met at the door by a grave and reverent sire, who interviewed the guide.

We had been told that we would have to take off our shoes (just here we noted the same pliancy observable in many of our own denomination when there is prospect of getting the almighty dollar). In some way the matter was compromised by putting on over our shoes large sandals made of straw. After paying 50 centimes each (equal to 10 cents in our currency), we entered a large room without furniture or other adornment, with stone floor, some matting, upon which a number of worshipers were kneeling and supplicating "Allah," their supreme being. There was an earnestness that bespoke sincerity, and an all-abiding faith. I could but think how few of us who would criticise are true to the creed we profess.

In a kind of lavatory adjoining could be seen men washing their feet and doing oddities unmentionable preparatory to worship.

After wandering about the building for some time I was accosted by one of the attendants, and was made to understand that one of my feet was uncovered. I had lost one of my sandals. I was rather uneasy for a while, not knowing what they might do with that unholy foot that had desecrated the temple. The guide found it, however, and "Richard was himself again." After leaving the "Mosque" the guide escorted us shipward through the business portion of the city, neat and cleanly, with hotels and stores creditable to a metropolis. But for beggars of unrivaled persistency I commend you to Port Said, for with a pitiableness, sincere or assumed, they dog your every footstep.

At the southern part of the city is a large cemetery, having stones with many hieroglyphics and inscriptions denoting the former locality, character and virtues of the dead. With the scholar are interred copies of his literary productions; with the soldier, his sword; with the statesman, a roll of his achievements for the good of the state, for presentation to "Allah."

Chapter 21

The passage through the Suez Canal was somewhat monotonous, but a continued reminder of bible history. On either side as far as the eye could reach the desert spread out its sandy atoms glistening in the sun.

Out of the canal we are in the Gulf of Suez, and in a few hours in the Red Sea, an interesting locality in ancient history. It is there we learn that Pharaoh and his hosts met their Waterloo (with the accent on the water) in the pursuit of the children of Israel. But here we find conflicting opinions. Some say that Pharaoh, arriving at the bank and seeing the impossibility of overtaking them, turned and retired; others, that there were shoal places in those far-away days where any one could cross; others, that they crossed on flats very like the ordinary modern mortal. But I do not accept this attempt to question the orthodox version, but will verify it as far as my observation will admit. The sea was likely red in those days, and has very properly retained its name on account of the locality being red-hot at times, or, perhaps, chameleon like, changes its color. This morning, however, it is a deep blue. As to Pharaoh and his hosts getting drowned, there cannot be doubt, if it was in its present condition and they attempted to cross on foot.

But this we do know, that the success of the "Children of Israel" in not being "overtaken" has been the prototype of father to son in every effort to do so from that day to the present. There is a serious view, however. Here the sea, sky and neighborhood of Jerusalem, pyramids, monuments and sacred traditions all conspire to have a solemn and awe-inspiring effect. Thousands of generations of men have lived and moved in the activities that engage modern humanity, but have passed like fleeting shadows, leaving only these sentinels as perpetual reminders. While the "Red Sea" sings in murmuring cadence that "men may come, and men may go, but I go on forever," doubly impressing us that

> *"So the multitude goes, like the flower or weed,*
> *That wither away to let others succeed;*
> *So the multitude comes, even those we behold,*
> *To repeat every tale that has often been told."*

But a truce to moralizing on the past. The children of Israel seem to have made and kept their record as "passengers." I was interested in the passage of a child of Ham. I am somewhat deficient in Bible history, and am without knowledge of the whereabouts of Ham's children at that time, or whether they had "crossing" to do; but if they possessed the proverbial character imputed to some of their offspring, antipathy to water, especially for lavatory purposes, I am of the opinion they took no desperate chances, "content to bear the ills they had than fly to those they knew not of."

Passing Hurich Island, a British possession, and having had a very pleasant passage on the Red Sea, we arrive at Djiboute, Abyssinia, the terminus of King Menelik's domain, the scenes of recent conflict between Italy and the King's forces, the "unpleasantness" resulting unprofitably to the Italians. There were landed from the ship many boxes of rifles and ammunition for the King's governor, who resides here. During the few hours we remained there, we were interested in and enjoyed the gathering of ten or fifteen native boys around the ship diving for centimes or francs thrown by the passengers, their dexterity as divers, securing every penny, was as clever as grotesque. They remained in the water six or eight hours during the ship's stay. A few hours brought us to Aden, a very strongly fortified appendage to the British Empire at the south end of the Red Sea. For armament and strategical locality it is the Gibraltar of the southern seas.

The rivalry of native boatmen for passengers and luggage to take ashore was appalling. When I say it surpassed a third ward political meeting in "ye olden times" in Little Rock I faintly describe it. Sunday morning; once more on the way; one more stop, and then to Tamatave, our destination.

Looking this beautiful morning on the foam-crest waves as they roll in sportive emulation, with a cloudless sky coming down on every side to kiss the horizon, shutting out human vision of all else beyond, one could not fail to be impressed with the greatness, the omnipotence of the Creator. This being but a speck of that vast whole, comprising the celestial and terrestrial aggregation, he, indeed, who regards this sublime workmanship as the product of chance and not that of a super-human architect and law-giver, by Whom every atom of nature is controlled, is more to be pitied than condemned.

To conclude our voyage, we have six or seven days of "innocuous desuetude." That is what I believe President Cleveland designated a monotonous and unprofitable period. I am not certain, however, and one should be careful in quoting great authors.

We pass the Gulf of Aden and enter the Indian Ocean, Rem Huffien Island to the right, and now appears the eastern coast lines of the continent of Africa. On that continent, I learn, lies the ashes of my forefathers. Peace abide with them, and may peace crowned with justice come to such of their descendants as are still the victims of dishonesty and inhumanity by enlightened and professedly Christian nations.

Travel by sea loses in interest as you recede or are midway between distant points. You somehow feel yourself located in the neighborhood of "Mahomet's coffin," and have a sort of a "don't-care-a-continental" atmosphere surrounding you, with nothing to arrest attention save the usual incidents of ocean voyage, with no land in sight. The constitutional promenade on deck before and after meals, with the French etiquette of raising your hat or cap as you pass; reading or lounging on sofas or reclining chairs; relating individual experiences of life or travel; criticising the conduct of others than yourselves; the welcome sound of the bell that calls you to meals; the last view of the sun as it bids you "good-bye," with its ineffectual rays, and gently sinks beneath the horizon; the rising of the moon, shedding its sheen of sparkling light on the dancing waves; retirement to your couch to listen awhile to the heavy breathing, and feel the pulse-beat of the iron monitor as it speeds you onward; finally to sleep, to dream of loved ones at home.

The suavity of the French is in notable contrast with the more taciturn deportment of the English; amiable contact has much to do with softening the asperities of life.

We are now crossing the heretofore much-dreaded equator—weather splendid, light, cloth suit not uncomfortable, but we are at sea and not on land. The forward deck is today given up to the sports of the sailors (the custom when crossing the line), and is now the center of attraction—running "obstacle races," the two competitors getting under, and from under a canvas-sheet held to the deck by a number of their fellows, and then running for the goal, picking up potatoes as they ran. Afterwards, with bucket of paste and paintbrush, lathering head and face, shaving with a large wooden razor the unlucky competitor—were a part of the amusements they imposed on "Old Father Time."

Arrived at Diego Suarez, on the northern port of Madagascar, a French naval station, having a land-locked harbor, providing good shelter and anchorage. The town is located on a plateau overlooking the bay. Many officers disembarked and a large amount of freight discharged. The resident population consisted of a medley from all eastern nations.

Anchored a mile off and in small boats, and after 20 minutes' rowing we were landed. A dozen stores, barracks and the hospital on the opposite side of the bay were the only objects of interest. The large amount of freight discharged indicated it to be a prominent distributing point for the interior. Leaving Diego and running down the eastern coast with land in view, mountainous and apparently sterile, we reach Tamatave and anchor in the bay.

The ship was soon boarded by a messenger from Mr. Wetter, the outgoing American Consul at Madagascar, and I was piloted ashore. The view of Tamatave from the ship was not prepossessing, and my walk through the city to the hotel was not inspiring. The attempt to dignify the six or eight feet wide alleys (which were the main arteries for travel) as avenues or streets, seemed ludicrous, and the filthy condition, the absence of all sanitary regulations in a province pretending a civilized administration, was to me a revelation. The natural sequence of such neglect was the visitation of the "Bubonic plague" a few months after my arrival and an immense death-rate. The alarm proved a conservator for the living, for the burning of the effected districts, widening the streets and enforcement of sanitary rules have tended to lessen its virulence, although it has been yearly in its visitations; for while foul surroundings are recognized as hot-beds for the propagation of the germs of this pest, recent experience has demonstrated that while cleanliness and rigid sanitary measures are less inviting, they are not positive barriers to its approach and dire effect. The "terror" originally supposed to be indigenous only to India, Egypt, and China, and so domestic in its habits as to confine its ravages to few precincts, now stalks forth as on a world mission—to Mauritius in Indian Ocean, to Japan, Brazil, Australia, Honolulu, and last and not least, interesting from an American point of view, are the stealthy footsteps of the unwelcome guest in the city of San Francisco, Cal. "While medical information relating to the plague is still less definite and extensive than it should be," says an eminent physician, "it is now well demonstrated that the disease depends upon a specific microbe."

It may be communicated from one person to another through expectoration, oozings from the mouth of dying persons, or through the excretions of the body. "The fears it inspires are well grounded, for the recoveries in a case of severe epidemics are only ten per cent. Of 126 cases reported from Manila from January 20 to March 30, 1900, 112 cases resulted fatally." In India, where the plague has been the most severe, the deaths from this cause have averaged 5,000 a week of recent years, a considerable amount of study has been devoted to the various phases of the plague, by physicians in Europe and the East especially, and a number have given their lives to the cause of medical science in attempts to find some method of successfully combating it. It is needless to say that no specific has as yet been discovered in its treatment, and ordinary curative measures have but little effect on its course.

In Chinatown, San Francisco, where it made its appearance, a rigid "cordon sanitaire" was established, and all outer intercourse prohibited. It is not believed that conditions are inviting in North America, although "the wish may be father to the thought."

The following brief expression relative to Madagascar and comment on Negro status in the following letter to the "Colored American," published in Washington City, may be in place:

Tamatave, Madagascar,
Aug. 5, 1900

Dear Friend Cooper

I have your favor June 14th last, in which you say you would like to have a line from me, that you "may let the friends over here know what you are doing." Well, here it is, line upon line, if not precept, etc. I am "still doing business at the same old stand," and doubt if I have anything to say regarding this "far-away post" that would particularly interest your readers, engrossed as I perceive they are in domestic phases and in the alignment of our recent acquisitions.

Regarding the physical development or moral progress of Madagascar, as you know it is now a French province, with a Governor General and staff, all appointees from France. The Government is doing considerable to open up the country by means of telegraphs, railroads, turnpikes and canals. At Paris they recently voted sixty millions francs (12 million dollars) for a railroad from here to Tananarivo, the capital, 200 miles from here, over a mountainous and broken country. The capital is situated on a plateau 5,000 feet above sea level, with a climate cool and bracing. Here at Tamatave a fireplace or heating stove in a house are unknown appendages. The Hovas for a long period were the rulers previous to the conquest and occupation by the French, who by diplomacy—

"force and iron will"—the means usually adopted by the strong when a coveted prize looms in the distance, added an immense territory to their colonial possessions. But perhaps in the interest of civilization the change is not to be deplored. The Hovas were a superior class of Madagascan people the rulers being men of education and ability, but not equal in quality or quantity to cope with the energy, wealth and military prowess of a power like France.

The mental and physical conditions of the great bulk of the natives were not, and are not, inviting; they were held by a mild system of slavery, a system that in substance still exists under French rule as to forced labor on public works. The severity of tasks and bad rum are said by a friendly society at Paris in its protest "to be fast decimating their number." The French Government, however, are establishing an extension of schools for the natives, where industrial training will be the marked feature, and which on yesterday, the occasion being an official visit the Governor was pleased to pay me, I took pains to extol; as you know industrial training is my pet. The General wisely remarking, "we wish first to place the present generation in a position to earn more money, so they will be able to give their offspring a higher education if they wish." The English, Norwegians from America, the Friends and other missions, are doing something for their educational and moral progress, but the appliances are meager compared with the herculean task that awaits them.

There is, however, this difference in the problem here. There are colored men occupying places of prominence as officials, as tellers in banks, clerks in counting-houses and merchant stores. Here it is condition, and not color, wealth and position, the "open sesame." On social occasions the brother in black is in evidence, without special notice of the fact, and, strangest of it all, on the following day the sun and other heavenly bodies seem to stand or revolve in their accustomed orbits. My health has been good, although the bubonic pest, periodical in its visitations, has been alarming in the suddenness of its destruction of life. In the spring it is again expected to alight without "healing in its wings." But I will not longer dwell on Madagascan peculiarities, many of which, as elsewhere, are not chastening. What I am interested in, and want to know about is, how you are getting on with the "old grudge?" If I judge correctly from the journals that reach me, that during my near three years' absence, its status, unlike renowned grape-juice, has neither dissipated or improved by lapse of time, and that lynching and disfranchisement still have the right of way.

The expansion of our sovereignty is fraught with complications, and onerous duties from the statesman, the zeal of the humanitarian, and of reformers and friends of equitable government, unflinching determination are required, that kindness and justice shall be ceded to the people thereof. But is the prospect for the dissemination or ascendancy of these virtues either bright or promising? If the exercise and enjoyments of these attributes are not granted to millions of the American household, is it reasonable to expect they will dominate abroad? There is reason for apprehension that our cousins in the East will find little change of despotic tendencies amid the rank and file of American adventurers. The philosophy of our system of government seems out of balance. Cicero wrote "that excessive liberty leads both nations and individuals into excessive slavery."

But amid the lights and shadows that environ the Negro, he is neither undeserving of the assistance rendered, and indispensable for educational development, which has been generous, and for which he is grateful, although handicapped by a prejudice confronting on so many avenues of industry, and forbidding his entry. Not undeserving for patient and non-anarchist in the realms of labor, his right to possess and enjoying equality of citizenship is written with blood and bravery on the battlefield of every war of the Republic where he "fell forward as fits a man." Munificent contributions of Christians and philanthropists, for missionary work abroad, are greatly in evidence, given with a self-complacency of duty done; but, however, fail to vivify the declining pulse-beat for equality before the law and justice at home. Manifestly there is an absence of that arraignment and condemnation of wrong done the weak, that contributed so largely to abolish the "corn laws of England" and slavery in the United States.

History is the record that it is the men of moral courage and heroism who by pen and voice, that sociality and gain cannot intimidate and combat evil in their very midst that "leave footprints in the sands of time."

I must close this letter, already too long. Don't regard me as a pessimist. I know that Bacon wrote that "men of age object too much," but the fact is, Cooper, it has been so long since I heard a Fourth of July hallelujah chorus that I am getting out of tune.

McKinley has been again nominated, I see, and doubtless will be elected, with a Congress in harmony, thus giving the party another lease of power, which, God grant, let us hope, may redound to the welfare of all the people. Say to my many friends that they are, "though lost to sight to memory dear."

Truly your friend,
M. W. GIBBS

Chapter 22

The Island of Madagascar was discovered in 1506 by Lawrence Almeyda, a Portuguese; but the Persians and Arabs are said to have known it from time immemorial. The island is divided into 28 provinces and is said to contain two hundred millions acres of excellent land, watered on all sides by streams and large rivers. Its two highest mountains are Vigagora in the north and Batistmene in the south, said to contain in their bowels abundance of fossils and valuable minerals. This island, situated near the eastern coast of Africa, with 300 miles of the Mozambique Channel intervening, is 1,000 miles in length and varying from 200 to 400 miles in width, and is supposed to have been in remote ages a portion of the continent of Africa and that the progenitors of its people were to that "manor born;" others that the channel was crossed in canoes and Madagascar populated.

Rev. W. E. Cousins, an English missionary, in a late edition of "Madagascar of Today," says that "its people are not on the whole an African people, and much of its flora and fauna indicate a very long separation from the neighboring continent. Particularly notable is the fact that Madagascar has no lions, deer, elephants or antelopes, which are abundant in Africa; the people generally are not Africans, but belong to the same family as Malays and Malayo Polynesians." How the Malayon came to be the predominant language has exercised the thoughts of many, Africa being not more than 300 miles from the west coast of Madagascar, whereas the nearest point, Malayon Peninsula, is 3,000 miles away. That the distinct type of African presents itself in large numbers of native population is beyond question.

For much of the following as to the religion, morals and customs of the Madagascar people, I am indebted to Rev. Cousins, the missionary above referred to, and a work entitled "Madagascar, or Drury's Journal," edited by Pasfield Oliver and published in 1729. Robert Drury was an English lad that ran away from home, was shipwrecked, and held in captivity by the natives for 15 years, and redeemed by Captain Mackett, commanding the "Prince of Wales" in the East India Company's service. Also to the "Island of Madagascar," by Abbe Alexis Rochon, a learned Frenchman, who visited the island in 1767 and made an extensive report.

Mr. Oliver mentions that there are authors who say that the religion of these people is Mahometanism, but he is at a loss to know from what they drew their conclusions, since their sacrifices and their antipathy to revelation; and, besides, at the only place where a Moorish ship (Mahometan) came, swines' flesh is eaten. These obviously show that there can be nothing in more direct opposition to it. There is no one circumstance like it, except circumcision, and that is well known to those learned in ancient history to have been common to some Eastern nations, even before the Jews had it, and where there is no reason to think the name of the Jews was ever heard, and we have more reason to think that the Jews derived a great deal from them instead of they from the Jews; that their religion is more ancient is evident for several obvious reasons.

First, by their regarding dreams and divining by them, which so early as the Mosaic law the Children of Israel were warned against.

Secondly, these people shave their hair all off in mourning for the dead. This Moses expressly commands the Israelites not to do, and the Jews do superstitiously observe this last and suffer their hair to grow in their mourning.

Thirdly, Moses commanded none but males to be sacrificed. On the contrary, these sacrifice cows for the most part. They have no burnt offerings but near their sepulchers, which with gum, burnt likewise, may only arise from a defense of cadaverous scents.

Fourthly, but the most remarkable instance of all is, that the "owley," which these Madagascar people divine by and procure most extraordinary dreams, is evidently the Ephod and Teraphin which the Levites used who lived in Micah's house (see Judges 17) and which the Israelites could never be wholly brought off from, though contrary to their law. Some have taken these Teraphin for images like a man, and there seems a show of reason in it from Micah, Saul's daughter putting one in David's bed to deceive her father's messenger, while he escaped. This, it is possible, alludes to some divination by the Teraphin which she used in his behalf, for Teraphin is the plural number; therefore, could not signify only one image; neither could the gods which Rachel stole from her father, Labon, be one god as big as a man, for she sat on them and hid them. The word is here in the original "Teraphin," although translated gods. Then, in Hosea, chapter 3, verse 4, "an image, an Ephod and Teraphin," are all mentioned in one verse, plainly showing that they are distinct things. It is further to be remarked that by this Teraphin they invoked the dead, which is exactly the same as these people do by the "Owley" always invoking the spirits of their forefathers, which is expressly forbidden to Israelites, and often sharply inveighed against by the prophets.

That these people had not their religion from any polite or learned nation is by their retaining no notion or meaning of letters, nor their having a horse among them, either for carriage or other use, which could never have been forgotten had they ever had it.

Mr. Oliver positively asserts that these Madagascar people came from Africa, and is certain on account of their color, while other writers think most of them to be descendants of Malays.

Captain Mackett, previously mentioned as the redeemer of Robert Drury from his 15 years' captivity, states that Devon (King) Toak, often told him they had a tradition of their coming to the island many years ago in large canoes; "but," says Captain Oliver, "let them come from where they will, it is evident that their religion is the most ancient in the known world and not much removed from natural religion, and whether the Egyptians and Canaanites had their religion from them, or that they are Egyptians originally, it had its rise long before the Children of Israel were in bondage, for Egypt was then a very polite country, and although idolators, they were not any more so than their neighbors before Abraham's time.

"The respect due from children to parents is taught them early by those parents and grows with them, besides the gratitude naturally arising to those who have fed and protected them when they were helpless infants. So it is no wonder to find a law there against cursing parents. The notion of the Being of one Supreme Author of nature arises from natural reflection on the visible harmony and uniformity of the universe and seeing that men and things did not produce themselves. The reverence due to this stupendous Being is only of a pious and rightly amazement, dread and respect. The testimony was everywhere uniform that where Europeans or Mahometans had not corrupted them they were innocent, moral and humane.

"Physically the island has lost none of its picturesque character, so vividly portrayed by Abbe Rochon more than a century ago, who wrote 'The Traveler,' who in pursuit of knowledge traverses for the first time wild and mountainous countries, intersected by ridges and valleys, where nature, abandoned to its own fertility, presents the most singular and varied productions, cannot help being struck with terror and surprise on viewing those awful precipices, the summits of which are covered with trees as ancient perhaps as the world. His astonishment is increased when he hears the noise of immense cascades which are so inaccessible that it is impossible for him to approach them. But these scenes, truly picturesque, are always succeeded by rural views, delightful hills and plains, where vegetation is never interrupted by the severity and vicissitudes of the seasons. The eye with pleasure beholds those extensive savannas which afford nourishment to numerous herds of cattle and flocks of sheep. Fields of rice and potatoes present also a new and highly interesting spectacle. One sees agriculture flourishing, while nature alone defrays almost all the expense. The fortunate inhabitants of Madagascar need not moisten the earth with their sweat; they turn it up slightly with a pick-axe, and this labor alone is sufficient. They make holes in the ground at a little distance from each other and throw into them a few grains of rice, over which they spread the mold with their feet. And what proves the great fertility of the soil is that a field thus sown produces an hundred-fold. The forests contain a prodigious variety of the most beautiful trees, such as palms of every kind, ebony, wood for dyeing, bamboos of an enormous size, and orange and lemon trees." The Abbe's picture is quite enchanting, for it seems that "every prospect pleases."

A view of Antananarivo, the capital of Madagascar, in the word-painting of Cameron, a war correspondent of the London Standard, is interesting. "Antananarivo was in sight and we could plainly see the glass windows of the palace glistening in the morning sun, on the top of the long hill upon which the city is built. It was Sunday, and the people were clustering along the foot-paths on their way to church or sitting in the grass outside waiting for the services to begin, as they do in villages at home. The women, who appeared to be in the majority, wore white cotton gowns, often neatly embroidered, and white or black and white striped lambas, thrown gracefully over their shoulders. The men were clad also in cotton, white cotton pantaloons, cotton lambas, and straw hats, with large black silk band. In the morning sun the play of colors over the landscape was lovely. The dark green hills, studded with the brilliant red brick houses of the inhabitants, whose white garments dotted the lanes and foot-paths, contrasted with the brighter emerald of the rice fields in the hollows. The soil everywhere is deep red, almost magenta, in color, and where the roads or pathways cross the hills they shine out as if so many paint-brushes had streaked the country in broad red stripes. Above all, the spires of the strange city, set on top of its mountain with a deep blue sky for a background, added to the beauty of the scene.

"It was difficult to imagine that this peaceful country, with its pretty cottages, its innumerable chapels, whose bells were then calling its people to worship, and its troops of white-robed men and women answering the summons, was the barbarous Madagascar of twenty years ago."

Mention of the form of government had by the Madagascar people and which is now being superseded by occupancy of the French and the introduction of laws of a civilized nation, may not be out of place. As far back as tradition will carry, there existed in Madagascar a kind of feudalism. Villages were usually built on the hilltops, and each hilltop had its own chieftain, and these petty feudal chiefs were constantly waging war with each other. The people living on these feudal estates paid taxes and rendered certain services to their feudal lords. Each chief enjoyed a semi-independence, for no strong over-lord existed. Attempts were made from time to time to unite these petty chieftains into one Kingdom, but no one tribe succeeded in making itself supreme till the days of Radam I, who succeeded in bringing the whole of Imerina under his government, and to his son, Radama, he left the task of subduing the rest of the island. By allying himself closely with England, Radama obtained military instruction and carried war into distant provinces. He ultimately succeeded in conquering many of the tribes and his reign marked the beginning of a new era in Madagascar. Indeed, only from his days could Madagascar in any sense be regarded as a political unit.

In one direction, however, the results of Radama's policy must be regarded as retrogressive. Before his reign no chief or king was powerful enough to impose his rule upon the people without their consent.

Opposition to rule, without the consent of the governed, has been the shibboleth with which liberty has rallied the votaries of constitutional government in all its reforms. It was the magna charter extorted from King John at Runnymead—the trumpet call echoing and re-echoing by hill and through valley in our Declaration of Independence. Before Radama, although rude and primitive in form, it was the basic principle cherished by the people of Madagascar. The principal men of each district had to be constantly consulted and Kabary, or public assemblies like the Greek or the Swiss Communal assemblies, were called for the discussion of all important affairs, and public opinion had a fair opportunity of making itself effective.

"A single tree does not make a forest, but the thoughts of many constitute a government," is handed down by tradition as one of the farewell sayings of their early kings, and is often quoted by the people. This was the spirit that existed in "ye olden time," but after Radama I. formed a large army and a military caste was created there was a strong tendency to repress and minimize the influence of civilians in public affairs, and men holding military rank have wielded the chief authority.

It was ever thus; for while the chiefs of victorious legions are received with strains of "conquering hero," have roses for a pathway canopied with waving flag and triumphant banner, there is not wanting a latent, reserved concern for the legitimate use of the franchise granted and whether vaulting ambition may not destroy the sacred inheritance they were commissioned to preserve. Military rank in Madagascar was strangely reckoned by numbers. The highest officers being called men of "sixteen honors," the men of twelve honors would be equal in rank to a field marshal, the men of nine honors to a colonel, and the man of three honors to a sergeant, and so on, through the whole series.

When any important government business had to be made known the men from 12 honors upward were summoned to the palace. Above all these officers stood the Prime Minister. His Excellency Ramiloiarivony. The supreme head of the state was the Mpanjaka, or sovereign, and every proclamation was issued in her name and was generally countersigned and confirmed as a genuine royal message by the Prime Minister. For three reigns, namely, from the accession of Rasaherina in 1863, Mpanjaka had been a woman and the wife of the Prime Minister. A general impression exists in England that this is an old Madagascar custom, but such is not the case. The arrangement is of quite recent date. The last Prime Minister (not being of royal blood) was content to be Mpanjaka, or ruler, and while all public honor was shown to the Queen, and her authority fully acknowledged, those behind the scenes would have us believe that the Queen was supreme only in name.

As a matter of fact, the Prime Minister, and even his supposed wishes and preferences, were the most potent forces in Madagascar. No one seemed able to exercise any independent influence, and time after time the men who showed any special ability or gained popularity have been removed, swept away as it were, out of the path of the man who had assumed and by his ability and astuteness maintained for thirty years the highest position in the country. There was, no doubt, a large amount of latent rebellion against this "one-man government," but those who were the most ready to grumble in private were in public, perhaps, the most servile of any. It is conceded that in many ways the Prime Minister was an able ruler, and compared with those who went before him was deserving of great praise.

He made many attempts to prevent the corruption of justice, and strenuously endeavored to improve the administration, and for many years had managed to hold in check the ambitious projects of French statesmen, and had shown at many times his interest in the cause of education.

But his monopoly as a ruler, the idea of omnipotent control, refusal to allow his subordinates to take their share of responsibility, like many similar instances which history records, loosened the bond of patriotic interest, love and integrity for country, and made easy the ingress of the French in subduing and appropriating the Island of Madagascar.

It has been stated that no account of Madagascar government would be complete that did not include a description of their system of "fanompoana," or forced service, which answers very nearly to the old feudal service, and to the system known in Egypt as "corvee." The tax-gatherer is not the ubiquitous person in Madagascar he is generally supposed to have been.

There were a few taxes paid by the people, such, for example, as a small tax in kind on the rice crop, and occasionally a small poll-tax, and money paid the sovereigns as a token of allegiance on many occasions.

Taxes of this kind were not burdensome. The one burden that galled and irritated the people was the liability to be called upon at any moment to render unrequited service to the government.

Every man had something that was regarded as "fanompoana." The people of one district might be required to make mats for the government, in another pots, the article required. From one district certain men were required to bring crayfish to the capital, charcoal from another, iron from another, and so on through all the series of wants. The jeweler must make such articles as the Queen would desire, the tailor use his needle and the writer his pen, as the government might need. The system had in it some show of rough-and-ready justice, and was based on the idea that each must contribute to the needs of the state according to his several abilities; but in the actual working it had a most injurious influence on the wellbeing of the country. Each man tried to avoid the demands made upon him, and the art "how not to do it" was cultivated to a very high degree of perfection. Many of the head men made this "fanompoana" system a means of enriching themselves, compelling the subordinates to serve them as well as the government. History does but repeat itself, as there are not wanting instances in our own country where certain heads of department "fanomponed" subordinates for private service.

In many ways are recorded the product of the fertile brain of these head men. For instance, the centurion, or head man of a certain district, gave out a notice in the church yard, on Sunday morning, or at a week-day market, that a hundred men would be required next morning to carry charcoal for the government. As a matter of fact, he required only twenty, but he knew that many would come to him to beg off, and as none would come empty-handed, his profit on the transaction was considerable. Another illustration was given Mr. Cousins by the British Consul. It was customary to send up mails from the coast by government runners, but English ideas being adverse to demanding unrequited service, the Consul had always sent the usual wages for the runners to the Governor, who pocketed the dollars and "fanomponed" the mail. But enough of this, as it has a flavor of our "Star Route Mail" disclosures, which startled the country some years ago, and conclude with a tribute to Tammany, as:

We arise to remark, and our language is plain,
That the Tweeds and the Crokers are of Malagash fame.

Chapter 23

The introduction and perpetuation of the Christian religion in Madagascar has been attended with vicissitudes, hopeful, discouraging, and finally permanent. The Catholics were the first to attempt to gain a footing on the southeast corner of the island. A French mission settled and commenced to instruct the natives in the Roman Catholic faith, and maintained a mission in spite of many discouragements for twenty years, and then came to an end. Protestants who a century and a half later carried the Gospel to Madagascar found it virgin soil. They found a people without a written language or knowledge of the Christian faith. Both in their literary and evangelical labors they had to revive a work that was not dying out, but to start de novo, and the London Missionary Society had to seek its own way to carry out its objects.

The men to whom it appears that the Madagascar people are indebted for their written languages and the first translation of the Scriptures were two Welshmen.

David Jones and David Griffiths—these two men were the pioneers of Protestant missions in Madagascar—the first in 1820, the second a year later. The main strength of these early missionaries was devoted to educational work, in which they were vigorously supported by King Radama I, and Mr. Hastie, the British agent. Besides this they began very early to make a translation of the Scriptures, and in ten years after the arrival of Mr. Jones in Antananarivo the first edition of 3,000 copies of the New Testament was completed, in March, 1830. At this time much progress had been made in the translation of the Old Testament. The account of the completion of it is interesting. Soon after the death of King Radama I, in 1828, the missionaries saw clear indications of the uncertainty of their positions; ominous clouds began to gather until the storm burst.

The edict of Queen Ranavalona I against the Christian Church was published March 1, 1835. A portion of the Old Testament translation was uncompleted. The missions were deserted by their converts, and they could procure no workman to assist; so with trembling haste they proceeded with their task, and at the end of June they had joy in seeing the first bound copies of the completed Bible. Most of these were secretly distributed, and seventy remaining copies were buried for safety in the earth—precious seed over which God watched and which in due season produced a glorious harvest. The translators were driven away, but the book remained. Studied in secret, and at the risk of life, it served during more than a quarter of a century of persecution to keep alive faith in the newly received religion; for, during all this time, to use the familiar native phrase, "the land was dark." At its commencement Queen Ranavalona (the Queen Mary of Madagascar), with all the force of her strong will, set herself to destroy the new religion. "It was cloth," she said, "of a pattern she did not like, and she was determined none of her people should use it."

The victims of her fury form a noble army of martyrs, of whom Madagascar is justly proud. The causes that led to the persecution are not far to seek. On the one hand, they were intensely conservative, clinging to ancestral customs; and on the other hand, a suspicious and jealous fear of foreign influence. The zealous work of the missionaries was believed by many of the Queen's advisers to be only a cloak to conceal political designs. The teachings of the foreigners were proving so attractive that their chapels were crowded, and the influence of this new religion was making itself felt in many families. Whither would all this lead? Was it to pave the way to annex the island to the English Government? The word "society" to a native ignorant of English would suggest a phrase of their own which sounds alike, viz: "sosoy-oty"—"push the canoe over this way." This to the ingenuous or suspicious mind of the hearers suggested the idea of pushing over the Government of Madagascar to those across the ocean who were supposed to be greedily seeking to seize it. This is seemingly absurd, but not too ridiculous to obtain credence with a people excited and suspicious.

The former King Radama showed his shrewdness in giving permission to the missionaries to reside in his country, for he expressly stipulated that some of them should be skilled artisans, so that his people might be instructed in weaving, smith-work, carpentry, etc. To this the society wisely assented, and a number of Christian artisans were sent out. The influence of these were of immense value, and to them is to be attributed much of the skill of the Madagascar workman of today.

There is no doubt that the manifest utility of their work did much to win for the mission a measure of tolerance from the heathen rulers of the country. One of the missionaries with great mechanical skill, in his "Recollections," states that Queen Ranavalona in 1830 was beginning to feel uneasy about the growing influence of foreign ideas and wished to get rid of the missionaries. She sent officers to carry her message, and the missionaries were gathered together to meet the messengers, and were told that they had been a long time in the country and had taught much, and that it was time for them to think of returning to their native land. The missionaries, alarmed at this message, answered that they had only begun to teach some of the elements of knowledge, and that very many more remained to be imported, mentioning sundry branches of education, among which were Greek and Hebrew languages, which had already been taught to some. The messengers returned to the Queen, and soon came back with the answer: "The Queen does not care much for Greek and Hebrew. Can you teach how to make soap?" (And if cleanliness is akin to godliness she was evidently groping in the right direction.) This was an awkward question to address theologians; almost as much so as "Do you know enough to come in out of the rain?" to some college graduates; but after a moment's pause Mr. Griffith turned to Mr. Cameron and asked him if he could answer it. "Give me a week," and it was given, and when the messengers again met at the close of the week a bar of tolerable good white soap, made from materials found in the country, was presented. This was entirely satisfactory, and the manufacture of soap was forthwith introduced, and is still continued to the present day. This bar of soap gained the missionaries a respite of five years, the Queen tolerating their presence on account of material advantage derived from the work of the artisans. In believing that industrial training, the knowledge to make things in demand, was the first necessary step for the elevation of her people, the Queen was eminently correct.

During the fifteen years (from 1820 to 1835) the mission was allowed to exist it was estimated that 10,000 to 15,000 children passed through school, so that when the missionaries were compelled to leave the island there were thousands who had learned to read, and thereby raised far above the mass of their heathen fellow-countrymen.

Dark Days—January, 1835, a formal complaint was presented to the missionaries by one of the Queen's officers against the Christian religion under six different heads. Excitement increased and opposition to the new teaching grew bolder. The Queen, in passing a native chapel and hearing singing, was heard to say: "They will not stop till some of them lose their heads."

On the first of March, 1835, the edict publicly prohibiting the Christian religion was delivered in the presence of thousands of people who had been summoned to hear it. The place of meeting was a large open space lying to the west of the long hill on which the city of

Antananarivo is built, and large enough to contain two or more thousand people. In the middle of the plain crops up a large mass of granite rock, on which only royal persons were allowed to stand; hence probably the name "Imohamosine," which means "having power to make sacred." There from time to time large public assemblies have been held, but never one of greater significance or of more far-reaching issues than that. Of this great "kabary," or meeting, notices had been sent far and wide. All possible measures had been taken to inspire the people with awe and to make them feel that a proclamation of unusual importance was about to be published. Queen Ranavalona seemed anxious to make her people feel that her anger was burning with an unwonted fury. It is stated that morning had scarcely dawned when the report of the cannon intended to strike terror and awe into the hearts of the people ushered in the day on which the will and power of the sovereign of Madagascar to punish the defenseless followers of Christ was to be declared. Fifteen thousand troops were drawn up, part of them on the plain and the rest in two lines a mile in length along the road leading to the place. The booming of artillery from the high ground overlooking the plain and the reports of musketry of the troops, which was continued during the preparatory arrangements, produced among the multitude the most intense and anxious feelings. At length the Chief Justice, attended by his companions in office, advanced and delivered the message of the Sovereign, which was enforced by Ramiharo, the chief officer of the Government. After expressing the Queen's confidence in the idols, and her determination to treat as criminals all who refused to do them homage, the message proceeded:

"As to baptism, societies, places of worship, and the observance of the Sabbath—how many rulers are there in the land? Is it not I, alone, that rule? These things are not to be done. They are unlawful in my country," said the Queen, "for they are not the customs of our ancestors."

As a result of this "kabary" 400 officers were reduced in rank and fines were paid for 2,000 others, and thus was ushered in a persecution which lasted a quarter of a century.

The Rev. William Ellis, on English missionaries, in his book entitled "Madagascar Revisited," states that the first martyr for Christ who suffered there in 1836 was "Rosolama." She was a Christian woman, between twenty and thirty years of age, bearing no common name, for Rosolama signifies peace and happiness. She was imprisoned at Ambotonakonga, the site of the first house built exclusively for

Christian worship in the country. A memorial church has been erected on the spot. When brought to the place she knelt down and asked a few minutes to pray. This was granted, and then her body fell, pierced with the spears of her executioners.

The second martyr, Rayfarolahy, a young man, suffered on the same place some time after. At the request of Rosolama when she was taken forth to death he had walked by her side to the place of execution and offered words of encouragement to her to the last. When brought to the place himself the executioners seized him and were about, as was their custom, to forcibly throw him down, he said to them calmly, "There is no need to do that; I will not cause any trouble." He also asked to be allowed to pray, and then gently laid himself down and received the executioners' spears. The measures taken to destroy Christianity were not at all times equally severe. The years that stand out with special prominence are 1835, 1837, 1840, 1849 and 1857. Of what took place in 1840 was depicted at the time in a letter written by Rev. D. Griffiths, who was then residing at Antananarivo. The nine condemned Christians were taken past Mr. Griffiths' house. "Ramonisa," he says, "looked at me and smiled; others also looked at me, and their faces shone like those of angels in the posture of prayer and wrestling with God. They were too weak to walk, having been without rice or water for a long time. The people on the wall and in the yard before our house were cleared off by the swords and spears of those leading them to execution. That we might have a clear, full and last sight of them, they were presented opposite the balcony on the road and at the entrance of the yard for about ten minutes, carried on poles by the executioners, with merely a hand breadth of cloth to cover them, they were then led away to execution. The cannon fired to announce their death was shattered to pieces, and the gunners' clothes burnt, which was considered ominous, many whispering 'Thus will the kingdom of Ranavalona Manjaka be shattered to pieces.'"

In 1849 what may be called the great persecution took place; not less than 1,900 persons suffered persecution of various kinds—fines, imprisonment, chains, or forced labor in the quarries. Of this number 18 suffered death, four, of noble birth, by being burned, and 14 by being thrown over the great precipice of Ampomarinona. It is not easy to estimate exactly the number of those who suffered the punishment of death in these successive outbursts of persecution. It is most probable the victims were between seventy or eighty. But these form only a small portion of the total number of sufferers. Probably hundreds of others died from their heavy irons, chains, or from fevers, severe forced labor, or privations during the time they were compelled to hide in caves or in the depths of the forests.

Notwithstanding the severe persecution much quiet Christian work was carried on in the lulls between storms—sometimes on hilltops, sometimes in caves, or even in unfinished tombs. Thus the story of the Covenanters was repeated, and the impossibility of destroying the Christian faith by persecution again shown. Through these long years of persecution the Christians were constantly receiving accessions to their ranks, and the more they were opposed "the more they multiplied and grew."

The year 1861 will ever be a period from which date results momentous in behalf of civil and religious liberty for the Negro. It was the beginning of the end of Negro slavery in the United States and the permanent establishment of religious freedom in Madagascar. Queen Ranavalona had a long reign of thirty-three years, but in that year it became evident she could not reign much longer. Natives give details of her last days. The aged Queen had for some time been suffering in health; diviners had been urgently consulted, charms and potent herbs had been employed, with no avail. Late in the summer of 1861 it became generally known that the fatal moment could not long be delayed. Mysterious fires were said to be seen on the tops of mountains surrounding the capital, and a sound like music was rising from Iatry to Andohalo. The Queen eagerly questioned those around her as to the meaning of these portents. But while the dying Queen was anxiously praying to the idol in which she placed her trust, there were those who whispered to the prince that the fire was the sign of jubilee to bring together the dispersed, and to redeem the lost, and so the event proved.

The aged Queen passed away during the night of August 15, 1861, and early on the morning of August 16 the news spread rapidly through the capital, and her son was proclaimed as Radama II. One of the first acts of the new sovereign was to proclaim religious liberty. The chains were struck off from the persecuted Christians and the banished were recalled. Many came back who had long been in banishment or in hiding, and their return seemed to friends who had supposed them to be dead like a veritable resurrection.

The joy of the Christian was intense. The long season of repression had at last come to an end. Now it was no longer a crime to meet for Christian worship, or to possess Christian books. On that first Friday evening some of the older Christians met and spent the night in prayer, and Sunday services were begun in eleven private houses; but these were soon consolidated into three large congregations. Radama II eagerly welcomed intercourse with foreigners and gave Christians permission to write at once, urging that missionaries be sent out, himself writing to the London Missionary Society making the same request. The society responded promptly with a large band of men and women missionaries, twenty or thirty thousand copies of the Bible, New Testament and tracts.

The result of three-quarters of a century of Christian work in Madagascar has been that the Christian religion has taken firm hold on the people. Manifest and noticeable are the number and prominence of church buildings in and around the capital. There are four stone memorial churches, built by the friends of the London Missionary Society to remind coming generations of the fidelity of the martyrs, and a very fine and well situated Roman Catholic cathedral in Ambodin Andaholo. Prominent as Christian agencies in Madagascar are "The Society for the Propagation of the Gospel," who sent out Bishop Kestel Cornish and James Coles; "The Norwegian Missionary Society," "The Roman Catholic Missionary Society," and "The Society of Friends in England."

To summarize, approximately there are now 110 foreign missionaries on the island; over 2,000 congregations, with a total of 400,000 adherents, which include 100,000 church members; while the Protestant schools contain 150,000 children. No statement of the Christianizing agencies and influences would be just or correct that did not include that of the Roman Catholic Church. "No one," it has been truly said, "can be long in Madagascar without learning to admire the self-denial, patience and heroic fortitude with which its work is carried on." It has been thus fittingly described, a few years ago, by an English visitor: "In 1861, when Catholic missionaries landed on the shores of Tamatave there was not a Catholic on the island; but little by little, by dint of unwearied labor, suffering and preaching, they won over not hundreds but thousands of pagans to the love and knowledge of our Lord and His truth, so that their pagan converts number over 130,000. They have built a magnificent cathedral, which is the glory and pride of Antananarivo. They have also 300 churches and 400 or more Catholic stations scattered over the island, where 18,000 children are taught and trained by a large and elevated staff of Christian brothers and sisters of St. Joseph, and 641 native teachers. They have also created industrial schools, where various trades are taught by two devoted brothers, Benjamin and Arnoad, and at Ambohipo they have a flourishing college for young Malagash. They have also on the island four large dispensaries, where thousands of prescriptions are distributed gratis to all who seek to relieve their sufferings. They have also established a leper hospital at Ambohivoraka, where the temporal and spiritual wants of 150 poor lepers are freely administered to, and have already opened another such establishment, in Betsilio land. Prison visitation, dispensing rice, clothing, and spiritual instruction to half-starved and naked prisoners under the Madagascar rule; their catalogue of books devotional, literary and scientific; a dictionary, all of which have been edited and published in the Madagascan language, are among the golden contributions for civilization by the Catholics in this far-off island continent in the Indian seas."

In referring to their labors, and to which, comparatively, I have made but brief reference, Mr. Cousins says: "To much in the Roman Catholic system we may be strenuously opposed; but to their zeal, their skill, their patience, their self-denial, we render the homage of an ungrudging admiration."

The foregoing were the labors and results of missionary effort up to the date of the French taking absolute possession of the island. It is to be hoped there will be no retrograde movement lessening the efficiency of these civilizing agencies. Although it is alleged that French control and influence in Tahiti and other South Sea islands have been averse to both morality and evangelical Christianity, and hence there are not wanting those who predict incumbrances in missionary work, now French authority is established. But in this age of progress along all the lines of human endeavor the French Government will undoubtedly see the justice and utility of governing with a regard to the advancement of these wards that the prowess of its arms have committed to its care. It is not unreasonable to expect, and the promise should be flattering, that with the European ideas of the proper functions of government, the incipient steps for the mental culture of the natives, present evidence of large expenditure and introduction of the most modern applications for the physical development of the island, the Madagascan people will attain in the future a higher degree of human advancement from contact with the civilization of the French than it was possible they could have under "Hova rule." And in this connection it is gratifying to note that "The Native Race Protection Committee," headed by Mr. Paul

Viollet, of the Paris Institute, in June, 1899, addressed an appeal to the Colonial Minister in behalf of the Malagash, entreating him to shorten the forced labor, to reduce the taxes, and to annul decrees, which greatly re-established slavery.

The appeal dwelt on the fearful mortality occasioned by forced labor on the roads, which threatened to reduce the most robust population of the highlands as to de-bar colonists from commercial and agricultural enterprises, and very pertinently asks "Is it not better to be without roads than without a healthy population?" The appeal also denounced arbitrary acts. "The native," it is said, "is arrested and imprisoned for months without a trial, and this with all the less forbearance, as the prisoner is always utilized as an economic laborer." The justice of this appeal and prompt reception and accord with the French conscience was evidenced in the public announcement to the natives by Gen. Gallieni, the Governor of Madagascar, a few months later, that forced labor would be discontinued after January 1, 1900, and thereafter they could work for whom they pleased, and if for government they would be paid wages agreed to.

It is needless to say that this proclamation was received by the natives with tumultuous rejoicing. Forced labor is now abolished, and the natives rejoice in a jubilee from a servitude the most galling.

Chapter 24

The adaptability of the Negro to conditions that are at the time inevitable has been the paladium that has sustained and multiplied him amid the determined prejudice that has ever assailed him. The Indian, unassimilating, combatted the prejudice of caste by physical force, and has been well nigh extinguished, while the Negro has bowed to the inevitable with the mental reservation to rise to a higher recognition by a persistent assimilation of the forces that disenthralled and exalted the Saxon.

The foregoing chapter, indicating the policy of the French in their occupation and dealing with Madagascar, the planting of a nation's authority and establishing a colony on the ruins of a weaker power, or of subject races, under the plea of humanity, or through the chicanery of diplomacy, has ever been the rule when territory has been desired by a stronger power. The proximity of Cuba to the States, and Spanish misrule of that island, and also of the Philippines, were the "open sesame," it is alleged, that beckoned the armed force of the United States to take possession. But in truth the Spanish jewel, Cuba, shone in the distance, "so near, and yet so far"—so near for mischievous complication, and so far for material and diplomatic control. With a vicious administration by a nation of decaying prestige were all elements promising success to the invader. The covert and dastardly destruction of the U. S. warship "Maine" in Cuban waters, the offspring of Spanish suspicion of American designs, was all, and more than required, to inaugurate a "causi belli" and complete the conquest of the island. To claim that these movements had their incipiency in a consensus of desire of the American people for justice to subject races, and was solely, or even mainly, on account of Spanish tyranny, is a statement that will not bear investigation for moral consistency. It being the very antipodes of their current behavior to a large class of citizens born beneath the pinions of their eagle of freedom at home.

For how does it happen that the alien Cuban and Filipino colored brothers are so much more entitled to protection and the enjoyment of civil and political rights than the colored American brother, that thousands of lives and millions of treasure must be expended to establish that humanity and justice abroad denied by these "world reformers" to millions of their citizens at home? Really, it would seem that to duty and the bestowal of justice 'tis "distance that lends enchantment to the view." "Wherever you see a head, hit it," was the slogan of Pat, at Donnybrook Fair, and wherever there has been a territorial plum ripe in its loneliness, and tempting in its lusciousness, there has not been wanting a "grabber." It was the French in Madagascar, the English in Africa, and the Americans in the Antilles. "O! civilization; what crimes are committed in thy name!" The record of our stewardship is in the tomb of the future for the coming historian to "point a moral or adorn a tale."

The acquisition of new territory, when honorably acquired, is ever attended with peculiar conditions and vicissitudes. The transformation of the population of which into a desirable element of the body politic depends much upon the wisdom of the statesman, and the insistence of moral rectitude on the part of the Christian and philanthropist whether it shall be a blessing or an evil to both parties in interest.

It is no secret that in many minds the motive and manner of acquiring the Philippines are open to much disparaging comment. We are charged with wresting by superior force that independence that a weak but heroic people were and had been for ten years struggling to attain from the Spanish yoke; that we, whom they hailed as an assistant and in good faith co-operated with in turn, became their hostile enemies and destroyed that identity as an independent entity for which they fought.

The conditions which confronted Aguinaldo as the leader of the Philippine revolution have been vividly described by a writer of English history: "With the statesman in revolutionary times, it is not through decisive moments that seemed only trivial, and by important turns that seemed indifferent; for he explores dark and untried paths; groping his way through a jungle of vicissitudes, ambush and strategem; expedient, a match for fortune in all her moods. Regardless of what has been called 'history's severe and scathing touch,' we cannot forget the torrid air of revolutionary times, the blinding sand storms of faction, the suspicions, jealousies and hatreds, the distinctions of mood and aim, the fierce play of passions that put an hourly strain of untold intensity on the constancy, the prudence, and the valor of a leader."

No one can read the state papers and proclamations of Aguinaldo without being impressed with his ability as a leader, the intensity of his patriotism and honesty of purpose depicted for the independence of his country from Spanish rule. The statesmanship he displayed, the intelligent and liberal conception of constitutional government, and the needs and aspirations of his people, are at variance with the allegation that the Filipinos were unfit for self-government.

Hence it is that men ask, "Would it not have been national nobility of a high order if as a protector we should have given them a protectorate instead of the ignoble action of shooting them down in their patriotic attempt?" Indeed, it remains to be seen whether absolute authority obtained by such means, together with current American usage of colored races, will not evolve the fact that they have but changed masters. For here in our own hemisphere our country's history continues to be rife with lawlessness at the bidding of a vicious sentiment, and in some sections it is the rule and not the exception. Free from the restraint of law-abiding localities in the States, the American adventurer of lawless propensity will have free reign in bullying and oppressing, and probable partiality in the administration of the law.

George E. Horr, the able editor of the "Watchman," under "Treatment to Subject Races," is pointed and timely when he says: "The Englishman who emigrates to an English colony finds that he comes under the same laws that apply to the natives; he is not a privileged personage, by virtue of the fact that he is an Englishman. Law is enacted and executed with absolute impartiality. In India a native and an Englishman stand exactly on the same plane before the law. Indeed, in many cases, an Englishman will be tried by an Indian judge. The British have not succeeded in winning the affections of the natives, but the natives are thoroughly convinced the Englishman will act justly. There will not be (in practice) one law for European and another for the native, as in too many cases in our own country there is one law for the white man and another for the black man."

But let us all work, hope and trust that the best of American Christianity and civilization may be equal to the emergency, giving the Filipinos a larger measure of liberty and civil rights than they had under the erstwhile rule of Spain.

Under a constitutional government it is premised that sustenance and valor for "amor patria" proceeds from the fact that its institutions are designed as bulwarks for the citizen's liberty, and that its political and economic features are such as guarantee equality before the law and promote an equal chance in the race of life.

That there is a degree of selfishness in his patriotism, and that government is revered only as a means to an end, is evidenced by revolutionary tendencies ever uppermost when there are reasons to believe that these benign purposes are being thwarted. But if for wrongs, the return be fidelity, for obloquy patience, for maltreatment loyalty, be a high type of Christian ethics, the reflex influence of which, we read, are God-like; surely the Negro has virtues "not born to die," presaging an endurance that must evolve out of this nettle discomfort, justice and contentment. For, as heretofore, in the last war with Spain, putting behind him his century of oppression in slavery, and the vicious discrimination since his emancipation, forgetful of all else save the honor and glory of the flag, there, as, always, he wrote his name high up on the roll of his country's heroes. "Our's not to ask the reason why; our's to do or die." To read the reports of commanders and other officers, and the narratives of bystanders, all attesting to a bravery invincible, causes the blood to tingle and the patriot heart to leap. We are making history replete with self-abnegation as we continue to bring to our country's altar an unstinted devotion and brilliant achievement. These take their places fittingly, and we should keep them in the forefront of our claim for equality of citizenship.

For it is declared that "not the least valuable lesson taught by the war with Spain is the excellence of the Negro soldiery". In the battle of San Juan, near Santiago, a Negro regiment is said to have borne the brunt of the battle. Three companies suffered nearly as seriously, yet they remained steady under fire without an officer. The war has not shown greater heroism. In the battle of Guasimas it is said by some of the "Rough Riders" themselves that it was the brilliant supporting charge of the Tenth Cavalry that saved them from destruction. George Rennon writes: "I do not hesitate to call attention to the splendid behavior of the colored troops." It is the testimony of all who saw them under fire that they fought with the utmost courage, coolness and determination; and Colonel Roosevelt said to a squad of them in the trenches in my presence that he never expected to have and could not ask to have better men beside him in a hard fight. If soldiers come up to Colonel Roosevelt's standard of courage, their friends have no reason to be ashamed of them. His commendation is equivalent to a medal of honor for conspicuous gallantry, because, in the slang of the camp, he is himself a fighter "from way back." I can testify, furthermore, from my own personal observation in the hospital of the Fifth Army Corps, Saturday and Sunday night, that the colored regulars who were brought in there displayed extraordinary fortitude and self-control. There were a great many of them, but I cannot remember to have heard a groan or complaint from a single man.

General Miles is quoted as favoring an increased number of colored soldiers in the United States service. He said that "in no instance had they failed to do their full duty in this war, or in the campaigns in the West; in short, they were model soldiers in every respect; not only in courage have they done themselves credit, but in their conduct as well."

When the Second Volunteer regiment of Immunes (white) became so disorderly in Santiago that they had to be sent outside to the hills for better discipline, General Shafter ordered into the city the Eighth Illinois regiment of colored troops, who had an unsullied name for sobriety and discipline, and enjoyed the thorough confidence of those in command. And the following brief compendium of Spanish war mention from a few of the leading press of the country is good reading. A soldier writing home to friends in Springfield said: "You want to see the Negroes; they let out a yell and charge, and the fight is over." Arthur Partridge, of Co. B, writes: "At first we got the worst of it, but we received reinforcements from the two regiments of colored infantry, who walked right up to the block house, against their whole fire; they lost heavily, but it put heart into everybody, and the way we drove those Spaniards was a caution. A colored man can have anything of mine he wants. When storming they yelled like fiends." Corporal Keating of Co. B writes: "The Negroes are fighters from their toes up. They saved Roosevelt at the first battle, and took one of the forts in the battle a few days ago."

Thomas Holmes, a Rough Rider, who hails from Newkirk, Oklahoma, was the magnet of attraction at St. Paul's Hospital, says a writer in the New York Tribune. "He is a handsome, stalwart fellow, full of anecdote and good humor, and popular all around. He was sitting next to Corporal Johnson, of the Tenth Cavalry, a Negro who still carries a Mauser bullet somewhere 'inside of me inside,' as he expressed it. 'The colored cavalry fought well, eh?' interjected the clergyman. 'Indeed they did,' said Holmes, fervently. 'That old idea about a "yellow streak" being in a Negro is all wrong. No men could have fought more bravely, and I want to tell you that but for the coming up of the Tenth Cavalry the Rough Riders might have been cut to pieces.' 'Oh, he is just talking,' said the colored man, who smiled like a happy child nevertheless."

Says the "Philadelphia Daily Press:" "At every forward movement in our national life the Negro comes to the front and shares in the advance with each national expansion. He does his part of the work, and deserves equal recognition. At Santiago two Negro regiments— the Ninth, in General Sumner's Brigade, and the Tenth, in General

Bates'—were at the front in the center of the line. With the rest they crested the heights of San Juan; with the rest they left their men thickly scattered on the slope, and since they shared in death every member of the race has a right to ask that in life no rights be denied and no privileges curtailed. The white regiments that connected them in that thin blue line, that slender hoop of steel which hemmed in more than its opposing number, may have held men who hesitate about this and that, contact with color; but on that Saturday afternoon and Sunday morning, when risk and peril hung heavy over the line, there was no hesitation in closing up on the Ninth and Tenth Regiments, because the men in them were colored. All honor to the black troops of the gallant Tenth."

Says the "New York Mail and Express:" "No more striking example of bravery and coolness has been shown since the destruction of the Maine than by the colored veterans of the Tenth Cavalry during the attack on Fort Caney of Saturday. By the side of the intrepid 'Rough Riders' they followed their leader up the terrible hill from whose crest the desperate Spaniards poured down a deathly fire of shell and musketry. They never faltered; the rents in their ranks were filled as soon as made. Firing as they marched, their aim was splendid, their coolness superb, and their courage aroused the admiration of their comrades. Their advance was greeted with wild cheers from the white regiments, and with an answering shout they pressed onward over the trenches they had taken close in pursuit of the retreating enemy. The war has not shown greater heroism. The men whose freedom was baptised in blood have proven themselves capable of giving their lives that others may be free. Today is a glorious 'Fourth' for all races of people in this great land."

The "New Orleans Item" gives its contemporary, the "States," the following spanking (with the usual interrogation, "Now will you be good?"): "The 'States' has evidently failed to profit by the beneficial lesson taught since the opening of the Santiago campaign. Had our esteemed contemporary been present in Richmond a few days since; when the form of a Negro soldier pierced by nine Mauser bullets was tenderly borne through the streets by four stalwart white infantry men, he would have heard the lustiest cheers that ever went up from the throats of the residents of the former capital of the Confederacy. Perhaps our anti-Negro friend would have learned wisdom from the statement of a member of Roosevelt's regiment, who declared in an interview with a press representative, that had it not been for the valiant conduct of the

Negro cavalry at Baguiri the Rough Riders would have found the routing of the Spaniards almost a hopeless task. The attack of the 'States' on the Negro soldier is vicious and unpardonable. There is no more intrepid or hardy fighter to be found anywhere than the much-abused descendant of Ham. He has dogged persistence and a determination to conquer which triumphs over all obstacles. He is aware of his social inferiority and never seeks to attain positions of eminence to which his valor and his spirit of daring do not entitle him. The 'States' presents one of the most rabid cases of negrophobia extant. It should seek an immediate cure."

Such indorsements from the white press of the country is not only timely, but for all time. History of his endurance and endeavor in peace, and his valor in war, stimulates his demand and strengthens his claim for equal justice. Such and kindred books as "Johnson's School History of the Race in America" should be prominent as household gods in every Afro-American home, that along the realm of time the vista of heroic effort "bequeathed from sire to son" may gladden hearts in "the good time coming;" for it is display in endurance, a vigorous courage, a gladsome self-control, a triumphant self-sacrifice, that mankind applaud as supreme for exaltation, and the highest types of self-abnegation for human advancement; for "before man made us citizens, Great Nature made us men."

Equally as in the realm of war has the race produced its noblemen in the arena of peace and mental development. For, if it be true that "the greatest names in history are those who in the full career and amid the turbid extremities of political action, have yet touched the closest and at most points the ever-standing problems of the world and the things in which the interests of men never die," our industrial educators are fittingly placed.

Of the ever-standing problem of the world, and in which mankind is ever alert, is the struggle for survival, and he that by inspiring word and untiring deeds leads the deserving poor and destitute to prosperity and contentment, is entitled to unstinted praise as a great human force directed to a high moral purpose. While an advocate for the higher education of as many of the race who have the will or means to obtain it, for the majority, after obtaining a good English education, it should be immediately supplemented by a trade, to labor skillfully, is its great want today.

The question has been asked: "Can any race safely exist in any country composed only of unskilled laborers and professional men? Must not the future leaders of our people come from the middle classes, from those who work and think?" Education to be of practical advantage must not only sharpen the intellect, but it must be of that sort that will enable them to engage in pursuits and avocations above those of mere drudgery; those that are more lucrative, and from which accumulate wealth. The school room must be the stepping stone to a good trade. The statement has been made (which may be problematical) that we have fewer, comparatively, very many fewer, mechanics of all kinds now than we had in the days of slavery. The master knew that the money value of the slave was increased in the ratio of his efficiency as a skilled laborer.

To the credit of Kentucky, Alabama, Arkansas and other Southern States, they have made generous provisions for industrial education by supplying machinery and the most modern appliances to teach skilled labor to those who prefer them to the white apron of the waiter or the grubbing hoe of the plantation. Of the students that graduate from our high schools and colleges there are those who have not the qualities of head and heart essential for teaching and preaching, including a love and devotion to those callings, and possibly would have been shining marks had their studies fitted them to grapple with the mercantile or industrial factors that promise a future more independent and lucrative.

The advancement of any race in morals and culture is retarded when poor and dependent. It is indispensable to progress that it has the benefit of earnings laid by. It is therefore to these industrial features that we must look for the foundation of advancement for the race. It will not be found at either extreme of our present avocations; neither the attainment of the professions, nor devotion to menial labor will solve the problem of the "better way." A greater number must be fitted to obtain work more lucrative in character and more ennobling in effect. Institutions of applied science and business pursuits seem to me the great doorway to ultimate success. Economy and industries of this kind will more rapidly produce the means to achieve that higher education for the race so desirable. Morality, learning and wealth are a trio invincible.

To content ourselves with denouncing injustice is to fail to enlist the economic features so necessary as assistants. For amid all our disadvantages we are to a large extent arbiters of our fortunes, for we can by an indomitable will dispel many, many seeming mountains that encumber our way. But we have much to unlearn, and especially that the road to financial prosperity is not chiefly the dictum of the facile mouth, but through the manifestation of skilled hands and routine of business methods, however much the mouth may attempt to compete, conscious of its wealth of assertion and extent of capacity. While it is eminently proper we should strive for the administration of equitable laws for our protection, it should be ever remembered that while local laws under our constitutional government are supposed to be the equity of public opinion, for us they are not sustained unless in harmony with feelings and sentiments of their environments. Our work as a dependent element is plainly to use such, and only such, methods as will sustain or create the sentiment desired by a fraternization of business and material interests. This we cannot do either in the arena of politics or the status of the menial laborer. For in the one, when the polls are closed, we are continuously reminded of "Othello's occupation gone." In the other, the abundance of raw and uncouth labor robs it of its vitality as a force to compel conditions.

Chapter 25

The spirit in which these "schools of trade" have been conceived, and the success of their conduct, indicate they have struck a responsive chord in the communities where local approval is a necessity. Constituting an agreeable counterpoise to the fixed determination of the white people of the South that within its purview the Negro, however worthy, shall not occupy political prominence. This, while diametrically opposed to the genius and spirit of republican government, may yet be the boomerang, beneficent in its return, redounding to his advantage by turning the current of his aspirations to trades and business activities rich with promise of material and ennobling fame. From this point of view history records the Jew as a shining example. The Negro, constitutionally buoyant, should be energetic and hopeful, for "there is a destiny that shapes our ends," blunt them however much by "damning with faint praise" or apology for oppression from whilom friends. In the darkest hour of slavery and ignorance came freedom and education. When lynchings became prevalent, lynching of whites made it unpopular; when disfranchisement came, debasing him in localities as a factor in civil government, came elevation and high honor ungrudgingly bestowed for heroic deeds by commanders of the national armies.

President McKinley, in his order for the enlistment and promotion of the colored soldier in the Spanish war, added additional luster to his page in history, it being an act the result of which has been of inestimable value to the race. Just and inspiring is the speech of Hon. Charles H. Grosvenor, of Ohio, delivered at the close of the 56th Congress, entitled "The Colored Citizen; His Share in the Affairs of the Nation in the Years of 1897 to 1900. Fifteen thousand participated in the war. The President's generous treatment of colored men in the military and civil service of the Government."

General Grosvenor commences with an exordium eloquent in succinctness and noble in generosity. "I cannot let pass this opportunity at the close of a long session of Congress, and at the end of three years of this Administration, without putting on record to enlighten future generations the history of the part which the colored citizen has had in the stirring events of this remarkable period. It is a period in the history of the country of which future generations will be proud, as are those of today, and as the colored citizens of the United States have participated nobly in it, it is but just to them that the facts be put on record.

"I want to speak of his part in the war in Cuba, in Porto Rico, in the Philippines. Would a war with Spain benefit the Negro? was a popular question for debate. Some thought it would benefit, others thought not. In many respects it has been a Godsend and beyond dispute a great benefit. If in no other way, 15,048 privates have shown their patriotism and their valor by offering their bared breasts as shields for the country's honor; 4,114 regulars did actual, noble and heroic service at El Caney, San Juan and Santiago, while 266 officers (261 volunteers and five regulars) did similar service and demonstrated the ability of the American Negro to properly command ever so well, as he does readily obey."

General Grosvenor then pertinently adds: "When we learn to appreciate the fact that three years ago the Negro had in the army only five officers and 4,114 privates, and that one year ago he had 266 officers and 15,048 privates, we must know that inestimable benefit has come to the race. Among the officers are to be found many of the brightest minds of the race. Fully 80 per cent of those in authority come from the best known and most influential families in the land. Their contact with and influence upon their superior officers will be sure to raise the Negro in the popular esteem and do an incalculable good."

Reference is made to disbursements to Negro officers and soldiers during the Spanish war, which he colates to be $5,000,000; adding the salaries of those employed in the civil service brings up to a sum exceeding $6,000,000 paid the Negro citizen. This, coupled with the high honor attached to such military designations as colonels, lieutenants and captains conferred upon him, shed a halo of generosity over President McKinley's Administration.

General Grosvenor is richly entitled to and received a just meed of praise for the great service he has done by putting this grand array of fact and heroic deed in popular form, and thereby strengthening the Negro appeal for justice and opportunity, while its pages are a noble contribution to a valor that will illumine Negro history for all time. It was most opportune, for the then pressing need to strengthen the weak and recall the recalcitrants who indiscriminately charge the party with being remiss in requiting and acknowledging the Negro's devotion. The well-earned plaudits for his bravery on the battlefield should widen the area of his consciousness, intensify conviction that mediocrity is a drug in every human activity, for whether in the professions, literature, agriculture or trades, it is excellence alone that counts and will bring recognition, despite the frowning battlements of caste. As we become more and more valued factors in the common cause of the general welfare, that the flexibility of American sentiment on conviction of merit will be more apparent we cannot but believe; for conditions seem to have surmounted law and seek their own solution, since the supreme law of the land seems ineffectual and local sentiment the arbiter, when the Negro is plaintiff.

In the first section of Article 14 of the Constitution we have: "All persons born or naturalized in the United States and subject to the jurisdiction thereof are citizens of the United States and of the several States wherein they reside. No State shall enforce any law which shall abridge the privileges or immunities of citizens of the United States." To neutralize this pronounced and unequivocal legislation we have the dictum of the Supreme Court of the United States that this constitutional right, so plainly set forth, can be legally abrogated by a State convention or legislature. While from the premises stated the conclusion may be evident to a jurist, to the layman it is perplexing; and while bowing in obeyance to this court of last resort, he cannot but admire the judicial agility in escaping the problem. He is reminded of a final response touching the character and standing of a church member of whom the inquirer wishes to know. The reply was: "Brother B. is quite prominent and well known here." "Well, what is his standing?" "Oh, very high; he is the elder of our church and superintendent of the Sunday school." "Yes, but as I am thinking of having some business dealings with him, what I want to know is, how does he stand for credit and promptness?" "Well, stranger, if you put it that way, I must say that heavenward Bro. B. is all right, but earthward he is rather twistical." Ordinaryward, the Supreme Court is all right; but Negroward, twistical.

For the law-abiding citizens of these Commonwealths we have this other, the second section of the same article: "When the right to vote at any election for the choice of electors for President or Vice-President of the United States, Representatives in Congress, the executive or judicial officers of a State, or the members of the legislature thereof, is denied to any one of the male inhabitants of such State being twenty-one years of age and a citizen of the United States, or in any way abridged, except for participation in rebellion or other crimes, the basis of representation thereon shall be reduced in the proportion which the number of such male citizens shall bear to the whole number of male citizens twenty-one years of age in such State."

If, as avowed, that it is for the welfare of such Southern States that they desire to banish the Negro from politics, can welfare be promoted or national integrity sustained by such rank injustice, as their Members of Congress occupying seats therein, or having representation in the electoral college based upon an apportionment in which the Negro numerically is so prominent a factor, and in the exercise of rights pertaining thereto, he is a nonentity.

"The Baptist Watchman" takes this unassailable position of this misrule: "Ex-Governor Northen, of Georgia, in his address before the Congregational Club the other evening, declared that the status of the black race in the South was that of permanent dependence upon the white race. The central point of his contention is that capacity to rule confers the right to rule. The white man can give the black man a better government that he can give himself; therefore, the black man should be glad to receive the blessing at the hands of the white man. For our part, we believe that, whatever specious defense on the ground of philanthropy, civilization and religion may be made for this position, it is radically repugnant to the genius of American institutions. If the men of the nation who are best qualified to rule have a right to rule, they themselves being the judge of their qualifications, England or Russia would be justified in attempting to impose their sovereignty on the United States, if they thought they could give us a better government than we are apt to give ourselves. Unless the doctrine is vigorously maintained that governments 'derive their just powers from the consent of the governed,' and not from the conceit of an aristocracy as to its own capacity, then we of the North will not find it easy to protest effectively against the disfranchisement of the Southern Negroes."

But the issue will not be made in opposition to a great national party that draws a large measure of its strength from the South till disaster from material issues compel. With the Republican party (as of a Christmas morning) "everything is lovely and the goose hangs high;" but discomfiture, sometimes laggard, is ever attendant on dereliction of duty. This usurpation, which should have been throttled when a babe, has now become a giant seated in its castle, compelling deference and acquiescence to an anomaly, reaching beyond the Negro in its menace to representative government.

And now, while from inertia the Republican party has been privy to this misrepresentation, prominent Northern leaders are trying to take advantage of their own neglect in an attempt to reduce representation in national conventions from Southern States, irregularly Democratic. But the friends of just government need not despond, for the political and industrial revolution which the war for the perpetuation of the Union and the basic principle of equity it evolved will continue to demand and eventually secure equal rights for all beneath the flag.

Chapter 26

Now, on the eve of my departure from Madagascar, and approaching four years of consular intercourse, I have only pleasant memories. My relations with General Gallieni, Governor-General of the Island, and his official family, have ever been most cordial. On learning of my intended departure, he very graciously wrote me, as follows:

Madagascar and Dependencies.
Governeur-General.
Tananarivo, 19th Mch., 1901

My Dear Consul

I learn with much displeasure of your early departure from Madagascar, and would have been very glad to have met you again at the beginning of May, when going down to the coast. But I always intend to take a trip to America, and perhaps may find an opportunity to see you again in your powerful and flourishing country, which I wish so much to know. I thank you very much for your kind letter, and reciprocate. I had always with you the best relations, and I could appreciate your friendly and highly estimable character, and regret your departure. I have read with great pleasure your biographical sketch, and I see that you have already rendered many valuable services to your country, where your name is known very honorably. Yours faithfully,

GALLIENI

Socially, as a member of the "Circle Francais", a club of the elite of the French residents, a constant recipient of its sociability, the urbanity and kindness of Messrs. Proctor Brothers, Messrs. Dadabhoy & Co., and Messrs. Oswold & Co., representing, respectively, the leading English and German mercantile firms in the island, contributed much in making life enjoyable at that far-away post. My official life in Madagascar was not without its lights and shadows, and the latter sometimes "paled the ineffectual rays" of belated instructions. Of an instance I may make mention. I was in receipt of a cablegram from the Department of State advising me that the flagship "Chicago," with Admiral Howison, would at an early date stop at Tamatave and instructing me to obtain what wild animals I could indigenous to Madagascar and have them ready to ship thereby for the Smithsonian Institute, at Washington, D. C. How I responded, and the result of the response, is attempted to be set forth in the following dispatch to the Department of State:

Consulate of the United States,
Tamatave, Madagascar; July 3, 1899

Mr. Gibbs to the Department of State.

Subject:
Madagascar Branch of Smithsonian Institute.
A Consul's "Burden."

Abstract of Contents:
Procuration of Live Animals, as per Order of the Department, and Declination of the Admiral to Receive Them on Board.

Honorable Assistant Secretary of State,
Washington, D. C.
Sir

Referring to your cablegram under date of May 22d last, directing me to secure live animals for the Smithsonian Institute, to be sent home on the flagship "Chicago" on its arrival at this port, I have to report that I proceeded with more or less trepidation to accomplish the same, the wild animals of Madagascar being exceedingly alive. With assistance of natives I succeeded, after much trouble and expense, in obtaining twelve, had them caged and brought to the consulate weeks before the arrival of the ship. This, I regret to say, was a misadventure. I should have located them in the woods and pointed them out to the Admiral on his arrival. At first they seemed to agree, and were tractable until a patriotic but unlucky impulse induced me to give them the names of a few prominent Generals in the late war. After that, oh, my!

The twelve consist of different varieties. One of the twelve seems a cross of panther and wild cat, and rejoices in the appelation of "Aye Aye."

On the arrival of the "Chicago," forthwith I reported to Admiral Howison my success in capturing "these things of beauty," and eternal terrors, and my desire that they change domicile. He received me with such charming suavity, and my report with so many tender expressions of sympathy for the monkeys that I got a little mixed as to his preference. Still joy-smitten, I was ill-prepared for the announcement "that it was unwise to take them, as it was impossible to procure food to keep them alive until the termination of the voyage."

It was then, Mr. Secretary, that I sadly realized that I was confronted by a condition. Over seventy years of age, 10,000 miles from home, a beggarly salary, with a menagerie on my hands, while bankruptcy and a humbled flag threatened to stare me in the face. There remained nothing for me, but to "bow to the inevitable," transpose myself into a committee of ways and means for the purpose of securing sleep for my eyelids and a saving to the United States Treasury. For while ever loyal to "the old flag and an appropriation," a sense of duty compels me to advise that this branch of the Smithsonian Institute is of doubtful utility.

With a desire to avoid, if possible, "the deep damnation of their taking-off," by starvation, several plans promising relief suggested themselves, viz: Sell them, turn them loose, or keep them at Government expense. I very much regret that the latter course I shall be compelled to adopt. My many offers to sell seemed not understood, as the only response I have yet received has been: "I get you more like him, I can." As to turning them loose, I have been warned by the local authorities that if I did so I would do so at my peril. A necessary part of diet for these animals is condensed milk, meat, bread, jam, and bananas, but they are not content. Having been a member of the bar, and retaining much veneration for the Quixotic capers of judicial twelve, on their desire to leave I "polled" them and found a hung jury, swinging by their tails; eleven indicated "aye," but the twelfth, with his double affirmative cry of "Aye, Aye," being equal to negative, hung them up. Meanwhile, they bid fair to be a permanent exhibit.

Under cover of even date I enclose account for animals' food and attention to June 30, and beg to say regarding the item of food, that I anticipate a monthly increase of cost, as the appetite of the animals seem to improve in captivity. I conclude, Mr. Secretary, with but a single solace: They may possibly eat off their heads, but their tails give abundant promise of remaining in evidence. Patiently awaiting instructions as the future disposition of these wild and wayward wards of the Government, I have the honor to be,

Your obedient servant,

M. W. GIBBS,

U. S. Consul

How and when "I got rid of my burden" and the joyous expressions of a long-suffering Government on the event, will (or will not) "be continued in our next."

Having asked for leave of absence, and leaving Mr. William H. Hunt, the Vice-Consul, in charge of the consulate, on the 3d of April, 1891, I took passage on the French steamer, "Yantse," for Marseilles, France.

Chapter 27

April 3, 1901

It was not without regret, that found expression at a banquet given me on the eve preceding my departure, by Mr. Erlington, the German Consul at Tamatave, that I took my leave of Madagascar, when the flags of the officials of the French Residency and flags of all the foreign consuls were flying, honoring me with a kindly farewell. A jolly French friend of mine, who came out to the steamer to see me off, said: "Judge, don't you be too sure of the meaning of the flags flying at your departure from Tamatave, for we demonstrate here for gladness, as well as for regret." "Well," I replied, "in either event I am in unison with the sentiment intended to be expressed; for I have both gladness and regret—gladness with anticipations of home, and with regret that, in all human probability, I am taking leave of a community from whom for nearly four years I have been the recipient, officially, of the highest respect; and socially of unstinted friendliness."

I found Vice-Consul Hunt had secured and had had my baggage placed in a desirable state room. The ringing of the bell notified all non-passengers ashore. After hearty handshakes from the Vice-Consul, German, French, and other friends, taking with them a bottle or two of wine that had been previously placed where it would do the most good, they took the consular boat, and with the Stars and Stripes flying, and handkerchiefs waving a final farewell, they were pulled ashore. The anchor weighs, and the good ship "Yantse" inhales a long, moist, and heated breath and commences to walk with stately strides and quickened pace—weather charming and the sea as quiet as a tired child. The next day a stop at the Island of St. Maria, a French possession, and on the fifth day at Diego Suarez, on the north end of Madagascar.

On the ninth day from Tamatave we entered the Gulf of Aden, and after some hours dropped anchor at Camp Aden, in Arabia. Mr. Byramzie, a Tamatave friend of mine, and of the London firm of Dadabhoy & Co., with a branch at Aden, came off to meet me and accompany me ashore. Camp Aden is a British fortification I cannot readily describe with reference to its topography or the heterogenous character and pursuits of its inhabitants. Nature was certainly in no passive mood when last it flung its constituents together; for, with the exception of a few circling acres forming a rim around the harbor, high, broken, and frowning battlements of rock, ungainly and sterile, look down upon you as far as the eye can reach. No sprig, or tree, or blade of grass takes root in its parched soil or stony bed, or survives the blasting heat. Scattered and dotted on crag, hilltop or slope, in glaring white, are the many offices and residence buildings of the camp. While in hidden crevices and forbidden paths are planted the most approved armament, with its "dogs of war" to dispute a passage from the Gulf.

In a dilapidated four-wheeler, drawn by one horse, after considerable time spent by my friend in agreeing on terms (concerning which I pause to remark that these benighted Jehus can give a Bowery cabman points on "how not to do it"), over a macadam road of five miles we reach Aden proper—the site of hotels, stores and residences with little pretensions to architectural beauty; the buildings are quite all constructed of stone, that material being in superabundance on every intended site; their massive walls contributing to a cool interior indispensable as a refuge from the blistering heat. Pure water for drinking is a luxury, spasmodic in its supply. I once heard an hilarious Irish song that stated:

> *"We are jolly and happy, for we know without doubt,*
> *That the whisky is plenty, and the water is out."*

This, I learn is the normal condition at Aden as to the relative status of whisky and water—a very elysium for the toper who could not understand why whisky should be spoiled by mixing it with water.

Rains are infrequent and well water unpalatable. Sea water is distilled, but the mineral and health-giving qualities are said to be absent. The water highly prized and sold is the rainwater caught in tanks. Hollowed out at the foot of the rock hills, there are numbers of peculiar construction, connected and on different elevations. But for the last three years the non-rainfall has kept them without a tenant. As I looked in them not a drop sparkled within their capacious confines; they are seldom filled, and the supply is ever deficient. The population is from 6,000 to 8,000, amid which the Parsee, the Mohammedan, Jew, Portuguese, and other nationalities compete for the commerce of the interior. The natives are of varied castes, the Samiles the most energetic and prevailing type. The inferior classes go about almost naked and live in long, unprepossessing structures, one story high, divided into single rooms, rude and uncleanly.

While at Aden I availed myself of the honor and pleasure of a visit to the American Consulate, and received a warm, jolly, and spiritual welcome from the incumbent, the Hon. E. T. Cunningham, of Knoxville, Tenn. Mr. Cunningham intended to stay at Aden for six months. Like "linked sweetness long drawn out," that period has extended to three years, and is now "losing its sweetness on the desert air." He stated that he was not infatuated with those "scarlet days" and "Arabian nights," and is seeking relief or placement amid more congenial surroundings, where distance (does not) "lend enchantment to the view." But I assured him the Department was as astute as selfish. It knows when it has a good thing, and endeavors to keep it. Mr. Cunningham has proved himself to be an efficient and trusted official. We parted with mutual hope of again meeting in "the land of the cotton and the corn."

On my way to the landing I passed many convoys of camels and asses, laden with coffee, it being one of the main articles of export. Arriving at the steamer and bidding my Parsee friend a last, long farewell, shortly we weighed anchor and away for a five days sail to Suez.

On the 17th of April, eventful to me, being my birthday, we arrived at Suez for a short stay, without time or inclination to go ashore. But, seeing the Stars and Stripes flying from a ship lying in the distance, I could not withstand the temptation. Jumping into a native sailboat that described every point of the compass with oars and adverse wind, I reached the United States cruiser, "New York." Capt. Rodgers and his gentlemanly officers gave me a very cordial reception, ensuring an enjoyable visit. Capt. Rodgers informed me that Lieutenant Poundstone was aboard, who knew me as a "promoter" for the Smithsonian Institute at Washington, he having been aboard the "Chicago" when it visited Tamatave, and when Admiral Howison declined to convey my "gay and festive" collection of wild animals to America. I would be most happy to see him. He soon appeared with pleasant greetings and recollections of Tamatave incidents. My stay from ship being limited, after a chat, mingled with sherry and cigars and an expression of regret from Capt. Rodgers that, not being in our "bailiwick," he could not give me a consular salute from his guns, he ordered the ship's steam launch, and, escorted by the Lieutenant, under our national banner, I soon boarded my ship. I was much indebted to Capt. Rodgers and officers for their charming courtesy.

Leaving Suez at mid-day, we shortly enter the Suez Canal—85 miles, with numerous tie-ups to allow other ships the right of way.

At 8 o'clock the following morning we dropped anchor at Port Said, a populous city of Arabia with 30,000 inhabitants, much diversified as to nativities, Turks, Assyrians, Jews, and Greeks being largely represented. The city is quite prepossessing, and seems to have improved its sanitary features since my visit four years ago. There are many charming views; an interesting place for the tourist, alike for the virtuous and the vicious, for those so inclined can see human nature "unadorned." Wide streets pierce the city, the stores on which are a continuous bazaar, lined with many exquisite productions of necessity and Eastern art. But I have previously dwelt on Port Said peculiarities.

Leaving Port Said on the 18th, our good ship soon enters the Mediterranean, and with smooth seas passes through the Straits of Messina, with a fine view of Mt. Etna, as of yore, belching forth flames and smoke, with Sicily on our left and Italy and her cities on our right. Again entering the Mediterranean, we encounter our first rough seas and diminution of guests at the table. Neptune, who had been lenient for 17 days, now demanded settlement before digestion should again be allowed to resume its sway. For myself, I was like and unlike the impecunious boarder, who "never missed a meal nor paid a cent," but like him only in constant attendance, for I could ill-afford to miss any part of the pleasure of transit or menu costing $10 a day—happy, however, that I was minus "mal de mer," seasickness. But this temporary ailment of the passengers was soon banished by another phase of ocean travel, that of being enveloped in a fog so dense that the ship's length could not be seen ahead from the bow—every officer of the ship alert, the fog horn blowing its warnings at short intervals, answered by the "ships that pass in the night" of fogs. The anxiety of the passengers that the fog would lift was relieved after 36 hours, and our ship hied away and reached Marseilles on the 23d. From there by rail to Paris. Ensconced again at the "Hotel Binda," the next day I visited the site of the great Paris Exposition. Few of the buildings were in their entirety, but what remained of the classic beauty of their construction shone the more vivid amid the debris of demolition that surrounded them. The French were not enthusiastic in relation to the financial benefit of the exposition.

A few days in Paris, and thence to Cherbourg to cross the English Channel to Southampton, London. This channel, which has a well-merited reputation for being gay and frolicsome, was extremely gracious, allowing us to glide over its placid bosom with scarce a tremor.

Chapter 28

This was my first visit to the land of Wilberforces and Clarksons of the seventeenth century, whose devotion and fidelity to liberty abolished African slavery in Britain's dominion and created the sentiment that found expression in the immortal utterance of Judge Mansfield's decision: "Slaves cannot breathe in England; upon touch of its soil they stand forth redeemed and regenerated by the genius of universal liberty." With my English friend, C. B. Hurwitz, as an escort, I enjoyed an excursion on the Thames, and visited many places of note, including England's veteran bank, designated as the "Old Lady of Threadneedle Street," and the Towers of London. One of these, the Beauchamp Tower, is supposed to have been built in the twelfth or thirteenth century, the architecture corresponding with that in use at that period, and lately restored to its original state. Herein are many inscriptions, some very rude, others quite artistic. It was during the restoration that these inscriptions were partially discovered and carefully preserved. They were cut in the stone walls and partitions by the unhappy occupants, confined for life or execution for their religion or rebellion in the thirteenth to the sixteenth century. Many are adorned with rude devices and inscriptions denoting the undying faith of the martyr; others the wailing of distress and despair. Five hundred years have elapsed, yet the sadness of the crushed hearts of the unhappy occupants still lingers like a funeral pall to point a moral that should strengthen tolerance and cherish liberty.

Leaving Southampton, London, on the steamship St. Louis, after an uneventful passage I arrived in New York, and from thence to Washington, D. C. After my leave of absence had expired, I decided not to return to Madagascar. For after nearly four years' dalliance with the Malagash fever in the spring and dodging the bubonic plague in the fall, I concluded that Madagascar was a good place to *come from*.

W. H. Hunt, the Vice-Consul, who had filed application for the Consulship, conditioned upon my resignation, was appointed. An admirable appointment, for the duties pertaining thereto, I have no doubt, will be performed with much credit to himself and to the satisfaction of the Government.

I was honored as a delegate to a very interesting assembly of colored men from 32 States, designated the "National Negro Business Men's

League," which met in Chicago, Ill., Aug. 27, 1901. Of its object and labors my conclusions were: That no better evidence can be produced that the negro has a good hold on the lever which will not only give a self-consciousness of latent powers, but will surely elevate him in the estimation of his fellow-citizens, than the increasing interest he is taking and engaging in many of the business ventures of the country, and the popular acquiescence manifested by the crowded attendance at every session of the meeting.

The President of the League, Booker T. Washington, expressed the following golden thoughts in his opening speech:

"As a race we must learn more and more that the opinion of the world regarding us is not much influenced by what we may say of ourselves, or by what others say of us, but it is permanently influenced by actual, tangible, visible results. The object-lesson of one honest Negro succeeding magnificently in each community in some business or industry is worth a hundred abstract speeches in securing opportunity for the race.

"In the South, as in most parts of the world, the Negro who does something and possesses something is respected by both races. Usefulness in the community where we live will constitute our most lasting and potent protection.

"We want to learn the lesson of small things and small beginnings. We must not feel ourselves above the most humble occupation or the simple, humble beginning. If our vision is clear, our will strong, we will use the very obstacles that often seem to beset us as stepping-stones to a higher and more useful life."

The enrollment of the members present was not completed at the first session, but the hall was crowded and 200 of those present were visitors in Chicago. Pictures and some of the product of Negro concerns decorated the walls, as evidence that the black man is rising above the cotton plantation, his first field of labor in this country. Pictures of brick blocks, factories, livery stables, farms and shops of every description owned by Negroes in many different States of the Union were in the collection, but the greater evidence of the Negro's development were the men taking part in the deliberations of the sessions. They are clean cut, well-dressed, intelligent, and have put a business method into the organization.

The Governor of the State and Mayor of Chicago were represented with stirring addresses of welcome. The convention was singular and peculiar in this: The central idea of the meeting was scrupulously adhered to; there was present no disposition to refer to grievances or deprivations. A feeling seemed to permeate the participants of confidence and surety that they had fathomed the depths of much that stood in the way of a just recognition of Negro worth and a just appreciation and resolution to "fight it out on that line if it took all summer," or many summers.

There were so many expressions so full of wisdom; so many suggestions practical and adaptable, I would, had I space, record them all here.

Theodore Jones, of Chicago, a successful business man, in concluding an able paper, "Can a Negro Succeed as a Business Man," said:

"The tone of this convention clearly indicates that the Negro will succeed as a business man in proportion as he learns that manhood and womanhood are qualities of his own making, and that no external forces can either give or take them away. It demonstrates that intelligence, punctuality, industry, and integrity are the conquering forces in the business and commercial world, as well as in all the affairs of human life."

Giles B. Jackson, Secretary of the Business League of Virginia, read a paper on "Negro Industries," showing what had been done toward the solution of the so-called "Negro problem." The Negroes, he stated, had $14,000,000 invested in business enterprises in Virginia.

William L. Taylor, President of the "True Reformers' Bank," of Richmond, Va., gave interesting details in an able and intelligent effort, of the aims and accomplishments of that successful institution, presenting many phases of the enterprise—its branch stores, different farms, hotel and printing department, giving employment to more than 100 officers, clerks, and employees. Dr. R. H. Boyd, of Nashville, Tenn., the head of the "Colored Publishing Company, of Nashville," employing 123 assistants, delivered an able address on the "Negro in the Publishing Business," which was discussed with marked ability by the Rev. Dr. Morris, of Helena, Ark.

All the participants are worthy of a meed of praise for their many helpful utterances and manly deportment. Prominent among them were Charles Banks, merchant and a large property owner of Clarkesdale, Miss., who spoke on "Merchandizing"; William O. Murphy, of Atlanta, Ga., on the "Grocery Business"; Harris Barrett, of Hampton, Va., on "The Building and Loan Association of Hampton, Va."; A. N. Johnson, publisher and editor, of Mobile, on "The Negro Business Enterprises of Mobile"; F. D. Patterson, of Greenfield, Ohio, on "Carriage Manufacturing"; Martin Ferguson on "Livery Business," small in stature, light in weight, but herculean in size and heavy in force of persistency, told how by self-denial he had gained a fair competency; L. G. Wheeler, of Chicago, Ill., on "Merchant Tailoring"; Willis S. Stearns, a druggist, of Decatur, Ala., in his address stated that 14 years ago there was not a Negro druggist in that State; now there are over 200 such stores owned by colored men in various cities of that State, with an invested capital of $500,000. Walter P. Hall, of Philadelphia, Pa., an extensive dealer in game and poultry, spoke on that subject.

And possibly as a fitting wind-up, as all sublunary things must come to an end, George E. Jones, of Little Rock, Ark., and G. E. Russel, of St. Louis, Mo., undertakers, spoke pathetically to their fellow-members of the League (I trust not expectantly) of the advance in the science of embalming and other facilities for conveying them to that "bourne from which no traveller returns." The session was "a feast of reason and a flow of soul" from its commencement until its close. And, as ever has been the case on our upward journey, there were women lighting the pathway and stimulating effort; for during the sessions Mrs. Albreta Smith read a very interesting paper on "The Success of the Negro Women's Business Club of Chicago"; a delightful one was read by Mrs. Dora Miller, of Brooklyn, N. Y.; "Dressmaking and Millinery" was entertainingly presented by Mrs. Emma L. Pitts, of Macon, Ga., the ladies dwelling on the great good that was being done by their establishments by teaching and giving employment to scores of poor but worthy girls, and thereby helping them to lead pure and useful lives.

I have given this exhibition of what the Negro is doing the foregoing space for encouragement and precept, because I believe it to be the key to unlock many doors to honorable and useful lives heretofore barred against us.

Chapter 29

L eaving Chicago, and having business with the President, I visited him at Canton, was kindly received, and accomplished the object of my visit, little thinking that, in common with my countrymen I was so soon to be horrified and appalled by an atrocity which bathed the country in tears and startled the world in the taking-off of one of the purest patriots that had ever trod his native soil.

The tragedy occurred at 4 o'clock p. m., on the 6th of September, 1901, in the Temple of Music on the grounds of and during the Exposition at Buffalo, N. Y. Surrounded by a body-guard, among whom was Secret Service Detective Samuel R. Ireland, of Washington, who was directly in front of the President, the latter engaged in the usual manner of handshaking at a public reception at the White House. Not many minutes had expired; a hundred or more of the line had passed the President, when a young-looking man named Leon Czolgosz, said to be of Polish, extraction, approached, offering his left hand, while his right hand contained a pistol concealed under a handkerchief, fired two shots at the President.

James Parker, a colored man, a very hercules in height, who was next to have greeted the President, struck the assassin a terrific blow that felled him to the floor, preventing him (as Czolgosz himself avers in the following interview) from firing the third shot:

"Yesterday morning I went again to the Exposition grounds. Emma Goldman's speech was still burning me up. I waited near the central entrance for the President, who was to board his special train from that gate, but the police allowed nobody but the President's party to pass where the train waited. So I stayed at the grounds all day waiting.

"During yesterday I first thought of hiding my pistol under my handkerchief. I was afraid if I had to draw it from my pocket I would be seen and seized by the guards. I got to the Temple of Music the first one, and waited at the spot where the reception was to be held.

"Then he came, the President—the ruler—and I got in line and trembled and trembled until I got right up to him, and then I shot him twice through my white handkerchief. I would have fired more, but I was stunned by a blow in the face—a frightful blow that knocked me down—and then everybody jumped on me. I thought I would be killed, and was surprised the way they treated me."

Czolgosz ended his story in utter exhaustion. When he had about concluded he was asked:

"Did you really mean to kill the President?"

"I did," was the cold-blooded reply.

"What was your motive; what good could it do?"

"I am an anarchist. I am a disciple of Emma Goldman. Her words set me on fire," he replied, with not the slightest tremor.

During the first few days after he was shot there were cheering bulletins issued by the medical fraternity in attendance, all typical of his early recovery, and the heart of the nation was elated, to be, a week later, depressed with sadness at the announcement that a change had come and that the President was dying. Never was grief more sincere for a ruler. He was buried encased with the homage and love of his people. William McKinley will live in history, not only as a man whose private life was stainless, and whose Administration of the Government was beyond reproach, but as one brilliant, progressive, wise, and humane.

Pre-eminent as an arbiter and director, developing the nation as a world power, and bringing to the effete and semi-civilized peoples of the Orient the blessings of civilized Government; as a leader and protector of the industrial forces of the country, William McKinley was conspicuous. With strength of conviction, leading at one time an almost forlorn hope, by his statesmanship and intensity of purpose, he had grafted on the statute books of the Nation a policy that has turned the wheels of a thousand idle mills, employed a hundred thousand idle hands, and stimulated every manufacturing industry.

This accomplished, in his last speech, memorable not only as his last public utterance, but doubly so as to wise statesmanship in its advocacy of a less restrictive tariff, increased reciprocity, and interchange with the world's commodities. His love of justice was imperial. He was noted in this, that he was not only mentally eminent, but morally great. During his last tour in the South, while endeavoring to heal animosities engendered by the civil war and banish estrangement, he was positive in the display of heartfelt interest in the Negro, visiting Tuskegee and other like institutions of learning, and by his presence and words of good cheer stimulating us to noble deeds.

Nor was his interest manifest alone in words; his appointments in the bureaus of the Government of colored men exceeded that of any previous Executive—a representation which should increase in accordance with parity of numbers and fitness for place.

THE FOLLOWING EXCERPTS FROM THE Washington Post, the verity of which was echoed in the account of the crime by the New York and other metropolitan journals on the day following the sad occurrence, gives a sketch of the manner and expressions of the criminal, and throws light on a peculiar phase of the catastrophe, that for the truth of history and in the interest of justice should not be so rudely and covertly buried 'neath the immature "beatings of time."

Washington Post: In an interview Secret Service Detective Ireland, who, with Officers Foster and Gallagher, was near the President when the shots were fired, said:

"A few moments before Czolgosz approached a man came along with three fingers of his right hand tied up in a bandage, and he had shaken hands with his left. When Czolgosz came up I noticed he was a boyish-looking fellow, with an innocent face, perfectly calm, and I also noticed that his right hand was wrapped in what appeared to be a bandage. I watched him closely, but was interrupted by the man in front of him, who held on to the President's hand an unusually long time. This man appeared to be an Italian, and wore a short, heavy, black mustache. He was persistent, and it was necessary for me to push him along so that the others could reach the President. Just as he released the President's hand, and as the President was reaching for the hand of the assassin, there were two quick shots. Startled for a moment, I looked and saw the President draw his right hand up under his coat, straighten up, and, pressing his lips together, give Czolgosz the most scorn and contemptuous look possible to imagine.

"At the same time I reached for the young man, and caught his left arm. The big Negro standing just back of him, and who would have been next to take the President's hand, struck the young man in the neck with one hand, and with the other reached for the revolver, which had been discharged through the handkerchief, and the shots from which had set fire to the linen.

"Immediately a dozen men fell upon the assassin and bore him to the floor. While on the floor Czolgosz again tried to discharge the revolver, but before he could point it at the President, it was knocked from his hand by the Negro. It flew across the floor, and one of the artillerymen picked it up and put it in his pocket."

Another account: "Mr. McKinley straightened himself, paled slightly, and riveted his eyes upon the assassin. He did not fall or make an outcry. A Negro, named Parker, employed in the stadium, seized the wretch and threw him to the floor, striking him in the mouth. As he fell he struggled to use the weapon again, but was quickly overpowered. Guard Foster sprang to the side of Mr. McKinley, who walked to a chair a few feet away."

Washington Post, Oct. 9: James Parker, the six-foot Georgia Negro, who knocked down the assassin of President McKinley on the fatal day in the Temple of Music, after the two shots were fired, gave a talk to an audience in the Metropolitan A. M. E. Church last night. He was introduced by Hon. George H. White. Parker arose, and after a few preliminary remarks, in which he thanked the crowd for its presence, he said he was glad to see so many colored people believed he did what he claimed he did at Buffalo.

"When the assassin dealt his blow," said Parker, "I felt it was time to act. It is no great honor I am trying to get, but simply what the American people think I am entitled to. If Mr. McKinley had lived there would have been no question as to this matter. President McKinley was looking right at me; in fact, his eyes were riveted upon me when I felled the assassin to the floor.

"The assassin was in front of me, and as the President went to shake his hand, he looked hard at one hand which the fellow held across his breast bandaged. I looked over the man's shoulder to see what the President was looking at. Just then there were two flashes and a report, and I saw the flame leap from the supposed bandage. I seized the man by the shoulder and dealt him a blow. I tried to catch hold of the gun, but he had lowered that arm. Quick as a flash I grasped his throat and choked him as hard as I could. As this happened he raised the hand with the gun in it again as if to fire, the burning handkerchief hanging to the weapon. I helped carry the assassin into a side room, and helped to search him."

Parker told of certain things he was about to do to the assassin when one of the officers asked him to step outside. Parker refused. He declared the officers wanted to get him out of the way. He said he helped to carry the assassin to the carriage in which the wretch was taken to jail.

"I don't know why I wasn't summoned to the trial," he said.

Parker said Attorney Penney took his testimony after the shooting.

"I was not at the trial, though," concluded Parker in an injured tone. "I don't say this was done with any intent to defraud me, but it looks mighty funny, that's all."

The above interviews with officers present agree with Parker's version of the affair, and whether the afterthought that further recognition of his decisive action would detract from the reputation for vigilance which they were expected to observe is a fitting subject for presumption.

At the time of the occurrence Parker was the cynosure for all eyes. Pieces of the clothing that he wore were solicited and given to his enthusiastic witnesses of the deed, to be preserved as trophies of his action in preventing the third shot. No one present at that perilous hour and witnessing doubted or questioned that Parker was the hero of the occasion. This, the better impulse, indicating a just appreciation was destined soon to be stifled and ignored. At the sittings of the coroner's jury to investigate the shooting of the President, he was neither solicited nor allowed to be present, or testimony adduced in proof of his bravery in attempting to save the life of the Chief Magistrate of the Republic. Therefore, Parker, bereft of the well-earned plaudits of his countrymen, must content himself with duty done.

Remarkable are the coincidences at every startling episode in the life of the Nation. Beginning at our country's history, the Negro is always found at the fore. He was there when Crispus Attacks received the first of English bullets in the struggle of American patriots for Independence; there in the civil war, when he asked to be assigned to posts of greatest danger. He was there quite recently at El Caney; and now Parker bravely bares his breast between the intended third shot of the assassin and that of President McKinley.

If this dispensation shall awaken the Nation to the peril of admitting the refuse of nations within our borders, and clothing them with the panoply of American citizenship; if it shall engender a higher appreciation of the loyalty and devotion of the Negro citizens of the Republic by the extension of justice to all beneath the flag, William McKinley will not have died in vain.

Chapter 30

Taking up the reins of the Administration of the Government, with its complex statesmanship, where a master had laid them down, President Roosevelt, heretofore known for his sterling worth as an administrator, and his imperial honesty as a man, has put forth no uncertain sound as to his intended course. The announcement that the foreign policy of his illustrious predecessor would be chiefly adhered to has struck a responsive chord in every patriotic heart. The appointment of ex-Gov. Jones, of Alabama, to a Federal judgeship was an appointment in unison with the best of popular accord. The nobility of the Governor in his utterances on the subject of lynching should endear him to every lover of justice and the faithful execution of law. For he so grandly evinced what is so sadly wanting in many humane and law-abiding men—the courage of his convictions.

"For when a free thought sought expression,
He spoke it boldly, spoke it all."

It is only to the fruition of such expressions, the molding of an adverse sentiment to such lawlessness that we can look for the abolishment of that crime of crimes which, to the disgrace of our country, is solely ours.

This appointment is considered eminently wise, not only for the superior ability of the appointee as a jurist, but for his broad humanity as a man, fully recognizing the inviolability of human life and its subjection to law. For the Negro, his primal needs are protection and the common liberty vouchsafed to his fellow-countrymen. To enjoy them it is necessary that he be in harmony with his environments. A bulwark he must have, of a friendship not the product of coercion, but a concession from the pulse-beat of justice. Such appointments pass the word down the line that President Roosevelt, in his endeavor to be the exponent of the genius of American citizenship, will recognize the sterling advocates of the basic elements of constitutional Government, those of law and order, irrespective of party affiliation.

This appointment will probably cause dissent in Republican circles, but it may be doubted if the Negro advances his political fortunes by invidious criticism of the efforts of a Republican Administration to harmonize ante-bellum issues. For while he in all honesty may be strenuous for the inviolability of franchises of the Republican household, and widens the gap between friendly surroundings, each of the political litigants meet with their knees under each other's mahogany, and jocularly discuss Negro idiosyncrasies, and tacitly agree to give his political aspirations a "letting alone." For, with character and ability unquestioned for the discharge of duties, the vote polled for him usually falls far short of the average of that polled by his party for other candidates on the ticket.

The summary killing of human beings by mobs without the form of law is not of late origin. Ever since the first note of reconstruction was sounded, each Administration has denounced lynching. All history is the record that it is only through discussion and the ventilation of wrong that right becomes a valued factor. But regard for justice is not diminishing in our country. The judiciary, although weak and amenable to prevailing local prejudices in localities, as a whole is far in advance on the sustenance of righteous rule than in the middle of the last century, when slavery ruled the Nation and its edicts were law, and its baleful influence permeated every branch of the Government.

Of the judiciary at that period Theodore Parker, an eminent Congregational divine and most noted leader of Christian thought, during a sermon in 1854, said:

"Slavery corrupts the judicial class. In America, especially in New England, no class of men has been so much respected as the judges, and for this reason: We have had wise, learned, and excellent men for our judges, men who reverenced the higher law of God, and sought by human statutes to execute justice. You all know their venerable names and how reverentially we have looked up to them. Many of them are dead, and some are still living, and their hoary hairs are a crown of glory on a judicial life without judicial blot. But of late slavery has put a different class of men on the benches of the Federal Courts—mere tools of the Government creatures who get their appointments as pay for past political service, and as pay in advance for iniquity not yet accomplished. You see the consequences. Note the zeal of the Federal judges to execute iniquity by statute and destroy liberty. See how ready they are to support the Fugitive Slave Bill, which tramples on the spirit of the Constitution and its letter, too; which outrages justice and violates the most sacred principles and precepts of Christianity. Not a United States Judge, Circuit or District, has uttered one word against that bill of abominations. Nay, how greedy they are to get victims under it. No wolf loves better to rend a lamb into fragments than these judges to kidnap a fugitive slave and punish any man who desires to speak against it. You know what has happened in Fugitive Slave Bill courts. You remember the 'miraculous' rescue of a Shadrach; the peaceable snatching of a man from the hands of a cowardly kidnapper was 'high treason;' it was 'levying war.' You remember the trial of the rescuers! Judge Sprague's charge to the jury that if they thought the question was which they ought to obey, the laws of man or the laws of God, then they must 'obey both,' serve God and Mammon, Christ and the devil in the same act. You remember the trial, the ruling of the bench, the swearing on the stand, the witness coming back to alter and enlarge his testimony and have another gird at the prisoner. You have not forgotten the trials before Judge Kane at Philadelphia and Judge Greer at Christiana and Wilkesbarre.

"These are natural results from causes well known. You cannot escape a principle. Enslave a negro, will you? You doom to bondage your own sons and daughters by your own act."

At the death of Theodore Parker, among the many eulogies on his life was one by Ralph Waldo Emerson, highly noted for his humanity, his learning and his philosophy. It contains apples of gold, and richly deserves immortality; for in the worldly strife for effervescent wealth and prominence, a benign consciousness that our posthumous fame as unselfish benefactors to our fellow-men is to live on through the ages, would be a solace for much misrepresentation. Emerson said: "It is plain to me that Theodore Parker has achieved a historic immortality here. It will not be in the acts of City Councils nor of obsequious Mayors nor in the State House; the proclamations of Governors, with their failing virtue failing them at critical moments, that generations will study what really befel; but in the plain lessons of Theodore Parker in this hall, in Faneuil Hall and in legislative committee rooms, that the true temper and authentic record of these days will be read. The next generation will care little for the chances of election that govern Governors now; it will care little for fine gentlemen who behaved shabbily; but it will read very intelligently in his rough story, fortified with exact anecdotes, precise with names and dates, what part was taken by each actor who threw himself into the cause of humanity and came to the rescue of civilization at a hard pinch; and those who blocked its course.

"The vice charged against America is the want of sincerity in leading men. It does not lie at his door. He never kept back the truth for fear of making an enemy. But, on the other hand, it was complained that he was bitter and harsh; that his zeal burned with too hot a flame. It is so hard in evil times to escape this charge for the faithful preacher. Most of all, it was his merit, like Luther, Knox, and Latimer and John the Baptist, to speak tart truth when that was peremptory and when there were few to say it. His commanding merit as a reformer is this, that he insisted beyond all men in pulpit—I cannot think of one rival—that the essence of Christianity is its practical morals; it is there for use, or it is nothing: If you combine it with sharp trading, or with ordinary city ambitions to glaze over municipal corruptions or private intemperance, or successful frauds, or immoral politics, or unjust wars, or the cheating of Indians, or the robbing of frontier natives, it is hypocrisy and the truth is not in you, and no love of religious music, or dreams of Swedenborg, or praise of John Wesley or of Jeremy Taylor, can save you from the Satan which you are."

Chapter 31

The accord so generally given to the appointment of ex-Governor Jones, of Alabama—a Gold Democrat, having views on domestic order in harmony with the Administration—to a Federal judgeship was destined to be followed by a bitter arraignment of President Roosevelt for having invited Booker T. Washington to dine with him at the White House. As a passing event not without interest, in this era of the times, indicative of "shadow and light," I append a few extracts from Southern and Northern Journals:

Shadow

In all parts of the country comment has been provoked by the fact that President Roosevelt, on Wednesday night last, entertained at dinner in the White House, Booker T. Washington, who is generally regarded as the representative of the colored race in America. Especially in the South has the incident aroused indignation, according to the numerous news dispatches. The following comments from the editorial columns of newspapers and from prominent men are given:

New Orleans, Oct. 19

The Times-Democrat says:

"It is strange news that comes from Washington. The President of the United States, for the first time in the history of the nation, has entertained a Negro at dinner in the White House. White men of the South, how do you like it? White women of the South, how do you like it?

"Everyone knows that when Mr. Roosevelt sits down to dinner in the White House with a Negro he that moment declares to all the world that in the judgment of the President of the United States the Negro is the social equal of the white man. The Negro is not the social equal of the white man. Mr. Roosevelt might as well attempt to rub the stars out of the firmament as to try to erase that conviction from the heart and brain of the American people."

The Daily States: "In the face of the facts it can but appear that the President's action was little less than a studied insult to the South adopted at the outset of his Administration for the purpose of showing his contempt for the sentiments and prejudices of this section."

The Dispatch says:

"With many qualities that are good—with some, possibly, that are great—Mr. Roosevelt is a negrophilist. While Governor of New York he invited a Negro (who, on account of race prejudice, could not obtain accommodation at any hotel) to be his guest at the Executive Mansion, and, it is said, gave him the best room in the house.

"Night before last the President had Prof. Booker T. Washington to dine with him at the White House. That was a deliberate act, taken under no alleged pressure of necessity, as in the Albany case, and may be taken as outlining his policy toward the Negro as a factor in Washington society. We say 'Washington society,' rather than 'American society,' because the former, on account of its political atmosphere, is much more 'advanced' in such matters than that of any other American city of which we know anything. The President, having invited Booker T. Washington to his table, residents of Washington of less conspicuous standing may be expected to do likewise. And if they invite him they may invite lesser lights—colored lights.

"When Mr. Cleveland was President he received Fred Douglass at some of his public entertainments—'functions,' so-called—but we do not remember that Fred was singled out for the distinguished honor of dining with the President, as Booker Washington has been.

"We do not like Mr. Roosevelt's negrophilism at all, and are sorry to see him seeking opportunities to indulge in it. He is reported to have rejoiced that Negro children were going to school with his children at Oyster Bay. But then, it may be said, too, that he has more reasons than the average white man to be fond of Negroes, since it was a Negro regiment that saved the Rough Riders from decimation at San Juan Hill. And but for San Juan Hill it is quite unlikely that Mr. Roosevelt would be President today.

"Booker Washington is said to have been very influential with the President in having Judge Jones put upon the Federal bench in Alabama, and we are now fully prepared to believe that statement.

"With our long-matured views on the subject of social intercourse between blacks and whites, the least we can say now is that we deplore the President's taste, and we distrust his wisdom."

The Enterprise says:

"It remained for Mr. Roosevelt to establish a precedent humiliating to the South and a disgrace to the nation. Judge Jones owes a duty to the South, to his friends and to common decency to promptly resign and hurl the appointment back into the very teeth of the white man who would invite a nigger to eat with his family."

Augusta, Ga., Oct. 19

The Augusta Chronicle says, in its leading editorial, today:

"The news from Washington that President Booker T. Washington, of Tuskegee Institute, was a guest at the White House at a dinner with President and Mrs. Roosevelt and family, and that after dinner there was the usual social hour over cigars, is a distinct shock to the favorable sentiment that was crystallizing in the South for the new President.

"While encouraging the people in the hope that the Negro is to be largely eliminated from office in the South, President Roosevelt throws the fat in the fire by giving countenance to the Negro's claims for social equality by having one to dine in the White House.

"President Roosevelt has made a mistake, one that will not only efface the good impression he had begun to create in the South, but one that will actively antagonize Southern people and meet the disapproval of good Anglo-Saxon sentiment in all latitudes.

"The South does not relish the Negro in office, but that is a small matter compared with its unalterable opposition to social equality between the races. President Roosevelt has flown in the face of public sentiment and precipitated an issue that has long since been fought out, and which should have been left in the list of settled questions."

Nashville, Tenn., Oct. 19

The Evening Banner says:

"Whatever justification may be attempted of the President's action in this instance, it goes without saying that it will tend to chill the favor with which he is regarded in the South, and will embarrass him in his reputed purpose to build up his party in this section."

Louisville, Ky., Oct. 19

The Times of yesterday afternoon says:

"The President has eliminated the color line from his private and official residences and with public office is hiring white Democrats to whitewash it down South."

Atlanta, Ga., Oct. 19

Governor Candler says:

"No self-respecting white man can ally himself with the President after what has occurred. The step has done the Republican party no earthly good, and it will materially injure its chances in the South. The effect of the Jones appointment is largely neutralized. Still, I guess it's like the old woman when she kissed the cow. As a matter of fact, Northern people do not understand the Negro. They see the best types and judge of the remainder by them."

Light

Philadelphia, Oct. 19

The Ledger this morning says:

"Because President Roosevelt saw fit, in his good judgment, to invite Booker T. Washington to dinner, strong words of disapproval are heard in the South. Mr. Washington is a colored man who enjoys the universal respect of all people in this country, black and white, on account of attainments, character and deeds. As the President invited him to be his private guest, and did not attempt to enforce the companionship of a colored man upon any one to whom the association could possibly be distasteful, any criticism of the President's act savors of very great impertinence. But, considered in any light, the invitation is not a subject for criticism. Booker T. Washington is one of the most notable citizens of the country, just because he has done noteworthy things. He is the founder and the successful executive of one of the most remarkable institutions in the United States, the Tuskegee (Alabama) Institute, which not only aims, but in fact does, educate and train the youth of the negro race to become useful, industrious and self-supporting citizens.

"Booker T. Washington is the embodiment of common sense and, instead of inciting the members of his race to dwell upon their wrongs, to waste their time upon politics and to try to get something for nothing in this life, in order to live without work, he has constantly preached the gospel of honest work, and has founded a great industrial school, which fits the young Negroes for useful lives as workers and teachers of industry to others. This is the man who was justly called by President McKinley, after he had inspected Tuskegee, the "leader of his race," and in the South no intelligent man denies that he is doing a great service to the whole population of both colors in this land. It is evident that the only objection that could be brought against association with such a man as that is color alone, and President Roosevelt will not recognize that prejudice."

The Evening Bulletin says:

"President Roosevelt night before last had Booker T. Washington, the worthy and much-respected colored man who is at the head of the Tuskegee Institute, as a guest at his private table in the White House. This has caused some indignation among Southerners and in Southern newspapers.

"Yet all the President really seems to have done was an act of courtesy in asking Mr. Washington to sit down with him to dinner and have a talk with him. As Booker T. Washington is an entirely reputable man, as well as an interesting one, the President doubtless enjoyed his company. Many Presidents in the past have had far less reputable and agreeable men at their table. If Mr. Roosevelt shall have no worse ones among his private guests, the country will have no cause for complaint.

"The right of the President to dine with anyone he may please to have with him is entirely his own affair, and Theodore Roosevelt is not a likely man to pick out bad company, black or white, for his personal or social companionship. The rumpus which some indiscreet Southerners are trying to raise because he has been hospitable to a colored man is a foolish display of both manners and temper."

Boston, Oct. 19

Commenting on President Roosevelt's action in extending hospitality to Booker T. Washington, President Charles Eliot, of Harvard, said:

"Harvard dined Booker Washington at her tables at the last commencement. Harvard conferred an honorary degree on him. This ought to show what Harvard thinks about the matter."

William Lloyd Garrison: "It was a fine object lesson, and most encouraging. It was the act of a gentleman—an act of unconscious natural simplicity."

Charles Eliot Norton: "I uphold the President in the bold stand that he has taken."

No Sympathy with Prejudice

New York Herald: The President has absolutely no sympathy with the prejudice against color. He has shown this on two occasions. Once he invited to his house at Oyster Bay, Harris, the Negro half-back of Yale, and entertained him over night. The other occasion was when he took in at the Executive Mansion at Albany, Brigham, the Negro baritone of St. George's Church, who was giving a concert in Albany and had been refused food and shelter by all the hotels.

Wasting Their Breath

Philadelphia Press: President Roosevelt's critics are wasting breath and spilling ink. There is an obstinate man in the White House. The cry of "nigger" will neither prevent him from continuing to appoint to any office in the Southern States the best men, under whatever color of politics, who can be found under current conditions, or recognizing in the hospitalities of the White House the best type of American manhood, under whatever color of skin it can be found.

That Dinner

New York Tribune: The Southern politician who criticises President Roosevelt's action in inviting Prof. Booker T. Washington to dine at the White House is likely to raise the query whether the manager of the Tuskegee Institute or himself is really the more deserving and genuine friend of the South.

Democrats have Changed Attitude

Glad of Booker T. Washington's Help in Securing Office.

Now Jeer Roosevelt

Berate President for Dining With a Negro.
Some Noted Occasions When the Alabama Educator Has Received the Plaudits of the South.

President Roosevelt has a fine sense of humor, and while he regrets that he has without malice stirred up a tempest in a teapot for the Southern editors by entertaining Professor Booker T. Washington at dinner, he cannot put aside the humorous side of the situation. It is only a few weeks since a number of white Democrats co-operated with Booker Washington in regard to the appointment of ex-Governor Jones to the vacancy on the Federal bench in Alabama, and Washington spoke for these white Democrats when he came to the capital and assured President Roosevelt that Jones would accept the appointment and that it would be satisfactory to all classes.

Washington had seen the President and had acted as his agent in interviewing Governor Jones and others as to the appointment. The Southern Democrats applauded the appointment of Jones, and they praised Washington for using his influence at the White House to secure such an appointment for a Democrat. Then they all spoke of Washington as a gentleman of culture, who had the refined sense to cut loose from the Republican leaders of the Negro party in the South and work in harmony with the best class of whites. Now they are abusing the President for dining with a "nigger."

Washington has entertained more distinguished Northern men and more distinguished Southern men at the Tuskegee Institute than any other man in the State, if not in the South. President McKinley and his Cabinet, accompanied by many other distinguished gentlemen, were the guests of Washington at Tuskegee two years ago, and they lunched at his table. Washington was the guest of honor at a banquet in Paris three years ago, when Ambassador Porter presided and ex-President Harrison and Archbishop Ireland were among the guests. This same "nigger" was received by Queen Victoria and took tea in Buckingham Palace the same year.

Invitation from White House

When he returned to this country Washington received invitations from all parts of the South to deliver addresses and attend receptions given by white people. He was received by the Governors of Georgia, Virginia, West Virginia and Louisiana. He spoke to many mixed audiences in the South, where whites and blacks united to do him honor. When the people of Atlanta wanted an appropriation from Congress for their Exposition in 1895 they sent a large committee of the most distinguished men in the South to the National Capital to plead their cause. Booker T. Washington was one of these distinguished Southern men. Congressman Joseph E. Cannon, Chairman of the Committee on Appropriations in the House, says that Washington by his force and eloquence secured that appropriation of $250,000 for the Atlanta Exposition.

The Southern people had only praise for him when he was arranging to take Vice-President Roosevelt to Tuskegee and Montgomery and Atlanta this fall, and they were eager to co-operate with him in entertaining such a distinguished visitor. They still hope to have President Roosevelt visit the South, and if he goes he will go as the guest of Booker T. Washington.

The President knows, too, that the real leaders of the South, white Democrats, do not sympathize with this hue and cry of Southern editors because Washington was a guest at the White House. Today the President has received many messages from Southern men, urging him to pay no attention to the yawp of the bourbon editors, who have not been able to get over the old habit of historical discussion of "social equality." Southern men called at the White House today as usual to ask for favors at the hands of the President, and they are not afraid of contamination by meeting the man who "ate with a nigger."

Amuses the President

President Roosevelt cannot help seeing the humorous side of the situation he has created by asking his friend to dinner, and he is pursuing the even tenor of his way as President without worrying over the outcome. He has, in the last two weeks, given cause for much excitement in the South. The first was when he appointed a Democrat to office and ignored the professional Republican politicians, who claimed to carry the "nigger" vote in their pocket. He was not disturbed by the threats of the Southern Republican politicians over that incident, and he is not disturbed by the threats of the Southern Democratic editors over this incident.

As to the Southern objection to dining, with a Negro, Opie Read, of Chicago, tells a story about M. W. Gibbs, who has just resigned his position as United States Consul at Tamatave, Madagascar. Gibbs is now in Washington on his way home to Little Rock. He resigned to give a younger man a chance to serve his country as a Consul. Here is the story Opie Read told about Gibbs dining with white men at a banquet in honor of General Grant in Little Rock:

In the reconstruction days a Negro by the name of Mifflin Wistar Gibbs located in Little Rock, Ark. He showed the community that he was keener than a whole lot of its leading citizens, who had kept the offices in their families for generations. Under the new order of things he was appointed Attorney of Pulaski County. His ability and the considerate manner in which he conducted his relationship with the whites gave him a greater popularity than any other colored man had ever before enjoyed in that place. His influence increased, until General Grant, then President, appointed him Register of the United States Land Office at Little Rock.

Gibbs' Speech the Best

"When General Grant visited our city a banquet was prepared, and it was finally decided that for the first time in the history of the 'Bear State' a Negro would be welcomed at a social function on terms of absolute equality. I was then editor of the Gazette, and my seat was next to that of Gibbs. The speaker who had been selected to respond to the toast, 'The Possibilities of American Citizenship' was absent. I asked Gibbs if he would not talk on that subject. He consented, and I arranged the matter with the toastmaster. The novelty and the picturesqueness of the thing appealed to me. Every guest was spellbound, and General Grant was astonished. Not only was the speech of the Negro the best one delivered on that occasion, but it was one of the most remarkable to which I have ever listened.

"The owner of the Gazette was a Democrat of the Democrats, and a strict keeper of the traditions of the South. Moreover, his paper was the official organ of the Democratic party, and we were in the heat of a bitter campaign. In spite of all this, however, I came out with the editorial statement that Gibbs had scored the greatest oratorical triumph of the affair. Perhaps this didn't stir things up a little. But the gratitude of Gibbs was touching. He is now United States Consul at Tamatave, Madagascar. In my opinion he is the greatest living representative of the colored race. We have been close friends ever since that banquet."

Booker Washington the Victim

(From the Washington (D. C.) Post,
October 23, 1901.)

Quite the most deplorable feature of the Booker Washington incident is, in our opinion, the effect it is likely to have on Washington himself; yet this is an aspect of the case which does not seem to have occurred thus far to any of the multitudinous and more or less enlightened commentators who have bestowed their views upon the country. Criticisms of the President are matters of taste. For our part, we hold, and have always held, that a President's private and domestic affairs are not proper subjects of public discussion. A man does not surrender all of his personal liberties in becoming the Chief Executive of the Nation. At least, his purely family arrangements are not the legitimate concern of outsiders. The Presidency would hardly be worth the having otherwise. The country, however, has a right to consider the incident in the light of its probable injury to Washington and to the great and useful work in which he is engaged.

IN CLOSING THIS PAGE OF "Shadow and Light" I am loath to believe that this extreme display of adverse feeling regarding the President's action in inviting Mr. Washington to dine with him, as shown in some localities, is fully shared by the best element of Southern opinion. Few Southern gentlemen of the class who so cheerfully pay the largest amount of taxation for the tuition of the Negro, give him employment and do much to advance him along educational and industrial lines, fear that the President's action will cause the obtrusion of his bronze pedals beneath their mahogany. Trusting that he will be inspired to foster those elements of character so conspicuous in Mr. Washington and that have endeared him to his broad-minded countrymen both North and South. The best intelligence, the acknowledged leaders of the race, are not only conservative along political lines, but are in accord with those who claim that social equality is not the creature of law, or the product of coercion, for, in a generic sense, there is no such thing as social equality. The gentlemen who are so disturbed hesitate, or refuse such equality with many of their own race; the same can be truthfully said of the Negro. Many ante-bellum theories and usages have already vanished under the advance of a higher civilization, but the "old grudge" is still utilized when truth and justice refuse their service.

Chapter 32

Washington, the American "Mecca" for political worshipers, is a beautiful city, but well deserving its "nom de plume" as "the city of magnificent distances;" for any one with whom you have business seems to live five miles from every imaginable point of the compass; and should you be on stern business bent, distance will not "lend enchantment to the view." It is here that the patriot, and the mercenary, the ambitious and the envious gather, and where unity and divergence hold high carnival.

Dramatists have found no better field for portraying the vicissitudes and uncertainties, the successes and triumphs of human endeavor. The ante-room to the President's office presents a vivid picture, as they wait for, or emerge from, executive presence, delineating the varied phases of impressible human nature—the despondent air of ill success; the pomp of place secured; the expectant, but hope deferred; the bitterness depicted in waiting delegations on a mission of opposition bent; the gleam of gladness on success; homage to the influential—all these figure, strut or bemoan in the ratio of a self-importance or a dejected mien. There is no more humorous reading, or more typical, than the ups and downs of office-seekers. Sometimes it is that of William the "Innocent," and often that of William the "Croker." The trials of "an unsuccessful," a prototype of "Orpheus C. Kerr," the nom de plume of that prince of writers, on this subject, is in place:

Diary of an office-seeker, William the "Innocent":

March 2d

Just arrived. Washington a nice town. Wonder if it would not be as well to stay here as go abroad.

March 4th

Saw McKinley inaugurated. We folks who nominated him will be all right now. Think I had better take an assistant secretaryship. The Administration wants good men, who know something about politics; besides, I am getting to like Washington.

March 8th

Big crowd at the White House. They ought to give the President time to settle himself. Have sold my excursion ticket and will stay awhile. Too many people make a hotel uncomfortable. Have found a good boarding house.

March 11th

Shook hands with the President in the East Room and told him I would call on a matter of business in a few days. He seemed pleased.

March 15th

Went to the Capitol and found Senator X. He was sour. Said the whole State was there chasing him. Asked me what I wanted, and said, "Better go for something in reach." Maybe an auditorship would be the thing.

March 23d

Took my papers to the White House. Thought I'd wait and have a private talk with the President, but Sergeant Porter said I'd have to go along with the rest. What an ill-natured set they were. Elbowed me right along just because they saw the President wanted to talk with me. Will have to go back and finish our conversation.

March 27

Got some money from home.

March 29th

Went to the White House, but the chap at Porter's door wouldn't let me in. Said it was after hours. He ought to be fired.

April 3d

Saw Mark Hanna, after waiting five hours. Asked him why my letter had not been answered. He said he was getting 400 a day and his secretaries would catch up some time next year. I always thought Hanna overestimated. Now I know it.

April 5th

Had an interview with the President. Was last in the line, so they could not push me along. When I told him of my services to the party, he replied: "Oh, yes;" and for me to file my papers in the State Department.

Said he had many good friends in Indiana and hoped they would be patient. Can he have forgotten I am not from Indiana? Probably the tariff is worrying him. Shameful the way the Senate is acting.

April 7th

Borrowed a little more money. Washington is an expensive town to live in.

April 11th

Senator X. says all the auditorships were mortgaged before the election, but he will indorse me for a special agency or a chief clerkship, if I can find one that is not under the civil service law.

April 12th

D—n the civil service law.

April 17th

Didn't know there were so many good positions abroad. Ought to have gone for one of them in the first place. That State Department is a great thing. Think I'll start with Antwerp and check off a few which will suit me. Wonder where I can negotiate a small loan?

April 19th

Got in to see the President and told him I could best serve the Administration and the party abroad. He said, "Oh, yes," and to file my papers in the Post-office Department, and he hoped his friends in Massachusetts would be patient. What made him think I was from Massachusetts? I suppose he gets mixed sometimes.

April 20th

Senator X. says there is one chance in a million of getting a Consulate; but if I will concentrate on Z town he and the delegation will do what they can. Salary, $1,000; fees, $87.

April 21st

Have concentrated on Z town. Got in line today just for a moment to tell the President it would suit me. He said, "Oh, yes," and to file my papers in the Treasury Department, and he hoped his friends in Minnesota would be patient till he could get around to them. Queer he should think I was from Minnesota.

April 26th

The ingratitude of that man McKinley! He has nominated Jones for Z town, when he knew I had concentrated on it. After my services to the party, too! Who is Jones, anyhow?

April 27th

I am going home. Senator X has got me a pass. Will send for my trunk later. It is base ingratitude.

William the "Croker," the other applicant for official favor, wanted "Ambassador to Russia," and while not attaining the full measure of his ambition, was nevertheless rewarded for his pertinacity. His sojourn in Washington had been long, and was becoming irksome, particularly so to the Senators and Members of Congress from his State, who had from time to time ministered to his pecuniary wants. But Seth Orton was noted at home and abroad for his staying qualities. He came from an outlying district in his State that was politically pivotal, and Seth had been known on several occasions by his fox-horn contributions to rally the "unwashed" and save the day when hope but faintly glimmered above the political horizon. For his Congressional delegation Seth was both useful at home and expensive abroad. That the mission for which he aspired was beyond his reach they were fully aware; that he must be disposed of they were equally agreed. After having adroitly removed the props to his aspirations for Ambassador, Minister Plenipotentiary and Consul, they told him they had succeeded in getting him an Indian agency, paying $1,000 a year. He was disgusted, and proclaimed rebellion. They appeased him by telling him that the appropriation for supplies and other necessaries the last year was ten thousand dollars, and they were of the opinion that the former agent had saved half of it. A gleam of joy and quick consent were prompt! Walking up and down his Congressman's room, pleased, then thoughtful, then morose, he finally exclaimed to his patron, "Look here, Mr. Harris; don't you think that $5,000 of the $10,000 too much to give them d—n nigger Indians?"

On the official side of colored Washington life, we see much that is gratifying recognition. The receipt by us of over a million dollars annually, on the one side, and the rendering of a creditable service on the other, while our professional and business status in the District is equally commendable, and much more prolific in the bestowal of substantial and lasting benefit. And on the domestic side we have much that is cheering, comprising a large representation of wealth and intelligence, living in homes indicating refinement and culture, and with a social contact the most desirable.

Mr. Andrew F. Hilyer, editor and compiler of "The Twentieth Century Union League Directory," in his introduction to that able and useful publication, says: "This being the close of the nineteenth century, after a generation of freedom, it was thought to be a good point at which to stop and take an account of stock, and see just what is the actual status of the colored population of Washington, the Capital of the Nation, where the colored population is large, and where the conditions are the most favorable, to see what is their actual status as skilled workmen, in business, in the professions, and in their organizations; in short, to make a study, at first hand, of their efforts for social betterment."

This publication contains the names, character and location of 500 business men and women. It is creditable to the compiler and encouraging for the subjects of its reference.

The colored newspapers of the District, several in number, are of high order, and maintain a reputation for intelligent journalism, and for energy and devotion to the cause they espouse are abreast with those of sister communities. The growth of Negro journals in our country has been marked. We have now three hundred or more newspapers and magazines, edited and published by colored men and women. The publisher of a race paper early finds that it is not a sinecure nor a bed of roses. If he is zealous and uncompromising in the defense of his race, exposing outrages and injustice; advertisements are withdrawn by those who have the most patronage to bestow. Should he "crook the pregnant hinges of the knee, that thrift may follow fawning," and fail to denounce the wrong, the paper loses influence and subscriptions of those in whose interest it is professedly established, and hence, as an advertising medium, it is deserted.

So, as for the publisher (in the words of that eccentric Puritan, Lorenzo Dow), "He'll be damned if he does, and be damned if he don't." He is between "Scilla and Carribdes," requiring versatility of ability, courage of conviction and a wise discretion, that he may steer "between the rocks of too much danger and pale fear," and reach the port of success. The mission of the Negro press is a noble one, for "Right is of no sex, and Wrong of no color," and God, the Father of us all, with these as its standard, to be effectual it must give a "plain, unvarnished tale, nor set down aught in malice." The white journals of the country often quote the Negro press as to Negro wants and Negro aspirations, and as time and conditions shall justify it will necessarily become more metropolitan and less exclusive, dealing more with economic and industrial subjects on broader lines and from more material standpoints.

Chapter 33

Howard University

Howard University was established by a special act of Congress in 1867. It takes its name from that of the great philanthropist and soldier, Gen. O. O. Howard, who may be called its founder and greatest patron. It was through the untiring efforts of General Howard that this special act passed Congress to establish a university on such broad and liberal lines as those that characterize Howard University.

This University admits students of both sexes and any color to all of its departments. The great majority of its students, however, are colored, and some of its graduates are the most distinguished men of the Negro race in America. It has splendid departments of law, medicine, theology and the arts and sciences.

Howard University is situated on one of the most beautiful sites of the Capital of the Nation.

Having two members of my family as teachers in the public schools of Washington City, I have learned considerable about them. They are said to rank among our best public schools, and are constantly improving, under the careful supervision of a highly competent superintendent, and a paid board of trustees. There are 112 school buildings in the city—75 for white and 37 for colored, the number being regulated according to population, about one-third being colored. New manual training schools have just been erected, for both races, and a growing disposition exists to provide equal (though separate) accommodation and opportunity. The colored schools are taught exclusively by colored teachers, the grade schools being conducted by the graduates of the Washington Normal School almost entirely. The M Street High School, a leading sample of the best public schools of the country, has a teaching faculty of twenty teachers, most of them graduates of our best colleges, such as Howard, Yale, Oberlin, University of Michigan, Amherst, Brown and Cornell.

R. H. Terrill, the present principal, is a graduate of Howard, with the degree of "Cum laude," and, after having won golden opinions from the board and attaches of the school for his scholarship and supervising ability, has been appointed by President Roosevelt to a judgeship of the District, and will assume the duties thereof in January, 1902.

All such appointments are helpful, coming from the highest ruler, and for place, at the fountain head of the Government, have a reflex influence upon much which is unjust. With each success we should beware of envy, the offspring of selfishness, which is apt to creep insidiously into our lives. We should crown the man who has achieved distinction and advise him as to pitfalls. "No sadder proof," Carlisle has said, "can be given by a man of his own littleness than disbelief in great men." There is no royal road to a lasting eminence but the toilsome pathway of diligence, self-denial and high moral rectitude; surely not by turning sharp corners to follow that "will-o'-the wisp" transient success, at the expense of upright conduct. Neither suavity of manner nor the gilding of education will atone for disregarding the sanctity of obligation, the violation of which continues to wreck the lives and blast the promise of many. By sowing the seed of uprighteousness, by unceasing effort and rigid frugality, the harvest, though sometimes tardy, will be sure to produce an hundred fold in Christian virtues and material prosperity. The latter is a necessity for our progress; for, say what you will about being "just as good as anybody," the world of mankind has little use for a penniless man. The ratio of its attention to you is largely commensurate with your bank account and your ability to further ends involving expenditure. Whether this estimate is in accord with the highest principle, the Negro has not time to investigate, for he is up against the hard fact that confronts the great majority of mankind, and one with which each for himself must grapple. Opportunity may be late, but it comes to him who watches and waits while diligent in what his hands may find to do. For, with all that may be said, gracious or malicious, of the "Negro problem," we are unmistakably on the upward grade, educationally and financially, while these bitter criticisms and animadversions will be the moral weights to steady our footsteps and give surety to progress.

Granting no excuse for ignorance or unfitness in a political aspirant, or for a religious ministry at the present day, we cannot but remember that our present lines in more pleasant places, both in Church and State, had impetus through the trying ordeal of toil, suffering and massacre during the era of reconstruction. Many, though unlettered, with a nobility of soul that oppression could not humble, were martyrs to their Christian zeal for the right and finger boards and beacon lights on the dark and perilous road to our present advanced position.

In concluding this imperfect autobiography, containing mention of "men I have met" in the nineteenth century, absence of many co-laborers, both white and colored, will be observable, whose ability, devotion and sacrifice should be treasured as heirlooms by a grateful people.

And now, kind reader, who has followed me in my wanderings—

"Say not 'Good night,' but in some brighter clime bid me 'Good morning.'"

A Note About the Author

Mifflin Wistar Gibbs (1823–1915) was an American-Canadian diplomat, judge, and lawyer. As a young man in Philadelphia he was involved in the abolitionist movement. In 1850 Gibbs migrated west during the gold rush and became a successful businessman in California. There, he founded *Mirror of the Times*, one of the first Black-owned newspapers in the country. In 1858 Gibbs moved to Victoria, B.C., where he prospered as a prominent community leader. In the 1870's he returned to the United States and became the first Black man elected as a U.S. judge, and eventually became a the first African-American diplomat.

A Note from the Publisher

Spanning many genres, from non-fiction essays to literature classics to children's books and lyric poetry, Mint Edition books showcase the master works of our time in a modern new package. The text is freshly typeset, is clean and easy to read, and features a new note about the author in each volume. Many books also include exclusive new introductory material. Every book boasts a striking new cover, which makes it as appropriate for collecting as it is for gift giving. Mint Edition books are only printed when a reader orders them, so natural resources are not wasted. We're proud that our books are never manufactured in excess and exist only in the exact quantity they need to be read and enjoyed.

bookfinity™

Discover more of your favorite classics with Bookfinity™.

- Track your reading with custom book lists.
- Get great book recommendations for your personalized Reader Type.
- Add reviews for your favorite books.
- AND MUCH MORE!

Visit **bookfinity.com** and take the fun Reader Type quiz to get started.

Enjoy our classic and modern companion pairings!

Classic & Modern